Also by Stephen Hough

The Final Retreat

ROUGH IDEAS

ROUGH IDEAS

Reflections on Music and More

Stephen Hough

FARRAR, STRAUS AND GIROUX

NEW YORK

Farrar, Straus and Giroux
120 Broadway, New York 10271

Grateful acknowledgment is made for permission to reprint an excerpt from
Night by Elie Wiesel, translated by Marion Wiesel. Translation
copyright © 2006 by Marion Wiesel. Reprinted by permission of
Hill and Wang, a division of Farrar, Straus and Giroux.

Library of Congress Control Number: 2019952369
ISBN: 978-0-374-25254-0

Our books may be purchased in bulk for promotional, educational, or business
use. Please contact your local bookseller or the Macmillan Corporate and
Premium Sales Department at 1-800-221-7945, extension 5442, or by e-mail at
MacmillanSpecialMarkets@macmillan.com.

www.fsgbooks.com
www.twitter.com/fsgbooks • www.facebook.com/fsgbooks

1 3 5 7 9 10 8 6 4 2

For Dennis
without whom many of these reflections
might be rougher . . . and more

Contents

Stage

Studio

People and Pieces

. . . and More

. . . and Religion

Introduction

Give me a rough idea . . . not as in a deliberately coarse or unformed one, rather one that has a beginning but not yet an end.

I spend a lot of my life sitting around – at airports, on planes, in hotel rooms – and most of this book expands notes I have made during that dead time on the road. Many of these jottings found their way into print, on paper or online, but others remained unfinished musings on scraps of paper or saved as files on the go on my iPhone: seeds, saplings, waiting to be planted or repotted or pruned.

Mostly I've written about music and the life of a musician (not always the same thing), from exploring the broader aspects of what it is to walk out onto a stage or to make a recording to specialist tips from deep inside the practice room: how to trill, how to pedal, how to practise. Other subjects appear too, people I've known, places I've travelled to, books I've read, paintings I've seen. Even religion is there: the possibility of the existence of God, problems with some biblical texts and the challenge involved in being a gay Catholic, and abortion. I've placed these reflections in a separate section so that readers allergic to such matters can avoid them and we can remain friends.

'How do you pronounce your name?'
   'Hough: rhymes with rough.'

FORUM

The Soul of Music

Great buildings catch the eye but great concert halls must catch the ear too – and not just as spaces in which to hear music. Rather they are meant to *be* musical instruments, their walls and ceilings and floors catching, mixing, projecting the vibrations, transporting them through the air to the ear. A fine acoustic does not just make the music created onstage sound better; it is part of the creative process itself. When I strike a chord, what I hear instantly affects how I will play the next chord. Pianists do not press down predetermined keys with predetermined weight; we spin plates of sound in the air, reacting with split-second reflex to their curve and quiver. Adjustments of pedalling and nuance, of rhythmic flexibility or rigidity, are as constant as the dart and dance of a juggler. We play a hall more than play *in* a hall.

Wigmore Street is a rather dull thoroughfare. Its buildings tend to be respectable and predictable. Above the shopfronts are offices with politely yawning windows, and the cheerful if not exactly cheap restaurants seem tolerated rather than celebrated. But then we reach number 36. Another shopfront it might seem, but no. Wigmore Street's mediocre Victoriana has lightened. There is a twinkle in the eye as you notice a glass awning. This crystal umbrella is more than a protection against occasional rain. To build with glass is architectural liberation, and to stand safely covered yet still under open skies is a form of ecstasy.

There are no bright lights outside number 36, nothing to distract one's continuing amble towards John Lewis or Selfridge's. Just, on both the east and west side of this glass awning, stencilled letters spelling WIGMORE HALL in one of the Arts and Crafts movement's more sober fonts. Now you know that you are standing outside a building that has resonated with music for over a hundred years.

Passing through the swinging wooden doors, inset with polished brass panels on which is also stencilled the name of the hall, you step into the outer lobby, a funnel through which all patrons pour. At the end of this corridor is the box office. A small window, as if from a country cottage lacking only a rambling rose, appears at waist level on the left. As you walk towards it only a hand is intermittently visible, dispensing envelopes containing tickets. It's hard to see who owns the hand, even as one reaches the aperture, for to see the face of the owner of the hand requires a rather undignified bending down, in the hope that your name is on the list, that your ticket is safely reserved, that you've come on the correct evening. To the right of the window is a door where a man in evening dress is usually found leaning. This is someone who can override the authority of the armless hand, someone who can make sure that reservations are honoured and that honoured guests are admitted with no reservations. Often the door appears empty until the final approach when a slim figure sidles out, smiling, knowing. He holds an envelope in his hand. The exchange is made. You're in.

Immediately past this door to the left is a staircase going up, leading to the hall's small balcony, which contains a mere 78 seats. I've sat up there a number of times and it has excellent acoustics and sight lines but it somehow has the feeling of last-minute admission, as if downstairs were oversold or you arrived late or there was a mix-up at the secret window. Or maybe it's the opposite, and this is the place for that special guest of the performer, or that celebrity who wants to remain incognito, or that jaded music professional who wants an easy exit in the event of a tedious evening. If a concert has not sold well, a fat, red rope hangs at the bottom of the stairs, blocking entry.

After the staircase there is a choice: left or right. Two doors leading into the holy of holies; no other way inside for the public in this small auditorium. Even if I'm sitting on the left side I nearly always enter by the right door, which is directly ahead of the street entrance. To enter by the left door, at the top of the basement staircase, suggests you have been loitering, or were in the loo, or were gulping down a gin and tonic in the bar. To go down to the bar during the interval is to be sociable; to go down there before the concert is to be . . . available.

And so to your seat: red velvet; straight back and sides. A hand in the gap and a gentle push down. Not too comfortable, so you can focus and concentrate on the music; not too uncomfortable, so you can focus and concentrate on the music for a long time. Glance around to see if you know anyone. Oh lovely, there's so-and-so. Oh dear, there's so-and-so. Turn back and look down. Thank goodness you bought that substantial programme book.

The stage is the centre of Wigmore Hall, its *raison d'être* and point of focus. It is also the dividing line between front of house and backstage. A concert is theatre – costumes, lighting, choreography – and its habits are not just thoughtless tradition. These customs can be the best preparation for the drama of the music to unfold – a reason, too, why we set aside special places for our concerts. As with churches, we use a separate building for this activity partly because we want to create a sacred space. A concert is a feast, a liturgy . . . a party even. It can be bad, but it should never be drab or routine.

In 1899 the British architect Thomas Edward Collcutt, having finished Britain's 'first luxury hotel', the Savoy, just over ten years earlier, was commissioned to design Wigmore Hall. It was his only concert hall. From the mid-twentieth century onwards acousticians emerged as a separate breed, commissioned by an architect to take his or her visual design and set it to music – scientists of sound. In earlier times the architect worked with the eye and hoped the ear would follow. It all appears to have been a matter of chance and tradition . . . and the shoebox.

This rectangular shape was traditionally used for concert buildings, the stage a heel at one end. And size didn't matter too much. As long as the proportions were right it would work. It has something to do with walls as arms embracing vibrations, enabling sound to be projected but contained. Wigmore's shoebox is small (a slipper fit for Cinderella herself), with every sound beautifully focused. Materials are important: wood is warm, to the touch and to the ear. Wigmore's stage is a curved cradle of wood, but out in the 545-seat auditorium are the heavier, grander materials of alabaster and marble. Indeed, despite its birth in the era of art nouveau, Wigmore Hall harks back to the Renaissance in style. There are candle sconces on the walls, and if altars were to project out between the flattened, pink-veined pillars, and oil paintings depicting the life of Christ or of the saints were to be hung above those altars, we might easily be in the private chapel of a minor Italian duke. But no, this is a solidly secular space. Indeed, the only iconography is the famous cupola above the stage, an exuberantly colourful mural entitled *The Soul of Music*.

This is in the Arts and Crafts style and was designed by Gerald Moira, later to become principal of the Edinburgh College of Art, and executed by the sculptor Frank Lynn Jenkins, who was much in demand as a creator of decorative friezes. The *Soul of Music* figure is gazing up at the 'Genius of Harmony' – a ball of fire with rays reflected across the world under a deep-blue but clouded sky. On the left a musician plays as if in a trance, seeking inspiration from beyond. 'Love' is there too, carrying roses. She apparently represents the idea that a musician's incentive must be love for art with beauty as the sole reward. On the right side is Psyche – the human soul – who inspires the seated composer to pen musical notes onto a scroll. The tangled nest of thorns that disturbs the perfection of this vision represents the possibility of humanity failing to live up to this artistic ideal – a choking by materialism. The whole image perhaps suggests music as religion. Such a message might well have shocked the post-Victorians who first received it, if they had not already been shocked by the erotic lurch of the *Soul of Music* figure, portrayed as a lithe, graceful, naked young man. This frieze is an unashamed display of exuberant naturalism in the pursuit of beauty and pleasure in music. On either side of the central cupola are two simpler rectangular paintings showing musicians responding successfully to the extravagant artistic suggestion of the central image.

Returning to the stage, what about Wigmore Hall's wings, the traditional theatrical term for the bits on the side where performers wait, often with extreme anxiety, for their moment to appear? Well, Wigmore's wings are more like two ears. On the back wall of the stage are two symmetrical doors for entry and exit. The door on the right, as you face the stage, through which every artist walks, is mysterious. Wherever you sit in the hall it is impossible to see clearly behind the door because of a twist in the space, and then a thick crimson curtain blocks further view. But on the left there is a yet more mysterious door. It looks exactly the same, but no. This is a sort of broom cupboard leading via some precipitous steps directly up to the Green Room. It's not used for public events. It's too informal somehow, too cramped, too prosaic for the stage. This left door is gauche. It's for Hilda Ogden rather than Maria Callas.

Leaving the stage and walking through the right door we reach (left, up and left again) the Green Room. I'm old enough to remember auditioning at Wigmore Hall when this was pretty much all there was backstage: a room with an upright piano and a few pieces of shabby furniture. It was merely a place to hang your hat and don your tails before playing your concert. It is a room in which I have experienced many conflicting emotions, from the tremble of nervous anticipation as I warm up on the well-worn piano to the exhilaration and relief at the end of a concert, a glass of chilled champagne in hand. 'Darling, what a performance!' 'I've never heard that piece played like that!' 'How do *you* think it went?' 'Dear, I'm speechless!' . . . some of the classic phrases expressing dissatisfaction or bitchy venom while still appearing to offer a crumb of praise to the hungry, self-doubting artist.

In 1992 a major restructuring added the Gerald Moore and Geoffrey Parsons rooms, rehearsal spaces named after two great accompanists – a reminder that Wigmore Hall has always had song at its heart, and that lieder require the piano to unfold the drama of a song as an equal partner. It also emphasises that Wigmore Hall is vitally, spiritually in the centre of Europe. So many of the thousands driven from their houses by jackboots found a home at Wigmore. It became a secular synagogue for those for whom the German language was a mother tongue, even if the Fatherland had made them orphans. Schubert, Schumann, Brahms, Wolf . . . comforting common currency for these refugees.

The hall was built by the piano manufacturer C. Bechstein, which had its London showroom next door. This performing space was originally named Bechstein Hall. During the First World War the passing of the Trading with the Enemy Amendment Act in 1916 meant that all the assets of the Bechstein company were seized, including the hall. It eventually re-opened in 1917 as Wigmore Hall and now, a century later, it flourishes as never before.

Buildings are homes to memories. 'If only these walls could talk,' we say. At 36 Wigmore Street, we might wish that they could sing.

'Our concert halls are like museums' – Yes, isn't that great!

I have a number of books by my bedside, ones I can dip into if only for a few minutes before I fall asleep. One of them is *Rendez-vous with Art* by Philippe de Montebello, Director of New York's Metropolitan Museum of Art for thirty-one years until 2008, and the art critic Martin Gayford. As I leafed through it the other night, seeing photos of some favourite paintings, I was struck by how some familiar artworks seem like dear friends. As the years pass it's as if we've grown old together. To contemplate these images again and again is constantly enriching and – so far – I've never felt jaded or bored by the repetition.

We look at a painting and it looks back at us. We stare at its detail with eyes of wonder as it strips away the varnish coating our own thoughts and memories. Great art in all its forms demands to be revisited. It requires time. To read a poem once is not to have read it properly. I opened at random at Titian's *Christ Carrying the Cross*, its combination of specificity and universality – Jesus of Nazareth, yes, but also every person who has ever helped or been helped in a moment of suffering – seemed to me to have depths of richness to last more than a lifetime.

In the musical world I often hear the complaint that concert life is dying because we have made our auditoriums into museums, repeating the same old chestnuts year after year. This can be true, but is it really a problem? I'm not suggesting for a moment that it's not important to have the opportunity to hear contemporary music or that we shouldn't be curious and passionate about neglected works and composers, but let's not disparage the classics in our permanent collections.

When I visit a museum, I want to be surprised and stimulated and even shocked. But I also want to see the familiar masterpieces – not because I feel comfortable with what I already know but because the greatest art will continue to surprise, stimulate and shock, time after time.

No one at London's National Gallery would suggest that Van Eyck's *Arnolfini Wedding* has outlived its interest and should spend some time in the storeroom but I have heard people say that they'd be happy never to hear a certain Beethoven work again. If a performer ever feels bored playing such well-known music then he or she is probably equally unsuited to playing newer works too. If Beethoven seems dull or old hat to us, then we need to listen to his music not less but more . . . more carefully, more intensely.

We might need to hang or light a painting better, display it alongside something different, rethink our education programme, communicate the painting's beauty and significance more imaginatively, even send it to a restorer, but let's not just remove it from the wall or apologise for it. A curator – of art or music – needs to have complete confidence in the collection. There will always be someone who is seeing a certain painting for the first time, hearing a certain piece of music for the first time, and for someone else it will be a chance to revisit a dear old friend.

Music in churches: magical ghosts or profane distractions?

Although churches were not designed for classical concerts, there is something magical about borrowing them for the evening. There are (friendly) ghosts in these buildings, smells of linen and wax, creaks from pew and sanctuary, strange shadows in cool, dusty corners, and so often, above all, acoustics that glow and pulsate, adding richness to the already rich sounds of the music. Strangely, it can be easier to lose the heavy weight of the ego where your performance is encouraged and appreciated but is not essential to the life of a building: a kind of bringing down to earth as the music itself soars to heaven.

In the past there were few secular concerts in places of worship. Strictly speaking, concerts are still banned in Roman Catholic churches – as I found out when I offered in vain to give a benefit concert in one in New York a number of years ago. However, I did play once in Bari, with the permission of the bishop, over the tomb of St Nicholas . . . Santa Claus himself. It was the Liszt B minor Sonata at a crushingly slow tempo owing to the extreme and resonant echo of the ancient stone. It's a strange experience to hear bar 35 still ringing in the air when your fingers are already playing bar 42.

These days many churches are not only venues for concerts but make superb recording spaces as well. Some are deconsecrated and others still thrive as places of worship. I've made dozens of recordings in them – St George's, Brandon Hill; Henry Wood Hall; Rosslyn Hill Chapel; All Saints', Finchley; All Saints', Tooting.

The words 'recording studio' conjure up the image of a soundproof room, its ceiling clad with foam, wires streaming from holes in ugly polystyrene walls, armies of microphones, triple-glazed windows – a sort of refrigerator sealed from the outside world in order to preserve the controlled sounds created within. With most pop music or electronic music the acoustic of the room should play no part in the final product; everything relies on post-production mixing. A bloom on the sound, because it varies and is unpredictable, is undesirable. But in classical music recordings the natural acoustic of the space is usually an important part of the process. Not only does a beautifully sounding hall encourage the performer(s) to play better, to relish the overtones, to savour the nuances, but it makes the final CD sound more natural. Classical music, and the instruments on which it is played, is organic – in more than one sense of the word.

Not having a sealed environment can have its drawbacks, however. The roar of a jet plane, the hum of a lawn mower, a distant car alarm have all on occasion forced me to stop in mid-flight. Years ago I was recording some Schumann in a church. We'd reached the sublime, rapt third movement of his *Fantasie* op. 17 when birds at the stained-glass windows began squawking with raucous pleasure. I'm sure that Robert and Clara at the height of their courtship were not so demonstrative. In the end – with ruined take after ruined take, time running out, and sanity at the point of shreds – I had to run out with a starting pistol (the engineer had thought of everything), shoot it into the air, then run back inside again to complete the recording. No glowing acoustic can compensate for such dramatic drawbacks.

On one of my CDs you can hear, if you listen very carefully, just for a few seconds, the gentle warble of external (chaste) birdsong. We left it there. It was the best take. It was unobtrusive. It was musical. It was organic.

Our wonderful, ageing audiences

Although most people turn up at concerts on their own or in couples, occasionally there can be a coachload, frequently of older people, more often than not from a nursing home. On one occasion in Canada a few years ago such a scene set me thinking.

I arrived at the venue that evening with some of the familiar worries most performers have in the hour before the curtain rises, and as I approached the stage door I saw someone being wheeled up the ramp to the front entrance from a bus parked outside. When I saw this man, my heart instantly lifted. It struck me as wonderful that he was there to hear Beethoven and I was the one who this evening was to bring that music to life. It sounds corny to talk about it being a privilege but that's exactly what it felt like. Ultimately to be a musician is to be a 'joy bringer': we are Jupiters, one and all! This old man in his wheelchair was a reminder of the fact, often lamented, that audiences for classical music concerts are mainly made up of the elderly, and that it seems increasingly difficult to attract young people to join us. But on that occasion such an observation seemed like a blasphemy. Greying audiences? I love them! With old age comes wisdom, patience, subtlety, contemplation . . . all qualities needed to appreciate great and complex music.

I've been playing professionally for over thirty years now and there's always been a sea of grey beyond the footlights. So what? A new grey has replaced the old grey. In the leisure of retirement or in the freedom from the responsibility of looking after children, people can finally find the time to go to concerts. Not that I want in any way to discourage young people from loving classical music and from joining us in the concert halls. In Asia especially it's thrilling to see large numbers of teenagers at concerts, clutching scores and taking photographs. For the young there should be as much education, encouragement, accessibility and affordability as possible . . . but not at the expense of making our seniors feel less welcome, as if we tolerate them only because we can't attract a younger, hipper audience.

Classical music should be a great equaliser, not just socially but also between the generations. The Beethoven concerto I was playing in Canada on that occasion was written two hundred years ago; there were people in the audience who were probably approaching their own century, and the conductor and leader were both showing me photographs of their infants at the post-concert dinner. Classical music across the ages: timeless, universal, ageless.

Dumping the interval

With an art so rich and cherishable it can be frustrating to be reminded of the limits to the appeal of classical music. There have been many suggestions about how people can be encouraged to discover this treasure: better education, more creative repertoire, lower pricing, ways to counteract elitism. But what about the logistics: the time a concert begins and how long it lasts?

At some point in the early twentieth century we settled into a pattern: concerts should start in the early evening and last roughly two hours with an interval in which either to drink a glass of wine or to visit the loo. Any shorter and we invite complaints from the audience; longer and we risk complaints, as well as overtime costs, from the backstage staff. I think it would be good to reconsider this convention if we want to refresh the experience of hearing great classical music live without resorting to gimmicks.

Traditionally in the UK concerts start at 7.30 p.m. and in the USA at 8 p.m. But on a recent recital tour I did in Australia the default time was 7 p.m. In Spain and Italy concerts can be at 9 p.m. or later. The St Louis Symphony has 10.30 a.m. concerts; the Atlanta Symphony has 6 p.m. concerts, and the pianist Vladimir Horowitz in later life would play only at 4 p.m. Rock around the clock indeed.

However, one thing common to them all is the interval – the fifteen-to-twenty-minute gap between the first half and the second half. For opera or ballet this is understandable: sets need to be changed, singers and dancers need to rest, the works being performed are long and have breaks written into them. But who decreed that a concert should last roughly two hours with a gap in the middle in order for us to feel we're getting our money's worth?

I think we should consider removing the interval and starting either earlier or later than at present: sixty to eighty minutes of music, then out. It might be objected that the interval is a time to socialise. But is this really true? Isn't it rather a time to scramble to the bar and at best begin a conversation that has to be cut short as you scramble back to your seat before the second half begins? The Los Angeles Philharmonic has 'Casual Friday' concerts when the orchestra plays a shortened version of that week's programme with no interval and no on-stage dress code. When I played one of these it felt charged with an energy that the traditional concert can sometimes lack. When you play for an appreciative, concentrating audience there can be a cumulative emotional effect in the hall as you all enter the powerful world of a composer's mind and heart. An interval's descent to chit-chat can bring everyone down to earth with a bump, requiring the engines to be started up all over again.

Another possibility would be to have two shorter concerts on the same evening, like sittings in a restaurant. A seventy-minute concert at 6.30 p.m. then another one at, say, 9 p.m.? It could be an exact repeat or have a slightly altered menu. It would be possible to choose to come to both concerts, with time for a proper meal in between, or to opt for the one that works best for the audience member. Concert halls with on-site restaurants could double the number of people they feed to the advantage of all, and we could have proper conversations with our friends rather than shouting a few hasty words over the hiss of the hand-dryer.

Classical music – for everyone?

I often hear it said that classical music is for everyone but I'm not sure I agree. Before I make enemies of all my friends and enrage all my colleagues, let me explain myself and explore this idea a little further. I want every door of access to music to be flung open. I don't want one pair of ears on this planet to be denied the opportunity to experience the ecstatic world of classical music – and certainly not through social or financial exclusion.

But the problem is not really with access. In Britain our auditoriums, orchestras and festivals put on concerts for every conceivable audience group, at every time of the day, sometimes in the most unlikely venues, streamed on multiple digital platforms, at prices that are more affordable than ever. Our broadcasters constantly play and explain music with energy and wit. On the phone in my pocket right now, in a matter of seconds, I could begin to listen to just about any symphony ever recorded, free of charge, in superb sound. The sheer accessibility of music today is mind-boggling. But in the end some people will just not respond to this art form we love – and that's just fine. There's nothing wrong with them and – more important – there's nothing wrong with the music.

Education, exposure, enthusiasm all play a part in developing new audiences, and many musicians and musical organisations are tireless and passionate in their determination to do so, but listening to great music requires an effort. People understand that playing an instrument, like excelling in sport, requires years of work and dedication to reach a level of expertise. What they might not realise is that, unlike with sport, when you can crack open your fifth beer, lie on the sofa and still enjoy the Wimbledon Finals on the telly, a Mahler symphony requires utter concentration to make its impact. It explores the most complex ideas and emotions. If the work is going to make any sense, the blood, sweat and tears of the composer must trickle down to the performers . . . and to the listeners.

Classical music audiences are not and should not be passive. They are an essential part of a performance; their attention amplifies the atmosphere on stage. It's a kind of psychic soundboard for the musicians. When we invite someone to come with us to a concert it's more like asking them to *play* a game of tennis rather than to watch a match. I do think we sometimes undersell classical music, especially to young people. We invite them to climb Primrose Hill when they are ready for Ben Nevis. Young people are, and always have been, attracted by complexity and a challenge. When I was at school I remember asking the English teacher, 'Which is the hardest book to read?' *Finnegans Wake* soon formed an impressive bulge in my satchel.

Classical music might not be for everybody but it is for millions more across the world than presently attend our concerts. What if each of us asked a couple of newbies to join us next time we go? Anyone for tennis?

Poking bows and spitting mouthpieces

I'm used to my profession being thought of as a luxury, something in which to indulge after the serious business of real life has been taken care of. Politicians in Britain – left, right and centre – have nodded at the arts with respect over the years (one even conducted symphony orchestras), but usually as a sideline to the main event, a cherry on top of the cake rather than deep in the very mix of the dough.

I know I'm biased but I think learning something about the history of the arts in schools is as important as learning about the history of kings and queens and presidents. How people live their imaginative, creative lives is vital in understanding how they make their brief time on the planet meaningful.

So much for theory; what about practice? Not so much 'music appreciation' classes, but rosin on a bow, reed in a mouth, fingers on keys. Many studies are now discovering that learning a musical instrument is something positive in itself – a discipline that helps a person to acquire skills of co-ordination, concentration and perseverance. It shares these with sport, of course, but there is more. What makes playing a musical instrument worthy of special attention is that its physical and mental complexities are a springboard to something beyond the tangible or the measurable. Unlike sport, music is not about winning, or keeping fit, or promoting your town or your school; it's about celebrating, to a level approaching ecstasy, the deepest human longings. At moments of acute joy or sorrow, men and women throughout history have sung or reached for musical instruments to express the inexpressible. When minds are taut with emotion, there seems to be an inner compulsive instinct to release and harness this tension through the measured vibrations in the air that we call music.

We can learn to draw, but our relationship with Rembrandt exists across a rope inside a gallery. We might understand a book, we might mutter its more melodious words under our breath, but reading, too, is a passive engagement. But playing a musical instrument allows us to touch the cloak of Beethoven. Without our fingers on the keys, his sonatas remain mere dots on a page – a soulless, soundless, unbroken code. Music flares into life only when you or I dare to strike the match. Our libraries, our museums, are sacred temples to be preserved with all our might, but the ability to play a musical instrument allows us to create a cathedral in any room where we might bow a violin or blow an oboe.

In a period of economic difficulty or social strife the arts don't just help us to cope, they call into question the way we live our lives. What makes a society happy, fulfilled, creative, law-abiding? Few would suggest that money can do this by itself. Discovering how to spend leisure time well could be as important in the effort to reduce crime as having extra police on the streets; increasing the population of concert halls might actually help decrease the population of prisons. As Pascal put it, 'The sole cause of man's unhappiness is that he does not know how to stay quietly in his room.' Few occupations pass the solitary hours more fruitfully than the playing of a musical instrument.

Children with genius levels of musical talent will always find a way to flourish, despite opposition or deprivation. Those from families where music is already present will have countless opportunities – even if a little coercion is sometimes involved – to learn an instrument. But what about all the other children? Political leaders need to be proactive here because change will not happen by itself. The ubiquity of low culture, the inaccessibility of instruments and teachers, peer pressure, schoolwork demands, the blare and glare of technology's latest gadgets – all of these make it more difficult for children to begin studying the cello or the horn, and to persevere beyond discouragement or boredom.

The most cursory glance at a music history textbook will contradict any nonsense about classical music being for the rich or privileged in society. In fact, most of the great musicians came from modest or often even seriously disadvantaged backgrounds. It is possible to combine an unflinching demand for excellence with a passionate insistence on equality of opportunity. This should become a norm in the early years of a child's schooling: a vast youth orchestra, a finely tuned machine for social improvement and enrichment, fuelled by communal cooperation. Up to a hundred individual personalities sitting within reach of a poking bow or spitting mouthpiece, forced to put aside their egos for the sake of a greater good.

Can you be a musician and not write music?

I have often written and spoken about the issue of pianist–composers, pointing out that until the Second World War it was virtually unheard of for someone to play the piano and not to write music as well. In the nineteenth century, arriving in a town to play only someone else's compositions would have provoked a raised and not entirely approving eyebrow. Every great instrumentalist was not a great composer, but each one wrote music, published music, performed his or her own music. Learning how to compose musical notes is no more difficult than learning how to write words; it is a technique. Actually it is something that is generally required at any music college in the form of harmony and counterpoint, and it is only a small step from harmonising a Bach chorale to writing one of your own.

When you reach Act III of Wagner's opera *Die Meister-singer von Nürnburg* you realise that the contest was not about winning the prize as a singer but as a *composer* ... and, indeed, as a poet too. It is Walther's creative originality and daring that exclude him from being accepted as a Master in Act I, just as it is the same qualities, finally recognised when the walls of prejudice are dismantled, that gain him the prize and the bride in Act III. The only character in the opera who is solely a per-former is the buffoon Beckmesser, who steals someone else's song and is unable to make sense of it, mangling it to great comic effect.

I hate the piling up of obligations but I do think that music students should be required to write music. We look at other composers' notes on the page in a different way when we have struggled to write our own. If we have spent time debating where exactly to place a certain dynamic marking or how to space a chord, I think we will look at those same issues in the music we play by others in a different, more intelligent way.

To answer the question in the title above: yes! I think it's obvious that there are many great musicians who have not writ-ten music. But I'm not convinced that they couldn't have; and if they haven't, I think they should have.

Can you be a musician and not play or read music?

Now, moving the argument in a different direction, do you have to play or sing in order to call yourself a musician? I mentioned this point to a friend once and he replied instantly, 'Of course! A musician is someone who plays music.' I'm not sure it's as simple as that, and I think this realisation could change the way thousands of people attend concerts or listen to recordings.

Everything hinges on how you define the word 'musician' of course. I have come across people whom I would happily call musicians, even though they might not even be able to read music. Unlike sport, where someone who has never sweated in action could hardly be called a sportsperson, the essence of music is something invisible, intangible. The playing of notes on an instrument is only the beginning of a connection with the inner world of the sounds. I have come across people whose profound alertness to music, whose instinctive, sympathetic resonance with its inner vibrations, is so acute that they seem to me to be not only musicians but great ones. Critics, novelists, poets, painters, actors, scientists, doctors . . . and many members of an audience can fit into this category.

To define a musician as 'someone who plays or reads music' doesn't hold water. Is the ability merely to be able to play a simple scale on a recorder or strum a few stray chords on a guitar a qualification? If not, at what point would someone *become* a musician? And what about those who, through serious injury, are unable to play any more? Are they 'ex-musicians'? No! To say, 'she used to be a musician' implies to me that the person is still playing but has lost that inner understanding of the spirit behind the sound waves.

Listening to music should always be an active process, and those who attend – pregnant verb – concerts, who listen, who respond, who treasure what they hear there, *are* musicians. They are the ones who do not let music wash over them like a bubble bath but who actively swim in the water. When vibrations in the air create vibrations in your soul, you're a member of the club.

Hidden musicians, hidden talents

When I was a student at the Royal Northern College in Manchester, I took organ lessons with the wonderful Eric Chadwick – an ebullient man, rather plump, glowingly pink-cheeked, always three-piece-suited, greatly jolly . . . and vaguely sad. He was one of those people whose enormous talents had been thwarted for various reasons and then buried for various reasons, mainly through circumstance and the lottery of a career in music.

One day, as I was having my lesson on the Hradetzky organ in the Concert Hall, he said to me, 'Would you like to hear what this organ can do?'

'Oh yes, Mr Chadwick.'

I slid off the bench and stood as he took his place. He sat still for a deafeningly quiet few seconds, selected the stops he needed, and then launched into the mighty *Sonata on the 94th Psalm* by Julius Reubke . . . from memory. It was a little as if my cleaning lady had suddenly removed her overalls to reveal a tutu in which she proceeded to dance the fiendishly difficult thirty-two *fouettés* from *Swan Lake*. It was a devastating display of power, an unleashing of frustration, an explosion of temperament that I remember to this day. He finished, a little more pink-cheeked than usual, with his waistcoat ridden up above his ample belly, and smiled with his usual gentle modesty.

'It's a good instrument, some wonderful reeds.'

It had been a performance of perfection, ready for prizewinning commercial release . . . but the overalls were already back in place, the tutu concealed once more.

The world is full of hidden musicians with hidden talents. Composers whose works sit in drawers or even just in their minds, instrumentalists who can play well only when no one else is around. Apparently even the great Polish pianist Leopold Godowsky was a mere shadow of himself in public (and in recordings), revealing his genius only at small parties for a few friends. Not to mention those hundreds throughout the ages who had within them a talent to match Beethoven's but had no access to the sort of opportunity or education that could make those gifts develop. And what would it have been, toiling in the fields on a farm a thousand years ago, to burn with his inspiration, before music notation was devised?

Don't listen to recordings

I have often made the point in masterclasses that students should not listen to lots of recordings of a piece they are learning. I'm always a little horrified when I hear a student say, 'My teacher told me to learn the Chopin G minor Ballade, so I went to the library and took out eight different recordings.' To me this limits a student's horizon even before the eye has been raised to it; it closes off paths even before the putting on of shoes. (Eight different editions? Well *that's* a different story!)

Of course, it was impossible to do this until recently. A conductor learning a Beethoven symphony in 1902 had to sit down at a desk or piano and . . . learn the score. The danger now is that we've become lazy and can merely absorb other people's 'Beethoven Experience' rather than living through our own. It's much harder work to draw the map ourselves, but I'm convinced we learn more about the inner topography that way, even if the first draft can send us on a false path or two. And it's from this *study* that we can go on to have original ideas that are neither copied nor capricious. I'm sure that the frequently heard claim that many young pianists today sound the same has a lot to do with the fact that they have not been allowed the time to make mistakes, and the leisure to correct them, in their hurry to claim the first prize in this or that competition. The fruit is picked and packaged and sold (and discarded) before the ripening process is complete.

On the other hand, recordings can be an invaluable resource when it comes to hearing and understanding how musicians played in the past. This is using recordings as a substitute for attending a concert, not as a crib sheet for the piece you happen to be studying. I'm aghast when a student playing Rachmaninov's Third Concerto admits that he has never heard the composer play. I don't mean students should copy his interpretation of that particular piece but they should know his general style of playing, his habitual choice of swifter tempos, his characteristic inflections and nuances. They can ultimately reject them if they like (musical style and taste is gloriously subjective) but from choice, not ignorance.

It's important to recognise that there is an apprentice stage to be undergone in study. I don't want to hear students, who barely play any Chopin at all, emoting their way through the A flat Polonaise in an arrogant, artificial attempt to be different – wobbly eccentrics before the centric has been established. In all the arts, early discipline and rigour create healthy roots that are invaluable for future growth. A firmly dug foundation allows the buttress the liberty to fly more extravagantly later on. Individuality comes only when there is a properly formed 'individual' in the first place.

Joyce Hatto and listening blind

'Hattogate' was the musical scandal of the season when it surfaced in 2007. Joyce Hatto was a pianist who, when she was old and ill, released a mountain of recordings of everything under the sun – over a hundred discs in a few years. The problem is that they were not by her. They were by lots of other pianists, all repackaged under the name Joyce Hatto. I have no sympathy for those who created the CDs and the falsehood behind them (and I don't want to recount here the long story that unfolded) but I do have more sympathy than many for the music critics who were deceived.

A few years ago I was at a radio station to give an interview. As I walked into the booth there was piano music playing. I listened for a few seconds and then asked, 'What's that?'

'It's *you*, playing Britten's *Sonatina Romantica*.'

Not only did I not recognise the pianist, but I had no idea what the piece was either. I hope it says more about one of Britten's less successful pieces than it does about my faulty musical memory, but it illustrated to me, with a blush at the time, that we hear things in different ways when we hear them in different circumstances.

The Joyce Hatto phenomenon, as well as being a perfect 'blind listening test', proved that when we listen to music we don't listen suspended in a scientific abstraction. Yes, there should be objectivity; yes, we can be culpably prejudiced in favour of artists we know and like, and against those we don't know or don't like; but the mysterious chemistry of music is immeasurable, and the magic of a great artist is more than mere notes vibrating in the air. We seek enchantment, we crave fantasy in musical performers. They are shamans taking us to another world, into another dimension.

Hatto, for a short while considered by some a pianistic genius, will now be remembered mainly as a fake. It's a pity because it seems she was unaware of the full extent of the deception and her own fingers had made some lovely records in earlier years.

Meaning what you sing

Does it make a difference to performers if they 'believe' the words they are singing? It is an interesting question and the issues are complex. We can start with a love duet. We do not expect 'Tristan' and 'Isolde' to mean the rapturous words they sing to each other in Act II of Wagner's opera; nor do we attribute the wickedness of a character on stage to the singer or actor playing the role. Sometimes he can be booed during the curtain calls but it would be manifestly ridiculous to tip a glass of beer over his head in the bar after the greasepaint and costume have been put aside. The artifice of the theatre is something we learn to accept and celebrate.

But there are deeper implications. When Elgar's *The Dream of Gerontius* was being performed in the years immediately after its premiere, many choir members objected to being made to sing its Popish words, 'stinking of incense' as composer Charles Villiers Stanford spluttered. A phrase from Cardinal Newman's poem such as 'Mary, pray for him' was deeply offensive to many Protestants, much as singing 'I believe in God' might be to a present-day atheist. Are such choral works simply pure music with words attached to enable the music to be sung by a human voice? Would the B minor Mass of Bach or the *Te Deum* of Dvořák (works written with fervent religious faith) be just as effective with words celebrating the glories of nature rather than of its Creator? Can we sing words in a foreign language with fervour but without comprehension? The story goes (I do hope it's not true!) that John McCormack once cited Hugo Wolf's 'Herr, was trägt der Boden hier' as one of his favourite songs but then was unable to tell the interviewer what the text was about. These are all interesting questions without simple answers, but one example changes the focus.

In 1939, the Austrian composer Franz Schmidt, at the end of his life and during his final illness, wrote a cantata celebrating the glories of Nazism. His 'German Resurrection' (*Die Deutsche Auferstehung*) was left unfinished at his death and, although completed by his pupil Robert Wagner, it is never performed, has never been recorded and it is almost impossible to find any information about it. It is like a member of a family who, in deepest disgrace, has been removed from the collective memory. We do know that it ends with the words 'Wir danken unsr'em Führer! Sieg Heil', which is obviously an odious (goose) step too far in a post-Holocaust world, however fine the music might be. Fortunately, I believe, it has been possible to continue to promote performances of Schmidt's other music, especially his Fourth Symphony, which is a glorious late-Romantic work. But words do make a difference, and *singing* them makes even more of a difference.

St Augustine is quoted as having said, 'He who sings prays twice.' This attribution appears to be apocryphal but there's no doubt that music adds a dimension to the communicative power of words. And yet, conversely, I do think that someone can sing passionately of belief in the Holy Ghost in a Mass setting while being utterly convinced that all religion is ghosts and nonsense.

Old pianists

The profession of concert pianist is one of the kindest to the elderly of any in human history. At the age of seventy-five, vocation or no vocation, a Roman Catholic bishop has to submit a letter of resignation to the pope; but the seventy-five-year-old pianist can start learning that Schubert sonata he never got around to playing before, and he can make his debut with it in that city he never got around to visiting before. Indeed, many musicians have found their careers have gone roaring into sixth gear in their eighth decade.

Shura Cherkassky, who from childhood played regularly in New York, moved from a nicely full 92nd Street Y to a crammed Carnegie Hall only at the age when most of his non-pianist contemporaries were moving into nursing homes. Although Jorge Bolet had had a long and busy career playing and teaching, it was only in the final decade of his life that he suddenly found himself moving into the fast lane, with a Decca contract and major engagements. By this point, perhaps, he was not always at his best, and he did muse once to one of his friends, 'I've been playing for decades. Why only now do they want to book me?' In his nineties Mieczysław Horszowski saw his Indian summer burgeoning into blossom, and Vladimir Horowitz had a very special final few years, a late bloom after a period when illness and the medication prescribed to overcome it had blurred his brilliance.

Perhaps only conductors can last as long as pianists. Singers' voices mature late and deteriorate early; wind players lose puff and firmness of the lips; string players develop wobbly bows and curdling intonation; but pianists, admittedly often with a notch or three less on the metronome, a careful choice of repertoire, and a note left out here and there, can go on forever.

Graham Johnson, the brilliant accompanist and scholar, once quipped, 'Old accompanists do not die, they just fake away.' Many solo pianists do better than that: they remain unfaded and unfazed to the end.

Gay pianists: can you tell?

Someone (a psychologist) wrote to me once saying that he'd heard a recording of my two *Valses Enigmatiques* and 'homosexuality came to mind'. He then went to my website, looked around a bit and . . . bingo! He said that he hoped I was not offended but he was intrigued that his 'way-out hypothesis was confirmed'.

Vladimir Horowitz once said that there were three types of pianist: Jewish, gay and bad. Actually I've known some that were all three, and instantly a plethora of those who fulfil none of these categories springs to mind, but is there something that makes Horowitz, Sviatoslav Richter and Cherkassky (to choose three completely contrasting artists) different from, say, Artur Rubinstein, Emil Gilels and Rudolf Serkin? Can you tell the first three were gay? It's certainly not the old stereotype of effeminacy – Richter is one of the most physically powerful and 'unglamorous' pianists of all time. But perhaps there is an intensity, a verging towards the edge, a barely checked hysteria (Horowitz's on his sleeve, Richter's under ironclad armour) that can sometimes be a clue.

Was the earlier period of repression and illegality – the fear of policemen waiting at the dressing-room door – a reason for the loneliness you can sometimes discern in this aching turn of phrase, or that camp corner of puckishness? Is our present age's increasing acceptance of gay people going to make such discussions irrelevant in thirty years' time? The fact that each of the three pianists I've mentioned was married to a woman is significant and marks them as being from a different era.

Shura Cherkassky, the only unequivocally 'out' pianist of the three, could play with both intense sadness and riotous campness in dizzying succession in his recitals, and it's hard to imagine him being the same artist if he had been heterosexual. His marriage lasted only a couple of years and, not long after his divorce, a woman came backstage to see him after one of his concerts. He greeted her warmly: 'Very pleased to meet you, madam. Have we met before?'

'Yes, Shura. We were married.'

Leaving politics out of concerts

I'm allergic to telling anyone what to do. I respect totally those who disagree with me but I don't think a concert is the place to make a political point.

To win souls rather than arguments is an idea that appealed to me in the years when I was considering entering the priesthood. Indeed, to lose an argument in humility, in patience, through kind hesitation, might well be the way to 'listen through' to a person's soul. I feel this religious point strongly in the context of a concert. When I walk onto a stage I face and then sit in profile to a group of people the vast majority of whom are complete strangers to me – with opinions as numerous as bums on seats. I want to be friends with my audience. I don't want to preach to them or to judge them. I want us all to rise above controversy and conflict through the transcendent voice of the composers whose music is being performed. If I speak to them – and to address a captive audience about politics or religion is always in the end to preach – I will be affirmed by some and rejected by others and a wedge that cannot be removed will have been created.

To win souls rather than arguments. To make friends out of strangers with sounds. When I have done that then maybe we can speak. And maybe I shall change my mind.

Telling tails: do special clothes make a difference?

Does the wearing of special clothes change what our bodies are able to do in them? Are our professional abilities affected by how we dress? It is a vast topic, which touches on almost every area of the psychology of our incarnate lives. Clothing is part of the way we make judgements about others and thus about ourselves. From the first makeshift crown placed on one of our ancestors' heads to the peaked hat and epaulettes of the pilot who flies us from city to city, clothes symbolise expertise and authority.

It is interesting that two groups, musicians and the clergy, have been re-examining the implications of their traditional costumes in recent decades. Since the Second Vatican Council, priests and members of religious orders have changed the way they dress. Almost no nuns today still wear traditional habits, and many musicians, particularly soloists, have stopped wearing the white tie and tails that were de rigueur for so many years. Both groups now desire a greater informality and have expressed this through dress reform. But are we better musicians or priests if we wear a particular costume?

I really think I play better when I change into something special – when I drape my jeans on the back of a chair in the dressing room rather than around my hips on the piano bench. And if torn jeans were to be my choice of stage apparel then I would pull on a different pair from the ones I rolled out of bed into twelve hours earlier. Wearing something special is not an empty formality. It is a tacit acknowledgement that something special is planned. It is our wedding attire for the composer.

But it doesn't *have* to be traditional, black, evening clothes. When tails were first worn on stage everyone in the hall was dressed the same. To be at a concert in 1909, whether as a performer or as a member of the audience, was to attend a formal event requiring a traditional costume. It's a curiosity that after the First World War audiences began to dress more informally but the musicians on stage continued to be clothed like Edwardian gentlemen – minus the ticklish whiskers. Over a longer time span something similar was happening with religious orders. Widows, nurses and nuns in many parts of the world dressed similarly until the mid-twentieth century, and St Francis did not wear a 'habit' but simply gathered some beggar's rags around him held in place by a piece of dirty rope. Stylisation came later.

A piano recital is theatre. The lights dim; a nine-foot black box is illuminated; there is a hush; someone expected by an audience of thousands to be a master strides out from the mystery of darkened wings and sits down. There is a moment of silence and then sounds fill the air. I still find this sequence thrilling. The timing of its execution is related to the timing of a dancer's leap or an actor's line. It is drama reaching back to human prehistoric storytelling around a fire.

There is a place for informality in both the concert hall and in ecclesiastical life – I often talk in a fairly intimate way to the audience from the stage; but there's also a place for formality and distance, and for the dress that underlines such separation. Indeed, sometimes when I'm in the audience myself, an opening night at the ballet perhaps, if I take a little more care than usual with what I'm wearing, my experience of pleasure and of concentration is enhanced.

We are inescapably creatures of ritual, and it isn't just common decency that discourages us from capering down the street stark naked. The human being lacks natural 'feathers' of attraction, unlike the peacock, and our mating calls have no set melody. In fact, they might well sound something like: 'Darling, I've got two tickets for a piano recital this evening. Keyboard side.'

Stephen, that was really *dreadful*!

When people come backstage after a concert to greet you, they are usually diplomatic and offer words of praise, which are embarrassingly fulsome or politely restrained or mysteriously mendacious. Very occasionally, though, honest criticism is not withheld and flows forth without scruple. Someone once came back after a recital of mine and said, 'Stephen, it's amazing how you coped with that piano. It had *such* a horrible, nasty tone.' Was it a compliment or an insult? I thought the piano itself was rather lovely.

I remember a long time ago – I must have been about thirteen – playing Liszt's *Vallée d'Obermann* for some friends at home. I finished the piece, putting all of my adolescent soul into the performance, and one of the musicians there said, in a quiet voice shaking with emotion, 'Stephen, that was really *dreadful*! I've never heard such a ugly, banging sound in all my life.' I can still remember how shocked I was to hear this said in front of a group of people but our guest was probably right. It was a watershed moment for me. I blushed, spent the rest of the evening playing only the quietest music, and began a lifelong search for beauty of tone at the piano.

Backstage, immediately post-performance, is not the appropriate place for unrequested criticism. On the other hand, there are masterclasses – forums where you expect to be criticised. There's something intimate about an individual piano lesson but the vibe is completely different when you expose yourself to the stare and scrutiny of a curious, often voyeuristic audience. I've given countless public classes over the years and I'm acutely conscious of trying to pitch my comments with maximum awareness of minimising any potential embarrassment for the student. It's too easy to show off when you are 'expert' for the hour and any demonstrations you might choose to give can stop at the first sign of difficulty. I've seen famous pianists and teachers mock, deride and destroy a vulnerable young player; it's a disgusting sight. Only if a student seems completely unwilling even to try one of my suggestions – especially if they play badly – do I up the amount of spice a little in the sauce of my criticism.

I am reminded of the story of the pianist Sheldon Shkolnik (a great pianist and a dear friend of mine, who died tragically early) playing his own *Sonatina* for Darius Milhaud at Aspen many summers ago. Judging from Milhaud's own music one might expect the French composer to have been fun, light-hearted and frothy. In the flesh, however, he was apparently rather dour and humourless, scowling balefully from his wheelchair. He was rolled up to Sheldon as he played. After the first movement came the terse comment: 'Beautiful.' After the second movement, again: 'Beautiful.' But after the third movement, a change of tune: 'Cheap.' Actually Shelley said he was happy to settle for two beautifuls and one cheap from the famous man.

Stuck in a hole or building a tunnel?

Between 1813 and 1820 Beethoven went through a fallow period and often found it difficult to compose. He wrote just one string quartet (op. 95), the *Hammerklavier* and two other piano sonatas, two cello sonatas and a song cycle. Admittedly, most of these are great works and many people would be happy to have composed such a string of masterpieces in a whole lifetime, but his output during those years was sparse compared with what had preceded and what was to follow.

I don't think Beethoven was blocked in the sense of lacking inspiration, but rather that he had reached a certain classical threshold. He was up against a wall through which he was compelled to battle with enormous artistic and spiritual effort.

One of the reasons composers such as Haydn and Mozart were able to be so astonishingly prolific was that they worked in fixed forms. When Haydn sat down to write a symphony or Mozart a piano concerto the templates were already laid out on their desks. Their genius was displayed as they worked against as well as within these forms, but it was an adjustment of the pocket or lapels, not a total redesign of the suit. Beethoven was always an eccentric tailor, but by the time of the works mentioned above he was *standing* outside, not just *thinking* outside the box. You don't finish writing a sonata such as the *Hammerklavier* on Tuesday and just begin another one on Wednesday. That monumental work was the mapping-out of a new continent, not the building of a new house.

The fecund templates of the Classical era are now in museums. The works they helped produce are, thank goodness, alive and well, but simply to use their patterns today, unadapted, would be to produce mere replicas. Beethoven already realised as much during those 'fallow' periods.

Caruso's garlic breath

Perhaps it's eccentric, but I can say categorically that the recorded performances that have inspired, delighted and influenced me the most in my life have been from 78 recordings – or at least ones I have heard in LP and CD transfers. I'm often asked which pianists I like most: no hesitation in the roll call of Alfred Cortot, Ignaz Friedman, Sergei Rachmaninov, Artur Schnabel and others from this period.

I had casually heard 78s played on original machines over the years, but one magical evening in Chicago I actually operated one for the first time, spinning some of my favourite recordings on a Victor Victrola. It was a deeply moving and revelatory experience. First of all, there's no electricity involved; the machine works entirely with a wind-up mechanism and acoustic vibrations. So used are we now to everything from heating to lighting to flushing toilets being controlled with an electronic button or sensor that to have a wooden box producing (literally) vibrant music seems, ironically, as astonishing as the latest technological advance.

Not only is it non-electrical; it requires 'playing' in a way that a forefinger's stab at a CD player or slither on a smartphone's screen doesn't. I was taken through the process: first you unscrew the old needle (they last for only one or two plays – that's less than ten minutes); then you insert a new one – soft, medium or loud depending on the thickness of the metal. After that you crank the wrench about twelve times, feeling the tension mount as it tightens. Then you flick the lever that allows the turntable to begin its 78 revolutions a minute. Now you are ready to swing the heavy apparatus housing the needle over to the disc and lower it into the hissing, scratching grooves . . . and out pour the most amazing, rich, immediate sounds.

On this occasion, Caruso was simply too loud to listen to standing directly in front of the machine. It was as if his own garlic-breathed vibrato was hitting you full in the face. But beyond the clarity and volume was the realisation that the vibrations Kreisler's violin made through the horn onto the wax grooves a hundred years ago were the very same vibrations resonating in the air of Chicago in the twenty-first century. In a strange way it was a more accurate, tangible representation of that particular violinist on that particular day than anything a digital format could produce. You could almost see the strings shiver, smell the rosin clouding from the bow, feel in your gut the quivering sounds.

To hear performers on these living, breathing machines is to imagine they are in the same room – the scratches on the shellac only wrinkles in a mirror of preserved music and memory.

Punctured rolls

I want to believe in piano rolls. The idea that we can insert an object into a present-day piano and hear long-dead pianists and composers perform again as if they were in the same room is a tantalisingly attractive prospect. It has a magical aura about it. But, I'm afraid, it's a conjuring trick, or – forgive me – a confidence trick.

There's a lovely anecdote of Schnabel being approached by one of the major roll-making executives.

'This new model is state of the art! We have developed a system that allows you to capture fully *sixteen* different types of nuances and shadings!'

Schnabel, with his famously dry wit, replied, 'My dear boy, I'm afraid that will be a problem. You see, my playing has seventeen.'

Before I assume the role of the heartless uncle who is about to remove the whiskers and red cloak from Father Christmas to the tearful dismay of a gullible child, let me begin by admitting that piano rolls can be a lot of fun. Their enthusiasts are often great company, with a keen sense of history and a devoted appreciation for piano music and the legends who have played it. I had a most memorable afternoon in Sydney once at the house of Denis Condon, who probably had the largest private collection of piano rolls in the world. We took out one after another, squinting at the fading labels and threading them into his old pianolas. You could feel the floorboards shudder as their ivory keys gnashed up and down at great speed, like so many teeth. The fact that some major figures – Mahler comes to mind – made rolls but not recordings does tug with some thread of fascination. But if someone tells me they've heard Paderewski play, on a piano roll . . . well, quite simply, they haven't.

Piano rolls are about as accurate in reproducing a pianist from the past as telling the time from shadows in the park. In the simplest terms, playing the piano involves pressing down keys that activate hammers that strike strings. Dampers lift to allow the strings to vibrate – automatically as every key is struck, or deliberately if the right pedal is depressed. All of this involves countless thousands of different physical movements: the pressure from lightest to heaviest, the touch from long to short, the weight and flexibility of finger, wrist, forearm, elbow, upper arm, shoulders, upper back – in every possible combination, and with constant adjustment of inflection . . . not to mention the eight different levels at which both right and left pedals can be engaged.

Every single one of these physical actions by different parts of the body will be affected by the particular piano in front of which one sits on that particular day. Moreover, every individual piano will sound different from month to month (even sometimes from day to day) depending on the humidity, the tuning, the voicing, the regulation, the pedal adjustments and so on. When I returned to Dallas after a six-month gap to continue recording my set of Rachmaninov concertos, the piano I had used earlier was unrecognisable. I would say that virtually every movement my fingers, wrists, arms or shoulders made on every note had to be different from six months earlier in order to produce the same sounds.

The fiction of the piano roll is to believe that if Paderewski made *these* (hundreds of thousands of) movements on *this* piano on 6 July 1923, we can simply take the data and feed it into a totally different instrument and, lo and behold! Paderewski plays again. It is simply not the case.

Even if we could use the very same instrument on which he had made the original roll it would actually be a different instrument, with new strings and hammers. These deteriorate with time, and to leave them on the piano unaltered would make the instrument sound even more different due to the inevitable ravages of rust and mildew. Even on a new instrument, routine voicing, in which the hammers are needled and shaped to achieve tonal evenness, will change the sound of a note completely. It is not that the *piano* sounds different, but that the *physical actions* made by a pianist on every piano are different.

The nuances a piano roll recorded were for one piano on one day, and cannot simply be transferred to another instrument on another day and be anything but an approximation. You couldn't even take a living pianist, get him or her to play the same piece on two different pianos, and get the same performance. The fingers, feet, elbows, wrists, arms, back and shoulders will all move in a different way in a constant adjustment of reflex on every instrument in every single bar.

Imagine a robot – under supervision, of course – driving from Manchester to Liverpool. You record exactly its feet, hand and eye movements for the whole journey. You then take that robot, with the carefully recorded data, and place it into another driving seat in another car on another day. It would certainly be a journey to talk about . . . if the passenger survived.

It's interesting that pianists whose playing had less rubato – Rachmaninov and Josef Lhévinne, for example – tend to fare better on rolls than those who played with more rhythmic freedom – for instance, Paderewski and Friedman, whose piano rolls are ghastly. This has to do with the fact that rubato and sound are inextricably linked. You can't take the *timing* of a rubato and separate it from the *nuance* of a rubato and have anything other than a mess. When working at the turn of a phrase in, say, a Chopin mazurka, we are splitting hairs of inflection and colour. If that F sharp is played a millisecond later it will need a slightly different weight of sound. To hear it inadequately on a 78 recording is frustrating, but true; to hear it approximated on a piano roll (on a different piano, different hammers, different strings, different dampers, different sound-board, different rim, different keybed, different action) is a travesty based on a total fiction.

Is there too much music?

Is there too much music surrounding us? As a musician I'm supposed to love music, aren't I? Can there really be too much of such a good thing? Well, leaving aside the ubiquity of record-ings and their sheer accessibility on the phones in our pockets (another fascinating topic), what about music as background, passive, decorative, filling a gap?

Vibrations have been hitting the air since that first mighty chord, the Big Bang, but 'music' suggests an ordering of those vibrations, a choosing and cherishing. The first sound of human music would have been random, then later seized on for its utility – a war cry perhaps. But gradually the rhythm and mel-ody carrying the message would have lingered separate from the words until the gradual discovery of music's allure indepen-dent of function: the war cry becomes a war song; and, closer to home, the whisper of music's lullabies, its lilt of affection, its tug of sadness.

The problem with present-day canned music is that it returns us to music as function. Instead of the specificity of a painting it becomes mere wallpaper, subject to a decorator's whim rather than a curator's choice – music as disposable noise to cover the embarrassment of silence, like some vibrating figleaf. As a constant nibbling from dishes of sweetmeats spoils the appetite for the main feast, so the ceaseless ring of synthetic music dulls the hearing for the real thing.

Music can entertain as well as elevate, but it shouldn't anaesthetise. Schubert's greatest love song was not one of many addressed to another human but 'An die Musik', a love song for songs themselves. Music should always be special, always chosen, always an elevation of the spirit.

Relics

Pianists use new tools. The sleek, standardised pianos on most major concert stages tend to be younger than a decade – but not always.

In the middle of Montana Peter and Cathy Halstead own a vast property. Tippet Rise Art Center is a sculpture park where the creations of man and nature intermingle in breathtaking harmony. But then, in the middle of it all, a small concert hall has been constructed, inside which a mere 150 music lovers can squeeze to witness its superb acoustics and cast their eyes beyond the stage through large windows to a view of paradise.

But for the pianist there is a further delight: a storage room like some rare wine cellar. Behind its doors are four superb nine-foot Steinways, three of which were expertly, lovingly sourced or restored by the great piano tuner Tali Mahanor. There is an ornate beauty from 1897 and two exceptional present-day examples, one built in New York and one built in Hamburg. But the special treat for me is the fourth.

Vladimir Horowitz was probably the most visible and powerful pianistic symbol of the second half of the twentieth century, at least in the West. Due to bouts of nervous illness he appeared and disappeared through a long career, his highly strung neurosis both feast and famine of his creativity. In the early 1940s he was a busy performer, and when he played and recorded with orchestra in those mid-century years he used CD-18, the piano now living in Fishtail, Montana. However, this instrument is not just special as the relic of a hero; its soul sings and soars today with a penetration of tone and deftness of inflection rare in the modern piano.

In the century before the war during which CD-18 was made, there were hundreds of piano manufacturers across Europe and America. Pianos were part of every home that could afford furniture, as ubiquitous as a sofa or a sideboard. Many companies were obscure then and have disappeared since, but some rode high in the Victorian era, not least the French firm Erard who gave one of its most extravagantly decorated instruments to Queen Victoria herself. Built in 1856, it was delivered to Buckingham Palace on 30 April that year. Monkeys and cherubs caper all over its gilded, mahogany case and, unlike the Horowitz piano, it really does feel like something from another era with its shallow action and reedy timbre. On one occasion at the Palace, when I started to play a Mendelssohn 'Song without Words' on its yellowing ivory keys, it was as if a magical aura was surrounding me. It wasn't hard to imagine the queen and her consort, Prince Albert, seated at the same bench, playing a duet by candlelight or accompanying each other in song in that velvet-curtained room.

Bechstein's fall and rise

Many of us have had the experience, perhaps an early and lasting memory, of seeing in the corner of some old aunt's living room a tall, heavy, black box adorned with an army of fading photographs and which, when opened up, displayed a line of yellow keys and the mysterious, tarnished letters: C. BECHSTEIN. While the Steinway gleams on the world's most glamorous concert platforms evoking the image of a new Rolls-Royce, the Bechstein seems rather to suggest that vintage car under blankets in the garage, either sparkling with care or a sad shell of rust and dust.

From the company's foundation in 1856 in Berlin until the Second World War, the Bechstein piano played a major role in European musical life, from concert venues to the salons of patrons and socialites, from the studios of famous artists and teachers – Liszt, Debussy and Scriabin used one when composing – to the practice rooms of students. However, decline was swift following the Bechstein family's association with Hitler, and the firm's location in the divided city of Berlin during the years following the war. The disintegration of the 1940s (its factory and supplies were destroyed by Allied bombing in 1945) and the uneven workmanship of the 1950s and beyond made the piano's continuing success an impossibility. In addition, good, cheap pianos from the Far East began to appear in the showrooms of the West, and, as with cars, offered a serious challenge in price and quality to the middle-range European instruments.

Taste, too, had changed in the post-war years. Audiences and ears were becoming used to the greater brilliance and penetration of the Steinway, especially in concerto repertoire, where it seemed a better match for the string section of the orchestra, now more frequently using steel rather than gut. The Steinway was always at the forefront in the development of the piano. The company was founded in 1853 in New York by Henry Steinway and three of his sons and within two years had developed the iron frame that came to be the standard skeleton for all subsequent pianos. There followed a stream of patents including the introduction of the Capo d'Astro bar in 1875 which enabled the piano to utilise larger, more powerful hammers, resulting in a bigger sound. These developments continued into the twentieth century and gave the Steinway its trailblazing image. The Bechstein's more delicate nuances and shallower, slower action-response made it less suitable for the new virtuoso techniques that composer–pianists such as Rachmaninov and Prokofiev were developing, and the recording studios had discovered that the clearer tone of the Steinway was more suitable for their ever-improving techniques. Once music colleges and concert halls turned almost exclusively to the Steinway a virtual monopoly came into being, justified only by that piano's extraordinary quality and beauty.

Earlier in the century there was a genuine variety of opinions about the relative merits of the great piano firms. A pianist such as Horowitz would reject the Bechstein as being better suited for chamber music, and he became a loyal Steinway artist from the start of his career. He was only once seen in public playing a piano other than a Steinway, when he played Scriabin's Bechstein in Moscow, the event captured by television cameras. On the other hand, Schnabel referred to the Steinway as being 'terribly loud' and insisted on taking two Bechstein concert grands plus a technician to America on a pre-war visit. After the Nazis had come to power and he was compelled to use Steinways in America he asked for their sound and action to be doctored and made closer to the feel of his beloved Bechstein.

Comparing the playing styles of these two pianists gives an over-generalised but valid indication of the differences between their preferred pianos. Many artists whose techniques had been developed on European pianos found the Steinway a challenge. Their whole approach to tonal control and colouring relied on the horizontal motion of the hand across a feather-light key rather than the greater vertical pressure required by the weightier actions of the American instruments. Moritz Rosenthal, the renowned Liszt pupil, is an interesting case in point. One of his trademarks was fast, fleet figuration exploiting extreme soft dynamics, and he claimed that it was impossible for him to achieve his effects on the Steinway piano.

Another wider social change is relevant to the collapse of many piano companies. The whole notion of the piano as an instrument for the home, a magnet drawing friends around it for evenings of amateur entertainment, quickly disappeared after the end of the war. The piano seemed like just another relic from the Victorian age; like an old armoire, it took up too much musty space in the suburban houses of the period. Its elephantine size, its jaundiced ivories, simply couldn't compete with the stampeding arrival of that smaller box, the television, with its bright, passive images. It was so much more appealing than Aunt Maud's arthritic fingers struggling with Chaminade's *Automne*, or Uncle Harry's repeated attempts to find *The Lost Chord*. So the pianos went to the antique shops, Maud and Harry went to the nursing home, and, suddenly, a chapter of European life was finished.

The piano seemed part of the baggage of Imperialism, and the guitar's six strings and keyboards that could be plugged in (requiring more sensitive ears to be plugged as well) suited the spring-cleaning mood of the age. So unfortunately the baby was thrown out with the Bechstein, and an unswimmable gulf was formed between the professional pianist and the now passive audience member, a gulf that has deeply affected concert life over the last few decades and seriously threatens its future as audience numbers decrease steadily.

So has the piano that was 'By appointment to His Majesty, Emperor William I of Prussia' gone the way of the country he ruled? Has that black box in the corner of the drawing room become its own coffin, awaiting only the death of its owner before it is dragged to the junk shop without even the last anointing of some furniture polish?

A friend recently played me a recording: some Ravel – gorgeous playing on a gorgeous piano.

'Who is that? It's beautiful!' I exclaimed.

'It's Andrew Tyson.'

'Ah, yes. He's wonderful.'

I went over to the computer to look at the details of the recording and saw that this young American pianist had recorded it on a . . . Bechstein. The venerable piano maker is obviously up and running again and making instruments that sound better than ever.

What kind of piano do you have at home?

This is one of those questions I get asked regularly. The assumption is that we pianists will own the piano of our dreams, that we will have searched out the equivalent of a Stradivarius, found a generous sponsor or saved up to buy it, and then will spend happy hours playing rippling arpeggios up and down its pearl-white keys.

The truth is that most musicians I know have pretty rough pianos at home, not to mention the sound systems on which they listen to music (and balance their coffee cups). It's not so much a question of the cost of a great concert grand, although I found it hard to discover the current price of a nine-foot grand Steinway on the internet: 'If you have to ask, you can't afford', perhaps? It's more that I find it hard to work well on a gleaming young beast and I prefer to be hidden away in a back room somewhere with a gnarled, weather-beaten old joanna. A concert grand is . . . a *concert* piano; for me it feels too much as if I'm on stage performing. Practising is the workshop, not the showroom. Also, I don't want to own an instrument that makes every concert-hall experience a disappointment . . . unless, of course, I can take it with me on the plane.

However, it is important to spend time on a fine, responsive instrument. Much of our practising will focus on colour, nuance, voicing and pedalling, and a worm-infested upright will be limiting, frustrating and damaging. In fact, for practice, better a bad grand than a good upright as the actions of the two are completely different. For my New York apartment I confess I chose floorspace over a Steinway and have a small digital Yamaha to keep fingers limber and notes memorised. It's surprisingly good, and with the volume turned low I can work all night in the city that never sleeps.

Lonely on the road

The nomadic aspect of constantly being on the road – hotel to hotel, airport to airport, dressing room to dressing room – is no great revelation, although its lack of glamour sometimes comes as a surprise to those who imagine the carpet always red, the car windows always darkened, and the hotel room always large enough to open a battered suitcase. But one aspect of the artist's homelessness is perhaps not fully understood. Concert life brings us many friends in many places . . . until we leave for the next city. It can be bittersweet indeed, as a week spent with people you love finishes abruptly, not to be experienced again for perhaps two years or more, except by email and phone. But then you de-plane in another city, collect your baggage once more, and throw your arms around another dear friend in another familiar place. Coping with this seesawing of emotional attachment and detachment (hugs of greeting, hugs of farewell) almost requires a 'technique', a tool for maintaining mental health on tour, a holding of friends in your heart while letting go of them with your hands. It forces on us an almost monastic discipline of indifference: married to none so that we can be intimate with all.

The pianist Gina Bachauer spoke once of a train journey she made one Christmas from one concert engagement to another, along a track of endless houses, all of them aglow with lights, families, fires and festivities. She said that she felt terribly lonely as she hurtled past these fleeting glimpses of idyllic hearthside scenes, but then she found comfort in the thought of a bigger family – the audience waiting to greet her at the next town.

When I don't play the piano

A concert pianist is someone who plays the piano in concerts. So far so good, although it might be worth adding the adverb 'regularly' to that description. Someone did once tell me that his Aunt Ada was a concert pianist. 'She had a lovely touch and played to great acclaim in a concert in our church hall – *Rustles of Spring*, I think.'

Much more time is spent playing the piano hidden away at home or backstage than in front of an audience. It's the training leading up to the Wimbledon Final, the solitary punchbag months before the blood flies into the roaring crowds at the World Heavyweight Boxing Championship. But between home and the stage there are many hours when I want to work and I can't. It's one of the greatest frustrations of my touring life that, unlike other instrumentalists, I arrive at a hotel without my instrument. There's that hour before dinner or the time spent twiddling thumbs before doing an interview when I would love to twiddle all ten fingers and check through a passage in my concerto or just get loosened up after a long flight . . . and I can't.

Or the effort involved in doing so can be enormous. A piano in the hotel is the best solution, as long as it's far away from prying ears – in an abandoned ballroom for instance. If the hotel is a quick walk from the hall then that's the next best scenario although, later in the evening, there's unlikely to be someone waiting just for me at the stage door. It has to be planned in advance and it's often hard to know my plans in advance.

Then the options start to get worse, a taxi ride to a distant hall in heavy traffic, for instance. Finding the venue itself is the first hurdle, but then, how to find the stage door? I've spent many occasions circling the building, rattling rusty handles, banging my fists against flaking doors, pressing antique buzzers, shouting through glass walls, leaving messages on voicemail . . . to no avail.

Sometimes a generous patron will invite me to use his or her piano. Now I don't want to sound unappreciative of such kind offers (and sometimes it's been the beginning of a wonderful friendship) but in my experience pianos in strange homes often come with cats and their dander, or rattling photo frames or vases of trembling flowers perilously balanced on piano lids, or an impossibly high bench, or a squeaky pedal. And worst of all is the person who, leaving the door ajar, says to me, 'Oh, I love the piano. Don't mind me. I'll just be in the next room if you need anything. What are you going to practise?' Then I freeze. I simply can't work if I know someone is listening to me. It's a bit like writing when someone is looking over your shoulder. Self-consciousness makes self-expression (and self-criticism) impossible.

So for a long time I oscillated between these various unsatisfactory formats until in more recent years I just stopped trying to practise on the road at all. But then a few seasons ago I started renting an electric keyboard if I stayed in a city for more than a couple of days. It was wonderful, saving time and making time so much more fruitful. I'd turn the volume down very low and work away at any time of the day or night. In some ways it was even better than a real piano. Like a ballet dancer at the barre, in just thirty minutes I could warm up, stretch the muscles, work at a few problem bars here and there and generally keep in shape without having to leave my room. Now when I don't play the piano it's because I don't want to.

Never mind the metronome, learn to use an alarm clock

I still panic when I think of the dress rehearsal I nearly missed with the New York Philharmonic back in 2005. I had set my alarm clock that morning for seven to give myself plenty of time to have breakfast, to be at Avery Fisher Hall by nine, and to be warmed up in time for the public rehearsal at ten. The problem was that I had mistakenly set the alarm for seven *p.m.* Just before nine I woke from slumber and lazily reached for the clock to check the time. Frozen panic . . . five seconds of utter disbelief . . . then the screech of engines kicking in as I leaped out of bed.

On this occasion, adrenalin had performed the task normally required of caffeine but the haystack that greeted me in the mirror that morning could not have greeted the audience at Lincoln Center. I showered, dressed, ran down the stairs (six flights, faster than waiting for the elevator), grabbed the subway (faster and more reliable than a cab), ascended the stairs from stage door to stage level in four or five lunging leaps. It was now about 9.54 and Mr Maazel was waiting in the wings to run through the overture. The orchestra was tuning; the audience was quieting their whispering (it looked like a full house, which is around three thousand people), and fifteen minutes later I was in front of the keyboard for the flurry of octaves that begins Rachmaninov's First Concerto. Since then I've always used a 24-hour clock.

Disgrace at a concert

I was once thrown out of a concert, along with a dozen friends and fellow students, for appalling behaviour. This is what happened.

It must have been 1981 or '82 when I was at Juilliard. A group of us, having had a few drinks and being en route to a party where we expected to have a few more, had been given free tickets to see the British pianist Ronald Smith play a recital at Merkin Concert Hall on West 67th Street in New York. Merkin is not a hall where anyone can hide. Sight lines to and from the stage, and all around the 449-seat auditorium, are crystal clear, and its intimacy is part of its charm. It was a huge and difficult programme: Bach–Busoni *Chaconne*, Chopin Études op. 25, and, in the second half, Alkan's *Concerto for Solo Piano*. We all settled down in one row, already a little giggly, and began to read the hastily photocopied programme notes. They were full of amusing misprints – although Chopin's étude in '*Eixths*' is the only one that I can still remember today. So before the pianist had even entered from the wings we were already buzzing and chuckling.

Then out walked Ronald Smith, and so began the evening's downward spiral of hilarity. He was wearing something along the lines of a blue jacket, red trousers, yellow shirt, and purple tie, and he sauntered towards the piano peering at the audience through spectacle lenses the thickness of glass bricks. A bemused butler's bow, an itchy shuffle to get comfy on the piano bench, and then he raised his left hand in the air at full arm's length and simply held it there – for what seemed like about eight seconds – before bringing it crashing down on the *wrong* chord of the Bach–Busoni. It was hopeless. A snort of laughter burst forth from one of our party and the seats began to vibrate with suppressed giggles. It was not that we were laughing at his playing, which was always interesting and in places wonderful, but just that the whole occasion was infectious with humour.

Throughout the first Chopin étude he teased out inner voices, many fascinating, but others perplexing, like jolts along a bumpy road; he ended the 'Butterfly' étude with an off-beat *lederhosen* slap on his right thigh; he played the opening single notes of the 'Winter Wind' étude with only one finger, somehow managing, occasionally, to catch more than one note per digit. But, the final mirth-inducing straw, he built up to the climax of the first half of the 'Octave' étude with crimson-inducing effort, the ferocious four chords before the (long) pause like a last paean of exertion: *DA DA DA DUM*, hands flung up into the air. He had planned a long, dramatic silence in those rests, but we did not allow that to happen. Our entire row burst out into audible hysterics. It was abominable behaviour, but, by that point, it was pretty much out of our control.

After the pianist had left the stage, and before the audience had left the auditorium for the intermission, a man two rows in front of us stood up. 'Ladies and gentlemen,' – a hush ensued, and he pointed at us with an angry, trembling finger – 'these students have behaved dis*grace*fully towards this great artist and I am going to ask them to leave the hall right now.' The whole audience stared at us and started a slow hand-clap of

disapproval as we stood up sheepishly, with the utmost embarrassment, and walked out. I admire this man's courage. We had
no excuse. And the irony is that, of the countless concerts I have
attended in New York, the chance to hear the man who, with
Raymond Lewenthal, *reinvented* Alkan play Alkan is one I am
really sorry to have missed.

Most of the strokes winners, none of them good enough

Occasionally, talking backstage with someone, I've mentioned
that I was playing a piece again soon – perhaps Rachmaninov's
Third Concerto.

'Oh, but you've played that before lots of times, and you've
made a recording of it,' has come the reply, as if it were merely
a matter of a quick glance through the score, a quick tinkle
through a few of the trickier passages and then I would be ready
to walk out on to the stage to face the orchestra's two shimmering bars of D minor semiquavers before playing the brooding
melancholy theme and the thicket of notes that follow.

There is a comparison to be drawn with a sportsperson. You
wouldn't say to Roger Federer, 'What? Are you training . . .
again? But you know how to hold the racket, you've played
so many matches, you're in good physical shape.' It's true that
replaying a complex piece is not as time- or nerve-consuming
as learning it for the first time, just as the ability to hit the ball
across the net is not something a great tennis player forgets, but
I find that the effort involved from beginning to learn a piece
to being able to play it from memory is about the same as it is
from being able to play it from memory to having it really 'ready'.
Learning the teeming demisemiquavers in the central section of
the third movement of the Rachmaninov is a mighty task, but

equal to it is striving to colour, to shape, to balance, to pedal each of those notes at will. It's a point I discuss sometimes with students who have just played a piece in a public class with total accuracy and brilliance: 'Great – but that's just the foundation on which you now need to build a real performance.'

The increments of improvement in this final stage for the pianist can be minuscule and the resulting frustration immense, but I imagine it's similar for Roger as his crashing serves thunder across the net in a monotonous, numberless series during training: most of the strokes winners, none of them good enough.

Staying power

Winning a competition is not a goal; it is putting the ball on the pitch, the keys in the engine. And the resulting opportunities from that first prize can come too soon and can be a liability. 'Carnegie just *loved* your debut recital, Freda. They want you to do a series, three solo recitals and a chamber music concert. What do you wanna play?' A curse for the talented youngster who has only one and a half programmes in her fingers: refuse to play and lose the chance (and the interest of a manager), or accept and risk undoing the debut's success (and the interest of a manager).

A young conductor can be in a slightly different position. He might be invited to an orchestra, sometimes as a last-minute replacement, and make a huge impression on his first visit. The charisma is palpable, the musical ideas fresh, the personality engaging, the repartee at the pre-concert talk or post-concert reception witty and charming, the concerts an enormous critical and public success. The management is on the phone the next morning: 'We'd like to book Maestro for two weeks next season and also for a small tour.' Sometimes this is the beginning of a major career that goes from strength to strength and the rest is history. Sometimes, however, by the second week of the re-engagement, or by that concert on the road in Des Moines, everyone realises that the first impression had been superficial. This conductor had a few winning pieces in his repertoire, but not enough to sustain interest. The charm of that foreign accent is wearing off; the raised left eyebrow when he says, '*Pianissimo*, dear hearts', begins to annoy everyone as each rehearsal lumbers past. The ferocious, shaking fist at the climaxes now seems meretricious rather than thrilling. Words whisper through the unforgiving corridors of musical bitchdom and a career that had flared up quickly fizzles out even more quickly.

The Russian crescendo

I first came across the term 'Russian crescendo' when Adele Marcus, one of my teachers at the Juilliard School, mentioned it in a lesson. She had been a student of and then assistant to Josef Lhévinne, one of the greatest pianists of the twentieth century, and the example she gave was the second subject of the first movement of the Second Concerto of Lhévinne's friend and fellow student Rachmaninov.

The Russian crescendo is an expressive inflection that has the inner intention of a crescendo (getting louder) but achieves it by getting softer. In the Second Concerto theme the phrase reaches – yearns – in an arch towards the top A flat but by backing off the arrival point it is made even more poignant and expressive. By the time Rachmaninov wrote his Third Concerto he was actually notating some of these Russian crescendos as diminuendos (getting softer) to make sure we didn't miss the point. Some can be seen in the first two pages of the piece.

I think this device, which is closely related to agogic accents, comes from the human voice. A singer will take a deep breath and start to sing a long phrase, and as the breath runs out there is a natural weakening of volume but without any weakening of expressive intensity. You are more likely to find examples of this shaping in ethnic folk or popular musicians than in the classical world. Russian crescendos, like Russian aristocrats, did not fare well as the Soviet years continued and most had disappeared completely by the middle of the twentieth century.

Fickleness of feelings

People are mistaken thinking that the creative artist uses art to express what he feels at the very moment of experience. Joy and sorrow are feelings expressed retrospectively. Without any particular cause for rejoicing I can be immersed in a mood of happy creativity and, conversely, I can produce, when cheerful, a piece saturated in gloom and despair. In short, the artist leads a double life: the ordinary human one and the artistic one, and moreover, these two do not always coincide.

Alexandra Orlova,
Tchaikovsky: A Self-Portrait

Tchaikovsky writes about a number of fascinating issues here: first, it adds to the evidence about whether or not he committed suicide. (I'm convinced he didn't; see pp. 184–5.) Then it addresses the often asked question of whether a composer needs to feel sad when writing sad music or happy when writing music brimming over with joy. (All the evidence is that mood has little impact on pen hitting paper.) Furthermore, it spills over to the performer and whether he or she needs to *feel* the music in a directly emotional way during performance. An actor will tell you that the worst thing to happen in a tragic scene is to be moved to tears on stage. It is no longer possible to act the role properly or to convey the play's emotions to the audience. The actor has – literally – 'lost it'.

To continue the train of thought: does 'expressive' music always need to be played 'expressively'? When we begin to learn an instrument and to learn the grammar of music, we not only acquire a battery of conventions – phrasing, articulation, flexibility – along with all the physical aspects of technique but we learn how to please our teachers . . . and eventually our examiners and jury members. This is inevitable but dangerous. I often hear in masterclasses a student who is self-consciously being 'musical', who is shaping melodies or rubatos in a way that sounds both artificial and, ironically, wooden. It is an issue in slow movements, especially when there seems to be a fear of doing nothing. Unless we pamper every beautiful moment, often with a seductive shrug of the shoulder or a lurch of the torso, it will cease to be beautiful, or – worse – the audience/ teacher/examiner might think we are unmusical.

I remember very clearly a certain lesson with Gordon Green when I was about twelve years old. I was playing the opening of the first movement of Beethoven's Sonata op. 110 and, just as I reached the decorative arpeggios at the bottom of the first page, he stopped me.

'My dear boy, this music is not beautiful. [*Pause for a deep draw on his smouldering pipe.*] It is sublime.'

I was responding to the superficial charm of the melody instead of reaching inside the flesh and bones to the very soul of the music. It is a lesson hard to learn as a young musician because it seems as if at the very moment when we have built up an impressive arsenal of expressive trinkets we need to start getting rid of them.

In our present age the baring of inner thoughts, emotions, neuroses, opinions, has become not only acceptable but in some ways mandatory. I don't want to return to an earlier time of repressive formality – and there is a fascinating wealth of rich, confessional literature – but there is a danger when we think that everything has to 'show and tell' in order to be telling. One recorded example that illustrates this is the first forty seconds of Rachmaninov playing his Third Concerto. This is a composer and pianist who was not afraid to wear his heart prominently on his sleeve but the deeply melancholy melody is played here almost rhythmically straight (and fast) with all of the expression refined into the most extraordinary tonal shading. We know from eyewitness reports of his playing that he sat completely motionless at the keyboard. I think what can be heard in this extract is another kind of stillness: emotion utterly distilled, and more powerful, more moving, because of it.

This one's happy, this one's sad

A research paper into music therapy came up with the following observation: 'Some online music stores already tag music according to whether a piece is "happy" or "sad". Our project is refining this approach and giving it a firm scientific foundation, unlocking all kinds of possibilities and opportunities as a result.'

I found this depressing reading and a further scrap of evidence that 'classical' and 'popular' music seem to be regarded as originating on different planets. Almost every great work in the Western classical canon would miss the mark of this too easy superficial definition. In fact, the first two minutes of the slow movement of Mozart's Piano Concerto in C K. 467 moves from 'happy' to 'sad' at least four times. Its happiness is full of the shadow of the sadness from three seconds earlier, and the next bars of sadness to come are even sadder because they suggest a later return of the happiness that was so terribly sad before . . .

It's depressing not just because of the reduction of art to a simplistic denominator, but because it suggests a measuring of life itself by too easy categories. Mozart's shifting clouds in front of the sun are actually closer to most people's experience of daily existence than the pap and pep pills of some pop music. Even if listening to Mozart might not cure someone's depression, at least it honestly addresses the fact that the human mind (and its dis-ease) is complex and subtle. It is a listening ear of compassion rather than Pollyanna's empty, unflinching smile.

What music makes you cry?

Adele Marcus led me to believe that she judged the worth of a performance by whether it made her cry – or at least produced a moistening of the eye. What makes this revelation from this deeply emotional woman all the more interesting is that she singled out the cool, detached, urbane English pianist Solomon as being the one who was most likely to have this effect on her . . . and she had lived through the golden age of great pianists, hearing them all repeatedly.

What is it in music that stimulates our tear ducts? Is it the association that certain pieces have, their vibrations reaching back to childhood? Or certain performances that uniquely touch us? Or the life circumstances that might have affected the composer? Are pieces in the minor key 'sadder' than those in the major? For me, when Schubert slips into the major in the slow movement of his final piano sonata (D. 960) it melts the tragic mood into greater human heartbreak. George Steiner puzzled why he was moved in an irresistible way by Edith Piaf's rendition of 'Je ne regrette rien' – a courageous admission from a man of the most sophisticated artistic sensibility. Many people weep their way through almost everything Chopin wrote, yet my friend and record producer Andrew Keener cites the Polish master as one of the few composers who never makes him cry. And then there are tears of joy. I have experienced these in performance with the coda of Brahms's First Piano Concerto (the D major, horn sunrise after the piano cadenza) and in the final movement of Beethoven's 'Emperor' Concerto, where the composer seems to fling a hat into the air in sheer exuberance.

Can atonal music make you cry?

Can atonal music move us, touch us, awaken in us emotions of a deep, human nature? I don't mean thrill or inspire admiration (I'm excited and stimulated beyond words by many wildly atonal works from Stockhausen to Jason Eckhard) but rather reach inside us and . . . well, reduce us to tears.

I am fully aware of simplistic traps that can arise in this discussion but there are some things worth pondering. First, almost no music is completely tonal or completely atonal. Since music notation began there has been a constant tension between the two: conflict with resolution or irresolution, with concord and discord living together in fruitful harmony. In fact atonality's greatest power comes precisely from it setting up such a dialogue. Pieces that *are* purely tonal are usually insipid – white on white. Similarly, pieces that are purely atonal are ultimately colourless – dirty brown on dirty brown, all the paints in the box mired in one indistinguishable puddle.

Purely atonal music is not expressionless. It can evoke anger and restlessness, although often in a fairly monotonous, shallow way. It can evoke humour, although generally of a cynical nature. It can evoke thrilling energy, but usually the sort found driving manically in rush hour on an emptying tank of petrol rather than in climbing a craggy mountain at dawn. Pure atonality's ultimate problem is its lack of reference points. If you take away the compass of tonality; the magnetic pull is annulled. You can fight against tonality with ferocious vitality or with anguished despair – much great music does – but if you remove tonality altogether you are punching the air, and you'll find you've forgotten what you were sad about.

So, to offer one possible answer to this question: perhaps *only* atonality can move us, but *only* in the context of the tonality it is struggling against, yearning for, or working around.

Symphonies under ice

Sibelius's Fourth Symphony is not a piece you can grasp fully in one or even in twenty hearings. In fact, that's the most amazing thing about all of his great works: however many times we hear this music, everything always seems new. But the Fourth is surely the most unsettling of the symphonies: unresolved, unfulfilled, the thematic material passed between instruments without eye contact or ownership. The final, non–*coup de théâtre* is the strange, mezzo-forte, chorale-like ending, which reminds us that it can be in the ordinary, middle-ground experiences of life where lurk the most searing depression and hopelessness. The eye remains dry in this piece because the tears just cannot, will not, flow.

The Fifth Symphony, after the enigmatic twists of the Fourth, seems a much straighter if not straightforward journey. Hearing them both back to back a number of seasons ago at the Royal Festival Hall with Osmo Vänskä and the London Philharmonic – craggy, rough-hewn, elemental readings, with a moss-off-the-mountains revelation of the works' towering peaks – I was conscious of a pricking of tears in my eyes as the Fifth Symphony finished. I tried to work out what it was that made this piece so overwhelming and it struck me that it was like a symphony under ice, as if a great Romantic work were being heard from a point of inaccessibility: tunes deflected and diverted by the frozen surface, fissures forcing the counterpoint to veer off at strange tangents, climaxes narrowly averted, melodies ungraspable. The famous swinging motive in the third movement, inspired by the composer seeing a flock of sixteen majestic swans in flight, is one of those examples. Only when it gushes into C major does it openly reveal its Romantic heart, flooding over us all the more powerfully for the moment's late arrival and brief duration. Even the final hammered chords, a six-time attempt to fell the tree, are prevented from full Beethovenian triumph by the anticipation of the timpani's grace notes. The ground is not totally solid under our feet.

Clothing the naked melody

Those ascending Sibelian swans in the Fifth Symphony's third movement – that swinging 'tune' once heard never forgotten – is an example of how we carry melodies in our heads, how we hold onto music with an inner humming, even when we cannot physically sing it. It *is* possible to sing that swinging motive but if we don't hear everything else that goes along with it in the score – the harmony of the glowing thirds, the shifting bass line, the orchestration with the brazen horns – it doesn't really make any sense.

The human brain remembers music in a most curious way. We hum this Sibelius tune as we leave the concert hall (and at full force when we get into our cars to drive home) and the brain seems to supply what's missing. The music has left an aura with it, a faint imprint, which is enough for us to relive the full moment with the sketchiest of material. Try this out with something familiar and simpler than the Sibelius example – maybe a hymn tune or pop song. Somehow, without being able to *identify* the harmonies, they accompany us as we sing; they have become an inseparable part of our recall of the music.

A different kind of example of the same principle is a piece such as the First Scherzo of Chopin. The outer sections of this piece are impossible to sing as they race by at breakneck speed and are outside the range of any human voice, yet we can still hold this music in our memories, in our hearts, as if it were a singable melody. This leads me to one of the main objections I have to some contemporary music. For me, great music should be able to be 'heard' after it's stopped sounding. The vibrations that were created in the air of the concert hall or on the recording must be 'cherishable'. When we listen to music we want some element of the piece to become a part of us. It is like reading a book. If we close the pages and nothing at all remains of what we've been reading, it is not unreasonable to suggest that we've been wasting our time. Ultimately if we cannot take away an aura from music, however complex the piece or indefinable the emanation, I don't think the music is really worth anything.

Two women, two songs: in and out of harmony

I love Brazilian popular music. I love its sultry sophistication, the lazy warmth of its harmonies, and its rhythmic beat, which breathes rather than batters. The most popular of its popular songs was born just after me, in the early 1960s, and Antônio Carlos Jobim's 'Girl from Ipanema' can still turn heads as if it were written yesterday. I've always loved this song and been fascinated by its harmonies, which somehow manage to combine complexity and subtlety with instant recognition and recall. It is an example of a melody that relies entirely on its harmony for its effect. Try singing it while removing the harmony from your inner mind. Or if you're near a piano, try playing it with the harmony the simple tune would naturally suggest, G major: it is utterly banal and worthless. But slide that harmony down a whole tone to F major and make of its opening Gs and Es major ninths and sevenths and you instantly smell the sun, the sand, the sea . . . and you see this inaccessible girl walk past. *Aaaah!*

So much for the seductively gorgeous 'Girl from Ipanema', and how that song relies entirely on its harmony to make any sense at all. Another song from the same era, the Beatles' 'Eleanor Rigby', could not be more different in every aspect. Not only is this poor, lonely woman unlikely to turn any heads, but it's hard to imagine the dank waterfront of the Mersey river being more different in every respect from the sultry beach in the suburb of Rio. And musically they are totally different too. If Jobim's song is meaningless without its harmonies, 'Eleanor Rigby' is unusual in needing no harmony at all to make sense. It is almost like Gregorian chant in its melodic self-sufficiency. Indeed, its E minor tonality sounds almost modal at times. The original recording, with its famous string quartet accompaniment, is an iconic track of the period, rough and rugged with a raw honesty that is hard to find in today's digital pop-music world. Father McKenzie laid more to rest in 1966 than the tragic woman who kept her face in a jar by the door.

Is New Age thinking bad for musicians?

Reading Bishop Richard Harries's book *God Outside the Box* I was struck by the following passage:

The German novelist Hermann Hesse wrote, 'When a man tries, with the gifts bestowed on him by nature, to fulfil himself, he is doing the highest thing he can do, the only thing that has any meaning.' This sums up succinctly the dominant idea of the twentieth century. Self-expression and self-fulfilment override all other considerations. This is related to new age spirituality because although conscious adherents to that movement may be relatively small in number, our whole culture is saturated with the idea of the self and its development. [Whereas true] fulfilment in life comes from giving oneself to what is worthwhile. It comes as a by-product of doing something else. We engage in something that interests us, let us say carpentry or gardening, and as a result find fulfilment. If we simply seek fulfilment in itself, it not only eludes but is likely to destroy us.

The 'pursuit of happiness' rather than the 'pursuit of the goods that (may) lead to happiness' is perhaps the deadest dead-end street in the modern age's sprawling moral metropolis.

There's much to be said in a general sense but is there anything that applies directly to music? I think there is, yet we are hit with an immediate question: isn't 'self-expression' what the arts are all about? Well, yes and no.

I have time for only one regular student but I do give public classes all over the world, usually organised by the orchestra or promoter where I'm playing. I would hate to return to an earlier authoritarian age when being 'seen and not heard' by your elders and betters was the order of the day, but I am often amazed at the unmerited self-confidence some students display. A good, healthy self-esteem seems often to have morphed into a carefree arrogance. I remember one student playing really dreadfully for me once: everything was weak, inaccurate, coarse, chaotic. As the performance ended I wanted to say something constructive that would be kind and encouraging, and I began by making a small suggestion of interpretation to get the ball rolling. He instantly shot back, 'Yeah, well I guess there are many ways of thinking about this piece. Your point is interesting but I prefer what I'm doing.' I said nothing then and I'll say nothing now.

We need a great dollop of self-confidence to walk out onto the stage and perform, not just to overcome the nerves involved, but to believe in the vision of the music we want to convey to the audience with passionate conviction. But self-confidence has to move away from self in order to be of any real value. It should ultimately be confidence in the music to be performed, and the gaze has to be outwards: a gift for the listener that the gift we possess makes possible. If it's all about *me* then all that's left on stage is *me*. The audience might still be sitting there but the communication music seeks – thirsts for, is made for – has shrivelled to impotence.

There is no greater school for self-absorption than the recording studio. (Let no one think I'm writing this from some pedestal where I've found all the answers. I begin each recording session on a surfboard riding waves of neurosis and anxiety.) Narcissus' reflection was blurred and brief in the old days of 78 recordings – a few minutes, much hiss and scratch, a faint (if glorious) hint of the real thing. But now the mirror of the playback is clean and even magnified. Today our rivals are ourselves – preened, polished, packaged – not our colleagues. The temptation when the red light is illumined to gaze, to obsess, to fuss, to be tortured by the hope for chimeric perfection, is overwhelming. I think we can hear it in live performances too, when many artists' anxious search for pitch perfection or laser-sharp accuracy hampers their ability just to *do it*. As Bishop Harries puts it, 'If we simply seek fulfilment ['perfection'] in itself, it not only eludes but is likely to destroy us.'

We might struggle for a lifetime even to begin to achieve such an outward-looking vision, but being aware of the thinness of the alternative is perhaps a helpful first step. Sorabji forbade performances of his works; Bach freely wrote for all to hear (and sing and play). I think there's a lesson in there somewhere.

Memory clinic and Mozart

A few years before my mother died, her memory was deteriorating, so I decided to take her to visit a memory clinic in Manchester. The doctor we saw, after asking various general questions, gave her a small test. As I was sitting there I did it too, and I was horrified how, when under pressure, the simplest things are difficult to remember. What year is it? Well, that was easy, but perhaps less so than in the days of writing cheques or letters by hand, when we would write that number numberless times until the year changed. What day is it? I panicked a little and it took about three seconds of oscillating between Wednesday and Thursday before I settled on (the correct) one. Then he gave us three words to remember, which he said he would ask us about later on. My mother couldn't remember any of them five minutes later, but I managed only two – because of the anxiety involved in the whole situation.

I've only ever had one serious memory slip in my career so far – early on, in the mid-1980s, in Mozart's Concerto in C K. 467. It was with the Bournemouth Sinfonietta (of happy memory) and I was in a state of utter exhaustion from the pressures of starting a career – learning the repertoire, travelling everywhere for the first time, constant jet lag, struggling to pay bills. The moment of amnesia happened when I took a wrong turn in the recapitulation of the first movement. With a solo recital such an occurrence would not matter too much; we can usually clamber our way out somehow to the next familiar passage. But the sudden descent of harmonic pots and pans to the floor as pianist and orchestra played along in different keys was hard to ignore or sweep out of the way. I decided that the best course of action was to pretend it wasn't happening, so I played on, trying to look calm. As it was the recap, the cadenza was around the corner – the bit where the pianist plays alone – so I headed for that, tumbling around with fumbled, threadbare figuration in the C major key of the movement. Finally the conductor stopped the orchestra and looked over in a panic – was it Wednesday or Thursday? – but I simply ignored him and played along serenely and merrily until I could start my solo passage. Finally! Of course, the conductor knew where to bring the orchestra in again at the end of it, so we finished the movement together.

A woman came backstage after the performance and said to me, 'I did enjoy that, Stephen. Pity the orchestra made such a mess in the first movement.' I am utterly ashamed to admit that I . . . well, I didn't *agree* with her, but I just smiled (and looked bashfully at my shoes). The cowardice of youth. But it's reassuring sometimes to remember that forgetfulness is not just for the older generation.

My terrible audition tape

In the spring of 1983 I saw a poster on one of the Juilliard noticeboards advertising the Naumburg International Piano Competition. I was twenty-one years old and finishing up my master's degree. I had no intention of trying to embark on a performing career at that point; my plan was to enter the doctoral programme and to learn repertoire. But as the early rounds of the Naumburg were going to take place inside the school building itself, and as I had all the pieces I would need in my fingers, I thought I'd enter on a lark. My teacher, Adele Marcus, who had won the Naumburg herself in 1928, thought it was a waste of time, but I decided, not for the first time, to ignore her advice.

I needed to make an audition tape – a cassette in those far-off days. There was no easy access to a recording studio but I did have a tape with me in New York from a recital I'd given a year or so before in Salford. I was fairly pleased with that concert, even though the piano was a clangorous old Bechstein. So after brunch one lazy Sunday afternoon a duplicate was made by holding my Walkman next to another cassette recorder that was playing my playing into the open room. It was at a friend's apartment and we had to keep quiet during the process or our voices would have been heard on the tape. Actually at the end we forgot for a moment and our chit-chat was recorded after the Chopin F minor Ballade's final chords had died away. This tinny hotchpotch of a tape (there were even some small blisters of silence in the middle of the pieces) was submitted in an attempt to be accepted into the competition. As you can tell, I *really* didn't care too much about winning.

After the event I heard the full story. My tape had been rejected, of course, but along with it I had had to submit two letters of reference. One of them was from the teacher of the Piano Literature course at Juilliard, Joseph Bloch, and apparently it was extremely and unusually positive. Lucy Mann, the executive director, phoned him up.

'Jim, we've rejected Stephen Hough from the competition. We liked his playing but the tape was terrible. But you wrote him such a glowing reference.'

'Let him into the first round, Lucy, and see how he fares in a live situation.'

She did, and one September morning I was having coffee in the Juilliard cafeteria with friends.

'Stephen, don't you have the Naumburg today?' said one of them.

I looked at my watch and realised I was due on stage in less than thirty minutes.

'I'd better go,' I said, putting down my coffee cup and heading off to play.

I wasn't expecting anything but I passed through to the second round. 'That's nice,' I thought. A day or so later I was on the same stage in the Juilliard Theater. The piano felt wonderful, I was still very relaxed, and later that day I heard that I'd passed through to the finals which were being held on the main stage of Carnegie Hall.

Now the nerves began to rumble a bit, but I was so bewildered by the successful journey thus far that I was happy just to have the experience of playing in that legendary auditorium: Beethoven's op. 111 Sonata first movement; Chopin's B minor Sonata first movement, Haydn's Variations in F minor, and Prokofiev's Sixth Sonata, last movement. I played the programme and then walked off the stage to see the pianist Jeffrey Biegel standing in the wings.

'Hi, Jeff, what are you . . .'

Then I realised. He was my 'orchestra' to play the first movement of Brahms's Second Concerto. The fact that I'd forgotten that I still had this monster to play destroyed all my anxiety. Laughing internally at the absurdity of it all, I walked out with Jeff on to that immense stage. Later that evening I received the first prize, which started a longer walk onto many immense stages since. No thanks to my tape, but many thanks to Jim Bloch's letter.

Quaver or not: should orchestras use vibrato?

Let me begin by emphasising in the strongest possible terms how much admiration and gratitude I have for all of those who have investigated and uncovered principles of performance practice over the past sixty years. Finding accurate source material, learning how to read it properly, taking composers' markings to heart and hand, and looking behind the notes on the page to the historical context in which they first sounded has revolutionised the way musicians play. Performance practice covers countless topics, most of which have been written about extensively, but there's one issue I'd like to raise: orchestral string vibrato – that wiggle of the fingers on the string that produces a quiver of pitch in the note being played.

It has become commonly accepted in the twenty-first century that until the post-war period string players did not use much vibrato. The evidence for this comes almost exclusively from early recordings from the first decades of the twentieth century. There is no doubt that string sections back then did not have the same constant vibrato that we tend to hear in present-day performances. But there is a problem with taking that particular historical practice and simply copying it now. There are three other crucial differences in string playing today that have to be taken into consideration.

First, before the Second World War most players used gut rather than steel strings. A gut string has its own internal quiver due to the irregularity of the natural material, whereas steel is naturally clean and 'cold' and in need of vibrato to warm up its sound. The cellist Steven Isserlis, who usually plays on gut strings, told me about a rare occasion when he was playing on steel. A certain soft passage, which he would normally have played with no vibrato to create a haunting, eerie sound, this time, on steel strings, came across as dead, synthetic and empty. He just had to use more vibrato than he would otherwise have done. It's one thing to remove vibrato in a period instrument group such as the Orchestra of the Age of Enlightenment, but it's another matter when the entire string section of a fully modern ensemble is playing on steel strings.

Second, string players tend to play more in tune today than they did in the early decades of the twentieth century and the general standard of rank-and-file orchestral playing is higher now. As whole violin sections play with a 'purer' intonation today there is a reduction in the complexity of colour – and in the number of pitches. Twelve violins, each playing with a slightly different tuning, will simulate a vibrato.

Third, there was a time when not only was pitch less uniform in a string section, but shifting to that pitch was less cleanly executed. Portamento – that gentle, expressive slide from one note to another – was a constantly employed technique. In fact, until the 1940s it is hard to find *one* melody recorded without one of these inflections. Today things are reversed: you can listen to a whole orchestral concert without hearing one portamento.

You can't re-create one aspect of olden style in isolation: you can't wear spats on sneakers. If you are seeking 'authenticity' in Romantic music – and there are many who argue that we shouldn't try – there is a need to learn again how to inflect the notes with the dialect of the period. This involves not just a removal of vibrato but an incorporation of portamento slides, agogic accents, characteristic rubatos, appropriate instruments and appropriate tempos. Otherwise the search for true character becomes truly a caricature.

Parlour songs

I love the repertoire of sentimental songs written for home consumption in a time when every house that had a kitchen had a piano. The greatest of these made their way to the stage and recording studio and their greatest exponent, John McCormack, made a recording of the 1908 ballad 'I hear you calling me' that sold 4 million copies.

In the 1990s I recorded a CD of a lovingly chosen selection of these songs with my friend the American tenor Robert White. Entitled 'Bird Songs at Eventide', this diverse collection shares an 'Edwardian' identity, dating from the late-Victorian years when Edward VII was waiting in the wings to the decade or so following his death, when the wings themselves were a memory, having been destroyed in the Great War. We cannot make fun of these songs when we perform them or listen to them. The slightest cynical smile or amused, knowing glance will destroy their magic completely. They come from a tradition where emotions were not trivialised and so could be sung about without shame or embarrassment. Although the tears had some sugar mixed with the salt, they could still be freely shed until the adolescent 1920s made crying unfashionable. This change of fashion was not without some justification, of course: there was something distasteful in indulging in the pleasures of tragic fiction when in wardrobes across the land there hung the fading clothes of millions of men, casualties not of changing fashion but of war's insane destruction, their owners' bodies lifeless under the mud of Flanders fields.

There is a profound nostalgia and a deep-rooted conservatism in this repertoire: 'That is no country for young men!' The young leave home, whereas these songs call us home, to take shelter from the storms of change and to take refuge from the thundering race of Time. They are shy of the modern age. Rather, with respect and affection, we have to enter their world, a more naive world, which the later twentieth century tended to leave behind. If we can do this for the length of a song we can, to our surprise, discover that this world, with its poignant, searing emotions, is not so alien after all, but is, in a strange way, still our home.

Breaking the law: a short speech for the Middle Temple

Thank you so much, ladies and gentlemen. I'm delighted indeed to have been invited to become an honorary bencher of the Middle Temple. But I think you've made a terrible mistake. You see, I spend my whole life *breaking* the law. It's not that I'm ignorant of it. No, I study it carefully, and then, with relish, I disobey. In front of tens of thousands of people every year. And, worse, I encourage young people to break the law too – in my teaching, in articles, in interviews. In fact, if a student of mine *fails* to break the law, if he or she meekly obeys it, I'm afraid the marks have to be reduced.

I'm referring, of course, to the laws of music, both the man-made ones and those presented to us by nature. Let's begin with the latter: specifically, the harmonic series. When I strike a C on the keyboard of the piano you are not just hearing that isolated note but a series of sympathetic vibrations rising up from it and forming the halo of a C major chord. Tonality exists as a law of nature whether we like it or not, but the fun began as musicians started to play with those rules. To shrink the major third in that harmonic series will give us a minor chord, a darker, sadder tonality . . . and so on, through thousands of years of musical history.

Once humans began to preserve musical vibrations in written form, they created laws and structures. Pleasing sounds were codified so they could more easily be recognised and repeated. An ugly interval sung in choir in a medieval monastery became a musical 'sin' to be avoided; and the worst offender, the tritone, which came to be known as '*diabolus in musica*', was a symbol of the greatest transgression – the forbidden interval. Liszt's *Dante Sonata* opens with a whole chain of tritones. The Devil is at the very gates of his imagined Inferno.

After humans began formulating rules of melody and harmony, they started to structure the *forms* within which they would resound. By the eighteenth century sonata form became the highpoint of Western musical order. No one respected this particular legal framework more than Beethoven – most of his compositions utilise sonata form – but no one was more audacious in bending and breaking its laws.

Lawless rebellion takes on a more subtle, devious shade with performers. The composer's score is made up of dots on a page representing instructions for performance – a sort of brief, I suppose. These are meant to be, and in general are, conscientiously observed. But certain effects cannot be written down, and decisions about nuance of sound and timing require a performer to make constant judgements about appropriate licence. How far can I go within the boundaries of respect for the composer's intentions? Can I change dynamics, alter notes or even make cuts?

Without structure, without rules, music's vibrations in the air would merely buzz around as if through open windows, impossible to grasp . . . or enjoy. But ultimately law is about freedom. We restrict one thing so that another more important thing can flourish. A firm starting place is the path to fluidity and creativity for a musician.

'Life is not a rehearsal,' it has been said. No, but it *is* an improvisation. And despite the themes given to us by Nature we each have to make our own variations. That search for the perfect balance between law and freedom, rigidity and flexibility – in music and in life – is perhaps, to borrow an analogy from that famous Victorian song, a search for the Lost Chord, that harmony we will get to hear only in heaven.

The Proms

The Royal Albert Hall – that 6,ooo-seat, redbrick spaceship parked to the south of Hyde Park – is home to the greatest music festival in the world. The First and Last Nights of the BBC Proms have become the artistic bookends of London's summer life: the First Night in the shadow of Wimbledon's last serve; the Last Night as deckchairs and sunglasses are reluctantly put away, one final burst of pomp before circumstances return to normal. Most cities take it easy in the vacant vacation-time; London brings out its *pièces de résistance*, night after night.

The perennial fluidity and invention of the Proms is a constant source of wonder. Its British identity is held as firmly as a bulldog's jaw, yet it presents more international artists, orchestras and works over its two-month duration than any other festival anywhere. It keeps alive the antiquated idea that live music heard in concert might still be an exciting way to spend an evening, yet the central role of the BBC – radio, television and internet – ensures as rich a feast of broadcasting as it's possible to imagine. 'Britannia rules the waves' . . . well, the *airwaves* at least during the season. The Proms are sheer good fun but also surprising, often challenging, never snobbish. The most seasoned concertgoer will almost certainly find something he has never heard before (not counting the many world premieres), but there are enough of the great standard classics to seduce the most innocent classical music virgin.

The Proms has an important social function too. We should not take for granted music's extraordinary power to unite, that spell of solidarity when over six thousand people are moved as if by one heart. To walk onstage into such a crowd, the noise of their applause reduced to breathless silence as the concert begins, is to experience a thrill hard to describe. The tingle in an auditorium as strangers share the experience of the same vibrations in the air renders all boundaries – at least for a while – irrelevant and somehow small, as if looking down on our blue planet from the distant sky.

Classical music has a special knack for putting certain things into perspective. To listen to or play music written up to five hundred years ago and still find its voice utterly contemporary is to experience a telescoping of human experience, a direct link to the wisdom and passion of the past. And, unlike some forms of entertainment, classical music is not escapism. We don't leave behind our deepest human longings for the length of a concert; rather we explore, with the composer, the most profound part of our being. Music heals. It is an antibiotic, not a painkiller.

The Royal Albert Hall seems as if it might have been constructed especially for this festival: it can give Mahler's 'Symphony of a Thousand' space to spare and yet the faintest whisper of a chamber choir's last breath meets the ear through the silence. However, the first fifty years of the Proms actually took place in the Queen's Hall, which was situated at the end of Regent Street, until it was gutted during an air raid on 10 May 1941. The last work to be performed there, earlier on that same fateful day, was Sir Edward Elgar's *The Dream of Gerontius*. How cruelly pertinent must the Demons' screaming chorus have seemed on the following, rubble-filled morning: 'Dispossessed, Aside thrust, Chucked down, By the sheer might of a despot's will, Of a tyrant's frown.'

The Proms moved to the Royal Albert Hall in the same year, and the same composer's rousing *Pomp and Circumstance March* No. 1 is still the theme song of the Last Night. Elgar wrote it only four months after the death of Queen Victoria, in May 1901, and it was a huge success from the beginning. A. C. Benson added verse to the central section's tune, and it became virtually a second national anthem in Britain: 'Land of Hope and Glory'. The irony of these overblown words is that their swagger and jingoism came at the very point when the empire they extolled was starting to crumble. The queen was recently dead, the Boer War was at its high point, and the government's 'wider still, and wider' policy was beginning to have a whiff of hysteria about it. 'God who made thee mighty, make thee mightier yet' was an unanswerable prayer.

It all had to come to an end, and it did – shuddering, splintering, splattering in two world wars. But what remains can be celebrated without shame or embarrassment. The Victorians created so many of the things we love and take for granted today, including some of the social and political mechanisms with which their worst mistakes could later be rectified. Flags can safely wave; voices can safely roar in praise of a long-gone empire, which is now only a memory: as real as the Prince Consort's golden statue on the edge of Hyde Park; as real as the extinct German duchies of Saxe-Coburg and Gotha, which were attached to his name.

Britain's true 'hope and glory' for me is its rich artistic life. The written and spoken word has always been the jewel in the crown, but Britain also excels internationally in film, dance, architecture, fashion, the visual arts and, of course, music. And not just as exports. Arts tourism and our educational establishments are magnets attracting visitors to Britain from across the world – culture as a unifying force conquering hearts without taking possession of lands.

It is important to realise how indivisibly pan-European the world of classical music is. Not only are our British orchestras, like our football clubs, full of 'foreigners' but it would be a significant challenge to exclude European music from the repertoire of the Proms. In the world of music education it is the same. My alma mater, the Royal Northern College in Manchester, was founded by Sir Charles Hallé, born in Hagen, Germany. He also founded the orchestra that bears his name and that was made internationally famous by a conductor with an Italian father and a French mother: Sir John Barbirolli. English musical life is stitched with European threads on every seam. Take Germany or France or Italy out of British culture and we would be left with rags.

'How shall we extol thee, who are born of thee?' asks the Elgar chorus. Awkward, because even our dear Queen Elizabeth has recent ancestors who were not born here. 'Go back home,' shout the bigots. Not outside the Royal Albert Hall, please. The mustachioed consort of Victoria would have to take the next boat back to Saxe-Coburg-Saalfeld. Their son, Edward VII, at whose request Elgar wrote 'Land of Hope and Glory', was three-quarters German. Queen Victoria, through her own background and her children's marriages, is the original European Union.

We see flags wave across the Royal Albert Hall on the Last Night in joyous celebration but they are by no means just Union Jacks. Dozens of nations are represented, a rainbow fluttering across the auditorium, a visible reminder of the universal appeal of this most British of festivals and a mirror of the eclecticism of the city and country in which it takes place, not to mention the enchantment of music's wordless communication across language barriers. The confidence of a healthy patriotism doesn't need to exclude. 'Festival', via its Latin roots, is a synonym for feast, an occasion when sharing is impossible to avoid. The Proms is the ultimate classical music feast and with ticket prices cheaper than a luncheon voucher, there's no excuse not to join in the fun. It is the feeding of the six thousand on the edge of Hyde Park.

STAGE

Once more onto the stage, dear friends, once more

The great British actor Simon Callow once drew a parallel between one of the famous speeches by King Henry in *Henry V* – urging, firing up, spurring his soldiers on to victory – and aspects of being a ham actor: 'Then lend the eye a terrible aspect . . . Now set the teeth and stretch the nostril wide.' As I thought about Simon's irreverent take on this passage (and actually a commander in the army does need some of the same magnetism as an actor), I saw that it contained insights for a musical performer too.

Once more unto the breach, dear friends, once more . . .

Once more – standing in the wings, summoning up energy, focus, inspiration. The consciousness of both a pleasing familiarity with the process but also a strange sadness if those wings are far from home.

In peace there's nothing so becomes a man
As modest stillness and humility . . .

In the practice room there is calm focus, self-criticism – we pare the score down, quietly delving into the composer's mind. There is peace off-stage, far from the crowds, free from nerves, away from the broadcaster's microphones.

But when the blast of war blows in our ears . . .

When the final backstage bell rings: 'Mr Hough, this is your on-stage call.'

Then imitate the action of the tiger;
Stiffen the sinews, summon up the blood . . .

Actually you should probably try to *loosen* the sinews, but the blood is usually rushing and the heart is usually beating fast.

Disguise fair nature with hard-favour'd rage;
Then lend the eye a terrible aspect . . .

That one's for the conductor.

Overall I think this speech gives a very good sense of the sort of energy and passion involved in performing music on stage.

A taxi driver once asked me what I did for a living.

'I'm a musician – a classical pianist.'

'Oh, I love classical music; it's so relaxing,' he replied.

This is one of the worst insults to serious music. It should be stimulating, exciting, moving, touching, exhilarating, life-changing . . . but never merely relaxing. I smiled at the driver and disguised my hard-favour'd rage with fair nature, holding hard my breath.

Bored on stage

Someone wrote to me once, 'How do you guys do it? Same programme night after night without variation. How could anything remain fresh after so many repetitions? Don't those of you who perform for our pleasure feel abused by this sort of monotony? Would you have it any other way?' He was referring to recitals and the sheer number of times a concert pianist plays a particular sequence of pieces.

I think I've learned more about this aspect of performing on stage from observing and thinking about actors than I have from musicians. No solo musician has a schedule of repetition like an actor in a successful play – sometimes eight shows a week, often in the same theatre for months on end. I at least get to perform in different halls, on different pianos. But one of the skills that makes a great actor is precisely the ability to walk out from the wings, every single time, with fire in the belly – every word and movement charged with electricity. With the greatest thespian there isn't the slightest hint of routine or boredom; every step, every line is alive.

For me this issue has a certain connection with two hard-working composers: Tchaikovsky and Britten. Both used to sit down every day and write. It was not a question of waiting for inspiration; the very act of picking up the pen was the short-cut to new ideas flowing from that pen. As performers we can't even allow for the *possibility* that the pieces to be played that evening might not be fresh. We walk to the piano as if to a liturgy. The music is there – all that remains is for us to be 'there' too. Of course, we can be physically or mentally tired, or even ill, and this can affect the *quality* of the performance, but it shouldn't really affect the *intention* of the performance. I've heard seventeen-year-olds sound jaded with a piece they've just learned, and seventy-year-olds bursting with fresh ideas about music they've played their whole lives.

Neurotic on stage

So much for maintaining inspiration when repeating the same repertoire many times; what about maintaining *sanity* in the same circumstances? What are some other factors to consider about playing music that is extremely familiar to us? Before looking at the mental health issue, here is a question and an assumption.

The question

In an interview once a journalist asked me if I felt differently about playing a familiar piece on stage than one that was unknown, and whether it affected the way I approached the performance. It was in reference to Mozart's Concerto in C κ. 467. It struck me, as I was about to answer, that every piece I play is equally familiar because I've spent the same amount of time working on each one of them. I know the obscure Saint-Saëns Third as well as the familiar Rachmaninov Third. I've certainly spent enough hours working on both! So I don't really feel I would approach one differently from the other.

The assumption

Then there is the assumption that an often performed piece is forever in the brain and fingers. Something that's difficult to do does not automatically become easy the more we do it. Witness the pocketing of that black snooker ball for the 10,000th time. Sometimes it can get more difficult, and here we encounter the neurosis of my heading.

With familiar pieces one has always to guard against both distraction and obsession. *Distraction*, because some passages become so much part of our motor memory that the notes tumble past via the reflexes without properly engaging the mind. Then if the focus changes for some reason, we can come totally unstuck. *Obsession*, because certain passages become feared over time, especially if they've caused a problem in the past. We can get a mental block about them, and then minutes before they arrive a certain panic arises. (Don't ask me to tell you which mine are.) Some people get a hang-up about a specific technique. They believe they can't play octaves, for instance, so every time a passage in octaves appears they expect to fall on their faces – and therefore they often do. Then there are the silly mind games performers can play with themselves on occasions. 'I'll bet the audience thinks I'm really involved in this passage, but actually I'm deciding whether to eat risotto or pasta afterwards.' 'What *was* the fee for this concert? Is that *before* VAT?' And so on. Overcoming psychological hurdles in concert life requires the same kind of willpower and discipline as not allowing oneself the possibility of being bored . . . and it is a lifelong challenge.

Nervous on stage

Maybe being bored or neurotic on stage has not crossed the minds of those who attend rather than give concerts. But being nervous – the paralysis in the wings, the butterflies in the stomach, the trembling leg, the thumping heart – is something anyone who has done anything in public can appreciate, whether it was that fumbled speech as best man at your sister's wedding or the Nativity play at school long ago when you feared dropping the frankincense. It all boils down to 'What will people think?' – that insatiable need for approval and admiration that reaches back to our childhoods and threatens to dominate our entire conscious lives.

For some, performance anxiety is a paralysis, either of the very ability to play or at least of the ability to 'play' – a carefree verb suggesting freedom, joy, exuberance, euphoria. But being onstage is, after all, an exposure to judgement, and one that we have initiated. In superficial terms, to have a career is to be better than others, or at least to be chosen over others on that particular occasion, a form of survival. Concert artists are always in a state of audition or examination. 'You're only as good as your last concert' is a malevolent taunt lurking at the back of our anxious minds, and no career is so firmly in place that the public's eye cannot tire and glance elsewhere. For an orchestral player the possibility of that split note is a daily 'interview' on which continued employment hinges. Is it any wonder that the name Richard Strauss strikes fear into the hardiest horn player's soul?

The pianist Egon Petri said that we would never be nervous if we were humble. One alternative to such Franciscan (or perhaps Puritan) self-awareness might be to have such utter self-confidence that the thought of failing does not even arise. A student I knew, when I was a student, apparently stood in front of a mirror before his concerto debut and repeated, mantra-like, 'You are the greatest pianist in the world; you are the greatest pianist in the world.' On occasion I have been so nervous that my doubts were raised more by the word 'pianist' than by the word 'greatest', although my experience of nerves on stage is generally found somewhere in between – a constant oscillation between sitting confidently on top of the horse, and the fear that the saddle is about to become dislodged.

Vladimir Horowitz used to say to himself, 'I know my pieces.' A good start to a rational assessment of the risks at hand. Unless we are incompetent at what we are meant to be doing onstage (and know it) the presence of anxiety is, strictly speaking, illogical. Another strategy, which was found effective by another pianist, was to imagine the entire audience naked. Perhaps a philosophical thought will help: five hundred years ago none of this existed, none of the music, the instruments, the concert halls . . . the critics. And five hundred years hence what is here now will probably have disappeared too. That speck of dust, *me*, on a planet that is itself a speck of dust. These are all ways to 'trick' the mind into relaxing and undermine the need to seek the approval of an audience.

Back to humility, and to a curious character with much power and influence in the Catholic Church at the beginning of the twentieth century, Cardinal Merry Del Val or, for the sake of completeness, Rafael María José Pedro Francisco Borja Domingo Gerardo de la Santísma Trinidad Merry del Val y Zulueta. Despite the aristocratic string of Latinate names (he was actually born in London) and despite a public career notorious for pulling puppet strings of powerful political reaction behind the scenes, he was by most accounts (when behind the scenes) a simple, humble man. A musician too. He wrote a prayer that someone sent me years ago, and which he was accustomed to recite every day after Holy Communion. Here are some extracts:

From the desire of being praised, deliver me, O Jesus.
From the desire of being preferred to others, deliver me,
    O Jesus.
From the fear of being humiliated, deliver me, O Jesus.
From the fear of being forgotten, deliver me, O Jesus.
That others may be chosen and I set aside, O Jesus, grant
    me the grace to desire it.
That others may be praised and I unnoticed, O Jesus, grant
    me the grace to desire it.

And, the final sting for a man who almost became pope in 1914:

That others may become holier than I, provided that I may
    become as holy as I should,
O Jesus, grant me the grace to desire it.

I once showed this prayer to a fellow pianist, and his response was: 'Well, if I could say that with conviction, I'd never care about anything, certainly not playing in front of an audience.' Another musician's response, half (but only half) in jest was: 'But if I really desired such humility, what would be the reason for going onto the stage in the first place?'

But what if we could actually *embrace* our nervousness? There are risks to being on stage of course, but dropped notes are not broken bones, a memory lapse is not a tumble to the ground. Most performers actually need a whiff of danger to be at their best, and the unpredictability of a live concert is part of its allure for the audience. Knowing that, if we're properly prepared, performance anxiety is a phantom of our imagination could actually serve as an injection of bravura, a challenge to the demons within, resulting in greater energy and concentration. I don't think any musician, unlike a trapeze artist, strikes the wires of a piano or draws a bow across a violin's strings primarily for the kick of an adrenalin fix but if 'ecstasy' means to stand outside ourselves, then what better ambition can there be as we stand in the wings of a concert hall than to leave self-obsession behind and take the audience on a journey across the high wire of Beethoven or the flying trapeze of Liszt.

Take a deep breath

So much for being nervous on stage – its psychological background and some psychological tricks to cure it. I discovered something extremely important recently: there can be a physical aspect to nervousness too. On those occasions when my nerves in performance have been greater than usual I had actually stopped breathing.

It seems very obvious but I hadn't really been conscious of it. Sometimes the passages in the pieces that had caused the nerves were physically demanding, setting up a vicious cycle: I would stop breathing, then I would start to get light-headed, making me a little panicky, which would make me more nervous, and so on. I can look back over years of concerts and remember specific instances when I have not played my best for this precise reason.

It's not just a matter of taking in a deep breath. It's exhaling that matters even more. The body will usually inhale as a reflex if we can concentrate on breathing out, which in turn is a metaphor for letting go – of anxiety, of nerves. Who would have thought that playing the piano involved not just the hands, wrists, arms, shoulders, back (and brain) . . . but the lungs too.

Routine on a concert day

A friend asked me recently what my routine is for eating and sleeping on the day of a concert. I remember reading Alfred Cortot's remark that, on tour, a good digestion and the ability to sleep were far more important than practising. How right he was. Once the suitcase is packed and the taxi is at the door, there's not much that can be done about the pieces due for imminent performance; if they are not packed in the brain and fingers by that point they never will be. But what is really important, and what must be attended to, is the mental and physical health necessary to hit the road.

Every concert day is slightly different. First of all, there are solo recitals, concerts when the responsibility lies on one pair of shoulders. If I've been in the city since the previous day, my ideal scenario is to work from around ten o'clock to one on the concert instrument. Gentle, unemotional practice, but not necessarily of the pieces I will be playing that evening. Then a substantial lunch (sushi is a favourite); then a walk where the spirit can soar, a park or a museum or a cityscape. After that a nap as if at nighttime – curtains fully closed, phones off, pillows fluffed – from about four. Around six, or two hours before the start of the concert, I get up and put on the kettle (I travel with one) and make a cup of good, strong tea. Then into the shower, dress and over to the hall to warm up backstage if there's a piano, or a drumming of cold, stiff fingers on a table top if there isn't. The lack of a dressing-room piano is the curse of a pianist. Then into concert clothes about ten minutes before I'm due onstage.

Orchestral concert days are quite different. Unless it's a tour – a different city every night with the same orchestra and repertoire – one fairly typical pattern is: arrive in the city on a Tuesday evening; main rehearsal either morning or afternoon on the Wednesday; dress rehearsal on the Thursday morning; concerts Thursday, Friday and Saturday evenings; leave town on the Sunday morning. The Fridays and Saturdays in this pattern are similar to a recital day. Of course, all sorts of things can change this arrangement: the matinee performance (anywhere between 10.30 a.m. and 4 p.m.); radio or press interviews; a sponsors' lunch; post-concert receptions; a masterclass at the local (or not so local) university . . . the list is long. And these are the ideal days, without the delayed flights, the fire alarms in the middle of the night, the unavailable (or unplayable) pianos, the nightclubs in the throbbing basement of the hotel at two in the morning, the malfunctioning bathrooms, the non-appearance of taxis. But just one anecdote for now: the broken zip on my concert trousers, which I discovered too late to mend. Yes, I played Brahms's Second Piano Concerto at the BBC Proms with only a safety pin preventing the audience from seeing the colour of my underpants.

Flying glasses

I now wear contact lenses most of my waking hours. It all started at the Juilliard School with a student recital I gave there at Paul Hall in 1982. I was wearing my usual nerdy glasses and working up a sweat in the last movement of Prokofiev's Sixth Sonata. The last furious page tore along to the concluding, hammering chords: *da-da-da-da-da-da-da-da-DA*! I flung my head back on the last '*DA*' and my glasses flew off my head, landing on the floor about ten feet behind me. It was a gesture that could never have been planned, a perfect moment of extra-musical drama . . . except that, after a few blind bows, I had to get down on my hands and knees, and crawl along the stage in search of them. I quickly located them, shakily threaded them into place behind ears and on nose, and got up to walk off the stage to a mixture of applause and roars of laughter. Then I realised that there was only one lens in the frame, the other had popped out with the impact. So my first curtain call began with me bending down yet again to reclaim the missing but thank-fully intact glass.

There was no repeating that humiliation. I had to get myself some contact lenses, and what a tremendous liberation they have been while playing the piano. No more steaming up or slipping down . . . or shooting back.

Page-turning: part of the performance

I made a journalist laugh once when I said that page-turning was a part of the performance. My point was that every phys-ical act done on stage has dramatic significance. Playing a con-cert is theatre. It's one of the reasons we usually wear different clothes when performing. It's part of an attempt to emphasise that a concert should never be routine. Music lifts us out of our regular state of mind; it takes us to an ecstatic state.

Consider, say, the slow movement of Schubert's B flat Sonata. If you raise your hands to the keyboard in a swift, jerky move-ment, you've ruined the music before it begins. The few seconds before the first hammer touches the first string are the moments of silence out of which music is born, the breath before the word is spoken. I dislike artificial movements at the piano but the body language required in this instance is a physical manifestation of an internal collection of thought and intention, a concentration that should cast a spell. And a hurried lunge at the score on the music desk by a thoughtless page-turner during a moment of musical repose and contemplation is a shattering discord, almost as painful as a fistful of wrong notes from the pianist.

As the page turns . . . or not

At the time of writing, for some strange reason of custom and historical precedent, it is still as expected for a pianist to use the score for chamber music as it is expected for him or her *not* to use the score for solo repertoire. So when we play an ensemble piece, unless we are adept with iPad and foot pedal, we need to use page-turners because a hasty, unaccompanied, tearing across of the page while faking the last left-hand arpeggio in a blur of pedal is not ideal. Although sometimes, with a photo-copier and a skilful use of Sellotape, a compromise can be made: a score can be patched together with enough space for stealthy, silent turns during the rests.

Most piano quintet performances, for instance, involve six people walking out on to the stage: five with or towards their instruments, and one carrying the score, trying to look as invis-ible as possible, making a beeline for the chair on the left of the keyboard, anxious not to be seen to be acknowledging the applause, adjusting the position of the seat far enough away from the keyboard to avoid a collision, but close enough to be able to see the score and to stand up to turn the page in time. To stand up to turn the page in time . . .

I remember a concert in St Wilfred's Church in Grappen-hall, Cheshire, with the cellist Steven Isserlis – with whom I have used more page-turners than anyone else. We were open-ing with Schumann's *Five Pieces in Folkstyle* op. 102 and a composer friend of mine, Stephen Reynolds, was sitting on my left, ready to turn the pages. Or at least, that's what I thought he was going to do. At the bottom of the first page of the first piece in the first minute of this full-length recital it seemed that something was wrong. I didn't sense his anticipation – that flexing of right arm, forefinger and thumb pinched and ready, buttocks inching to the edge of the seat, all poised for a calm elevation in the direction of the music desk. Out of the corner of my left eye I could see that he seemed to be enjoying one of the splendid stained-glass windows glowing serenely in the evening light. Four bars to go, three bars to go, two bars to go, one bar . . . Panicking, I was just about to turn my own page when I felt a flash of energy. He leapt up and ripped the page over, sending the music (and almost himself) flying – off the desk – back onto the desk – cockeyed – straightened out – flattened down – pushed to the right . . . and then he sat down again, in a terrible fluster. The thought popped into my mind that every page of the concert might be like this (there were about a hundred more to go) and the slapstick burlesque of that possibility made me burst into silent giggles. Two minutes into the concert and I was shaking with laughter, my arms weak, my eyes blurring over. Steven was playing away but, noticing that my robust forte had fizzled out to a wimpy piano, he turned around to see what was going on. His lips twitched as he was about to lose it too but we were both nervous enough at that early stage of the recital to pull ourselves together, and Stephen (with a 'ph', but not the pianist) got the hang of it by page 2.

There was another occasion with another composer friend turning pages. One of my first recordings, released in the US as *My Favorite Things* and in the rest of the world as *The Piano Album I*, was recorded at the 92nd Street Y in New York. Lowell Liebermann agreed to come along and listen, as well as to turn pages for a couple of pieces where I had decided to use the score. One in particular was the Mélodie in E minor by Ossip Gabrilowitsch. It's a tender and rather serious piece, but for some reason Lowell and I had been on the edge of a giggling fit for at least half an hour before we came to record that track. I hope it won't spoil it for any potential listeners to know that during that entire piece (I think there were three or four takes) we were both in *stitches* of laughter with Lowell ending up rolling on the stage of the Y after he'd turned and as I played the last page. If the final bar's rest seems *slightly* shorter than it might be, it is because, although both of us burst out into snorting fits of laughter as the melancholy E minor tonality shed its last tear of regret, the producer was just able to save the take by fading out a little early.

There was another memorable occasion when Lowell was turning pages for me, but this time it was more bemusing than amusing. I was going to record the two Brahms clarinet sonatas with Benny Goodman. It was the last year of his life and, sadly, he died before the recording sessions could take place. In fact, he had seemed quite ill when we were rehearsing, and at the try-out concert in New York's Century Club things did not improve. We started the E flat Sonata and it was extremely shaky. Then Benny stopped mid-flow and asked for a window to be opened as he felt breathless. After a minute or so we started again, but neither Lowell nor I knew quite where he was in the score. He would play his bit and then, instead of waiting for my solo bars, just skip to the next clarinet passage. It was a bit like chasing after a hat that the wind was blowing down the street. I'd have to jump ahead, guessing where he was, and my page-turner would have to try to find the place too. It was a hair-raising performance and, at the end, Benny made a little speech: 'Ladies and gentlemen, I'm sure you want to join me in thanking my pianist for this evening – Mr Stanley Gruff.'

The musical page-turner

The relationship with a (human) page-turner for the two-hour length of a concert is something quite intimate. Not only is one's musical life in their hands, but their physical proximity is quite close, and the chances of direct and indirect interference are plentiful. After all, the armpit of a page-turner and the nostrils of a pianist are never more than six inches apart at those crucial moments when the latter's musical attention needs to continue seamlessly overleaf. Slightly less unseemly than such an olfactory assault are the billowing, dizzying wafts of, say, Guerlain's Shalimar which can cause a momentary trance as they emanate from a diaphanous frock on the loose. I have had a turner who appeared to look on her role as an opportunity for open flirtation, as dress, necklace, bracelets and breasts all hung in an ensemble of (attempted but unsuccessful) seduction.

But during one recording session, when George Tsontakis's masterpiece *Ghost Variations* was on the bill, a body part of the page-turner was crucial and welcomed . . . her ears! In the control room we had a great engineer, a great producer, and the great composer himself. And, at the piano, someone who had studied the piece for over a year with love and total dedication. At one point when I stopped playing there was a moment of silence. The young student who was turning pages said to me, quietly, modestly, tentatively, 'Excuse me . . . shouldn't that note be an F natural not an F sharp?' She was right, and no one else had noticed.

A crucial tip when playing with the score

Playing chamber music with the score, unless you use an iPad, means using a music desk. This involves something seldom thought about, even by pianists themselves, but it's something of surprising importance.

When the music desk on a modern piano is fully erect you have an inch-thick piece of wood blocking the sound from the ear of the pianist. Try it sometime. Play first with the desk up, then with it down: it makes an enormous difference. But when playing with a cellist (or a seated string quartet) it is even more significant because it blocks their sound as well – a wooden barrier affecting not only the way the pianist creates colours but also the balance between instruments. As a simple rule you will play (or speak) more loudly than you realise if you can't hear yourself properly.

The solution is to have the music desk at an angle so that your ears are above the wood-line but you (and your page-turner) can still see the score. On newer instruments there is usually a setting for the desk to rest like this, but in the past I've had to resort to using clamps from a woodwork shop to create this lower setting.

In the past our more decorative ancestors unwittingly had a solution to this problem. Their elaborately carved desks had enough holes in them to let the sound float through. If your aunt is old enough and she still has her Bechstein baby grand from 1892 you will probably recall seeing this. Of course, it was a nightmare to dust . . .

As far as I know, only the magnificent Australian piano from Stuart & Sons maintains this design feature or, for that matter, maintains the finish of real wood rather than the polyester, acrylic finish we usually see gleaming on our concert platforms. What about it, Messrs Steinway, Yamaha, Fazioli?

Out of the cockpit

A composer sitting in the audience while his music is being performed may be central to the occasion, yet he has absolutely no control of it himself. Most of the time when I'm involved in a concert it is on stage – fingers on keys, body in direct connection with the instrument, eyes in contact with the musicians and conductor. A soloist is always in the cockpit, even if occasionally I have been forced to be a co-pilot on the journey. But as a composer, once the rehearsals are over, everything is out of my hands. It's exhilarating to hear people play music to which one has given birth, but it's not always plain sailing in the nursery.

I once sat with a composer friend of mine at a premiere of a work of his that was so badly played I could sense him sliding into his seat in embarrassment. The air was thick with dismay and I was sharing in it. 'Well, at least you can have another first performance of the piece because tonight we didn't hear the piece you wrote,' I suggested, by way of consolation.

Another composer friend told me about a performance when the solo pianist insisted on playing his piece from memory. 'Maybe it would be better to use the score. No one will mind,' suggested my friend gently, his attempt at tact bubbling underneath with panic.

'Oh no, I know the piece. Much better to play from memory.'

You've guessed it. In the performance the pianist got totally lost in one section and began making it up, ribbons of the wildest rubbish, a cacophony of banality, for what seemed to the composer like minutes. The piece ended and the composer had to acknowledge the audience's polite applause with an equally polite bow.

Humiliation and vomiting at the keyboard

Wayne Koestenbaum's book *Humiliation* was delicious. The tiny chapters are bite-sized dishes (in more than one sense) and all is a-sparkle with wit and insight – sometimes lyrical, sometimes brutal, never dull.

At one point, about a third of the way in, my teacher Adele Marcus makes an unnamed cameo appearance. The story goes that she was so overcome by nerves just after the Schumann Concerto's opening whiplash orchestral E and the piano's zigzagging chords, which simply beg to be smudged, that she vomited onto the keyboard. The author says this took place in London, I had always thought it was in Aspen, but the story has been repeated too many times for it not to be true. The author observes, 'Vomit on the keyboard – that image symbolises, for me, the always possible danger of the body speaking up for its own rights, against the stringent demands of the mind's wish to construct a plausible, attractive, laudable self for other people to admire.'

Wrong notes can be part of the acceptable rough and tumble of a romantic interpretation. They can even seem daring and exciting and carefree. But stopping . . . forgetting . . . blanking: this is the ultimate humiliation in a public space, in front of an audience. Actually I think that Adele Marcus was most likely afraid of *forgetting* in the Schumann, not just of striking false notes or misjudging phrasing or pedalling.

The requirement for pianists to play everything from memory has probably called a halt to many careers that would otherwise have flourished. From the first time we have to play in front of our fellow students at the earliest age we face the roulette of public performance: adulation = red squares; humiliation = black squares. And at the end of the evening it is the pianist's ability to *remember* the notes, that would appear to take him or her to the cashier with a light tread and heavy pockets . . . or the other way round.

Nothing that makes a performance great has anything to do with memory – except remembering to be at the hall in time to play the concert.

Stage fright and playing from memory

We have Liszt to thank for the unwritten but firmly held rule that the pianist must play that recital without a score. Chopin would not have approved; he chastised a pupil once for playing a piece from memory, accusing him of arrogance. In the days when every pianist was also a composer, to play without a score would usually have meant that you were improvising. Playing a Chopin ballade from memory might look as if you were trying to pass off that masterpiece as your own. No wonder Chopin went on the attack. But from the late nineteenth century onwards, as non-composing pianists gradually became the norm, using a score implied that you didn't know the piece properly and began to suggest a lack of professionalism.

It is a rich topic of many facets and people defend both sides of the argument passionately. What is for sure is that there have been pianists, maybe of transcendental gifts, who have failed to have careers because they felt ill at ease without a score. One of the most common comments I hear from audience members after a concert is 'How on earth do you remember all those notes?' It is well meant, and not really a question but a sigh of perplexed admiration, but is memory really that impressive? Is it an essential part of the pianist's toolkit? Does it have an artistic dimension or is it more like sight-reading – a skill of no particular musical relevance. Some artists can sight-read anything but have nothing to say about the music that races past under their accurate fingers; others (famously Josef Hofmann) cannot sight-read at all. Some learn quickly and others (famously Dinu Lipatti) take a long time to digest a new work.

Some arguments for using the score

1. It takes away the fear of forgetting, liberating the mind to concentrate on the music itself.
2. It enables the player to play what's really there – to examine anew the message left in code by the composer. There is a parallel with a monk who, even if he knows the Psalter by heart, will still read it from the Breviary. It is a humble acknowledgement that life is too short to know a complex text completely.
3. It allows for greater variety of repertoire. One of the reasons Sviatoslav Richter began playing from the score in older age was that it enabled him to play a greater number of pieces. There is no question that, unless your memory is freakish, you will not be able to play all the pieces you would like to if they all have to be memorised.
4. It makes the act of playing totally focused on the music being produced, not on the skill (or not) of remembering. In certain works we have to find tricks to distinguish slight differences of phrasing or note patterns – often abstract issues having nothing to do with the content of the music.
5. The fear of forgetting influences repertoire choices. I'm sure that Fauré's glorious piano pieces fail to appear as regularly as they should on concert programmes because they are so difficult to memorise.

Some arguments against using the score

1. It takes away the total physical freedom of simply walking onto the stage, sitting down and playing. Now that pianists usually play other people's music (and no one pretends that the Schumann *Fantasie* is a newly composed work) we do actually want it to seem as if something is being created on the spot. It's part of what makes hearing familiar music seem fresh.

2. It risks someone playing something that is not properly prepared. When we memorise something we have to learn it 101 per cent. If we can sight-read well and the notes are not complicated, there's always the danger of presenting something half-baked to an audience.

3. It spoils the theatrical event like a script in an actor's hand. Performing on stage is not just about what we are hearing, but about what we are seeing. There's no question that someone seated at a 9-foot concert grand, playing a ferociously difficult piece with no score in front of him is an impressive sight.

4. There are many practical negatives involved: insufficient light to see the pages; the need for a page turner (or electrical device); the inability actually to look at the score during an awkward passage where the eyes are required to guide the fingers on the keys; the visual distraction for the audience of as many as two hundred page turns in an evening's performance; the sound-blockage of the music desk.

There are many issues involved in nervousness in front of an audience, not just memory, but if you get a performer talking in a rare moment of complete honesty one of the principal reasons you will hear over and over again for stage fright is the fear of forgetting. The terror of suddenly not knowing where you are, an obvious wrong entry, that blackout, the orchestra and you in a train wreck of harmonic collision and confusion. It is one of the reasons some pianists start to conduct; it is one of the reasons others choose to focus on chamber music when the use of a score is acceptable; it is one of the reasons still others go into early retirement and start to teach; it is one of the reasons some artists play the same repertoire season after season; and I often wonder whether Glenn Gould's premature move away from the concert stage to the recording studio had something to do with a gradually failing memory. Ironically it might have been one of the reasons Liszt himself retired from active concert life. There is a letter dated December 1855 in which he replies to a request from the mayor of Vienna to play at his Mozart Festival:

> I have nevertheless a request to make – that you would be kind enough to excuse me from the performance of the Mozart Concerto which has been so graciously planned for me, and that this piece may be given to another notable pianist. Apart from the fact that for more than eight years I have not made any public appearances as a pianist – and many considerations encourage me to cling firmly to this negative resolve – the fact that my complete attention as director of the festival will be required may prove, in this case, to be my sufficient excuse.

I think all pianists need to learn how to memorise and to play from memory. To go through music college and always use the score seems to me to be missing an essential part of the formation process. Memorising is part of the discipline of learning the instrument and learning the music written for it. But I do think there comes a point (and not just in extreme old age) when we should feel free to play with a score without censure or comment. The only guideline should be the quality of the interpretation.

The only time (to date) I use a score, apart from chamber music, is to play my own music. Well, I wouldn't want people to think I was improvising, would I!

Bad self-consciousness as the death of good self-confidence

People often complain that modern recordings and performances are less convincing, less exciting, less moving, than those of an earlier generation. Singers, pianists, conductors – there seems to be a freshness in earlier generations that is often lacking today. It's a dangerous argument and our preferences can be the result of a nostalgic longing for the crackle of a 78 record or the Brilliantine in a sepia photograph, but there is *something* about this point that strikes me as true.

I once happened to see a video from 1946 of Tito Gobbi as Tonio in Leoncavallo's *I Pagliacci* and it started me thinking about this topic again. For all of the art (and artfulness) of this extraordinary clip, it struck me as completely devoid of self-consciousness – the sort of looking inwards to assess quality as the performance progresses or, worse, to have an eye to the assessment of quality the audience might be making. He . . . *sings*. Out of the lungs, out of the heart, his voice free to resonate at its best. Ironically, self-consciousness when performing leads not so much to arrogance as to timidity and fear: will I hit that high note? Is my low tessitura as good as X's? Is my voice at its peak now or is it in decline? And at the very point that these thoughts start to smoulder there comes physical as well as mental tension, reducing the ability to do the very thing about which one is worried.

This is not meant in any way to undermine the great singers (or pianists or conductors) of today. I could have chosen examples of fine performances from many names, and such psychological blocks are nothing new, but I'm sure that our present times and the omnipresence of recording equipment and the internet have made things worse. There is an artist who has become so paranoid about tape recorders in the audience that he has had physical confrontations with the public and has called in the police. I understand his worries. A concert one wants to live for that magical evening alone arrives with breakfast the next morning on YouTube and exists forever.

This issue goes beyond accuracy or technique. Tempos are also part of the problem. If I play this fast it will sound more impressive; if I play this slow it will sound more profound. There are performances of slow movements – in Schubert or Mahler, for instance – when the choice of tempo seems self-regarding not self-giving. I'm not suggesting a shrinking-violet approach or a pruning of individuality or eccentricity or even outrageousness, but to eliminate bad self-consciousness can be a path to achieving good self-confidence . . . and thus maximising our abilities on stage.

Beautiful bloopers: the joy of making mistakes

I came across a tweet once by Upen Patel: 'Don't let a bad moment ruin your day. Think of it as a bad minute, not a bad day and you'll be OK.' And it led me to think about playing concerts and to think about playing wrong notes.

When Vladimir Horowitz made his triumphant return to the stage in 1965 after over a decade of retirement, depression and illness, the anticipation was enormous, as were the expectations. He chose to begin his Carnegie Hall programme with a burst of Bach arranged by Busoni – that sparkling spritz of the high C major triad that opens the Toccata, Adagio and Fugue BWV 564. This moment has gone down in musical history because he hit an audible, strident wrong note in the first seconds. The tightrope frayed and the audience inwardly gasped as they looked up at the highly strung pianist's wobble. All was well soon afterwards, but somehow that blemish, with its hint of human fallibility, made this fine performance even greater.

There has been an increasing anxiety in recent years about wrong notes. It's partly the sanitised perfection of edited studio recordings, partly the competitions that fill the years of study and then afterwards seem the only gateway to a professional life, but also perhaps a more general digital way of thinking about everything. We live in a world with straight edges, with spell checks, with on/off switches. Computers don't do approximation or ambivalence. I'm happy about the precision of the pilot who flies me to my concert destination but once I reach the stage I want to fly free. And when mistakes come in a performance it is essential to brush them away instantly like so many flies.

I remember a conductor once stopping a rehearsal and turning to the violin section in frustration: 'I wish some of you would play out of tune for once. Everything's so tentative, so cautious. Let go, for heaven's sake!' In masterclasses I have listened to someone playing along note-perfectly, with dull, faceless monotony. Then . . . a botched chord, a bum note, and a visible wince on the face. I've sometimes pointed out (I hope kindly) that this was the most interesting moment in the performance. Not because it broke the boredom of 'perfection' for the listener but because it allowed for a momentary release of tension in the performer. The first scratch on those new shoes is annoying but how much better they look and feel as the leather creases and moulds and becomes supple.

My teacher Gordon Green once told me that he had sat with the great Hungarian pianist Annie Fischer as she reluctantly watched herself on a TV broadcast. She flinched as if in pain at every slightly misjudged phrasing, or at some passage she would have wished to inflect differently, but then there came a moment when she had had a memory lapse and had come obviously unstuck. She beamed at Gordon, delighted and proud of the deft way she had extricated herself from the potential train wreck.

Which snooker player has always pocketed every ball? Which tennis player has never had her serve called out? In performance aim for perfection, yes – but accept the mistakes when you fall short.

Can wrong notes be right?

Two of the most important things I think a teacher needs to encourage in a student are to lose the fear of inaccuracy and to be freed from the addiction to imitate recorded performances. They are related. The CD is seen as the perfection to strive for; if our concerts sound like that then we are getting it right. Wrong. If concerts are to be reclaimed as the place to hear music at its greatest, then they have to offer the audience more than a recording with an uncomfortable seat and a pricey ticket. We need to sense a connection with flesh and blood, with those who are our neighbours in row F in the balcony but more so with those whose pores are sweating onstage. And there will be mistakes. We've paid for them when we attend a live concert. A great performer will go for it, will take risks. The reaching beyond oneself, the utter commitment, the focus on things that *really* matter will result in mishaps. It is someone attempting the highest mountain with grazed, bloodied knees, not someone stepping onto an escalator in leather soles.

That doesn't mean we should aim at *inaccuracy*. Florence Foster Jenkins, the doyenne of dodgy divas, was *trying* to sing in tune even if it was her failure to do so that gained her such a huge following. Her execrable intonation was the result of an unmusical ear and an uncooperative throat. What I'm writing about is an entirely different thing. You can hear prime examples of it sometimes in the playing of Alfred Cortot – a towering pianist, who, through a careless (in the sense of carefree) musical vision, seemed simply not to worry that the notes on the keyboard failed occasionally to match those on the printed page. No matter. Like a bruised eagle he still soared higher than most.

Two problems remain. First, to learn a piece requires us to care immensely about every detail: every note, every nuance, is important. Yet at the point of performance something greater has to happen: a shift of focus, a broader scope, a letting go. Perhaps it's a little like preparing a parachute on the ground with the utmost attention and concentration so that we can exit the airplane with a leap of confidence when the moment arrives.

The other problem is with music no one has heard. A Beethoven sonata is one thing, but if we are attending a premiere of a newly composed work we do want to hear what the composer has written. Sometimes a change in harmony by just one note creates the very poignancy that can break the heart. Notes are words in music, and the wrong word can alter the meaning of a sentence completely.

Speaking of which, the pianist Martin Roscoe was reviewed once by a major newspaper in the days when reviews were telephoned through rather than sent via email. 'The immaculate pianist, Martin Roscoe' became 'the inaccurate pianist, Martin Roscoe' on the news-stands the following morning.

Clap between movements? Please!

Before a performance of Tchaikovsky's Second Piano Concerto in San Francisco, the conductor David Robertson and I gave a short talk to the audience about the piece they were about to hear. One of the last things David said before we began the performance was: 'If you enjoy the first movement then please applaud.' People were obviously a little shocked, and there were a few embarrassed giggles. Isn't it forbidden to clap before the end? Won't people think I'm ignorant? I don't want to be the only one. *My* only worry was that they might actually not like what they'd heard, but now feel obliged to clap anyway!

The reason why humans hit the palms of their hands together if they like something is probably buried in the mists of prehistory. Some audiences stamp too, or scream, or whistle, or shriek . . . or occasionally boo. In Holland there is the famous 'standing ovation', seemingly given to all, regardless of quality or level of appreciation. There are slow, rhythmic handclaps too, although with a positive connotation in musical settings, unlike in politics. These responses have more to do with the *audience*'s participation in what is happening on stage than with boosting the egos of the musicians. To experience passively something that is moving, touching, exciting or thrilling demands *some* active outlet if we're not to burst.

There are certain movements in the repertoire that absolutely demand applause. In piano concertos, off the top of my head, there are the first movements of both Brahms concertos, Rachmaninov's First and Second, Grieg, Tchaikovsky's First and Second . . . and so on. The list is long. The most interesting example for me is the third movement of Tchaikovsky's Sixth Symphony, which seems to call for an ovation like nothing else on earth. What do we do? Sometimes the conductor is so absolutely determined to stamp out the public's enthusiasm that he or she will start the final movement without a breath, with the applause still ringing in the auditorium. I have been at performances of this work when the opening bars of the last movement were completely inaudible because of this. But how much applause should you allow? Should the conductor leave the stage to take curtain calls and treat the final movement as a substantial encore? Obviously not, but a burst of steam from the pot before continuing is virtually essential – and would have been the tradition at the time of the first performance.

Once, though, I experienced an extreme exception to my present argument. I played a recital at Notre Dame de Fidélité, a Benedictine Abbey of nuns situated in Jouques, fifteen miles north-west of Aix en Provence. It was in the depths of summer and the stout, oak doors were open to the lavender fields. On my right as I sat at the piano, as usual, was the audience, but on my left, behind iron bars in flickering candlelight, were the barely visible faces of the nuns in their habits. Sviatoslav Richter discovered this little jewel of a church and was the first person to play here. The small series they held was to raise money for a new building for the novices. It was a conventional recital format . . . except that there was to be no applause at all during the entire concert. In this setting it was understandable, and, as it turned out, quite magical, almost like an erasure of ego and anxiety, and an embrace of the world outside the music, an inner world that was the very source of the music. As the final ghostly bars of Schumann's *Kreisleriana* tripped down the keyboard, dancing into the distance, I played the last, almost inaudible bass notes into a cave of silence. I stood up, acknowledged the audience with a slight bow, and walked away, the final sounds only an echo in the memory on the warm, perfumed night breeze.

Don't feel you *have* to clap between movements

In some places, notably the BBC Proms, applauding between movements has become almost customary. Is this a new trend sweeping across the world or just the local enthusiasm of the vast crowds sitting and standing in the Royal Albert Hall?

In a way I'm pleased because, as I discussed above, there are works where applause between movements would have been expected by the composer, is appreciated by performers, and is a cathartic release of tension for the audience. But . . . one summer a few years ago, during a performance of Bruckner's Seventh Symphony, I became uncomfortable when about a quarter of the audience (that's over a thousand people) applauded after *every* movement. It seemed as if their hand-clapping was virtually routine. It was not a letting off of steam from a pressure cooker of emotional intensity; rather it came across as conventional, polite and, in the event, almost divisive. It felt as if, well, the movement had finished, better clap a bit before the next one begins – an alternative to scratching one's ear or shifting one's legs. These patches of lukewarm applause were especially puzzling after the slow movement – that long stretch of majestic sorrow, with its heavy cloak of brass chords sound-wrapped around the hall. Appreciation would have been much more effectively displayed with the breathless weight of silence.

What about applause in the *middle* of a movement? That was as common in classical music as it still is at the ballet or after a great jazz solo. Jazz musicians would be puzzled and hurt if the crowd did not cheer, whistle and clap at these cadenzas: 'Were we really off form tonight?' Any ballerina would throw her *pointe* shoes at her dressing-room wall in frustration and disappointment if her 32 *fouetté* turns in *Swan Lake* did not receive a roar of approval. Hans von Bülow, perhaps the most 'serious' pianist of the late nineteenth century, known for his strict adherence to the score, wrote that he never played Beethoven's 'Emperor' Concerto without receiving applause at the end of the opening cadenza (which is only three minutes into the piece).

Perhaps this is going too far in music where the unfolding of a piece's narrative is as important as any details along the way, but nevertheless I think we should let our audiences loose to enjoy the concerts they have paid to attend, to express their appreciation when and how they want to, and thus to go back to an older, authentic tradition of concertgoing, the tradition of Mozart, of Chopin, of Liszt, of Brahms . . . and of just about everyone else.

Ample amplification

People who do not go to classical concerts are often amazed to learn that the pianos we play are never amplified in an ordinary concert setting. So used are they to everything in life being connected in some way to a microphone – singers, guitarists, priests – that the idea of something ringing in the air, supported only by the natural resonance of wood and wire, is beyond belief. When microphones are seen pointing into a piano's lid onstage, they are recording or broadcasting the sounds, not amplifying them, even in the largest indoor auditoriums. Actors today are often inadequately trained to project their voices to the back of a theatre; pop singers without a mike are barely audible beyond the front row . . . it's a matter of technique. For a classical pianist to be heard above a full orchestra in every corner of a 3,000-seat hall requires years of study and work. We have to learn how to use the whole body to form and project the sound from the instrument to the furthest pair of ears. Interestingly, this is different for jazz musicians; unless the performance space is very small, amplification for them is de rigueur. The technique for a jazz pianist is more often hands and forearms producing either light-fingered nonchalance, a chunky, angular thrust, or battering rhythmic violence – and mikes are built into the equation. For the classical pianist, the power of shoulder and back-weight involved in playing huge chords against eighty players in an orchestra is actually diminished by amplification. The sound loses tension when it lacks a literal and figurative ceiling, and it rides too easily, too glibly, over the sonic mountain.

One afternoon a few years ago, I was walking around Seville and I came across some flamenco dancers in one of the squares. I love flamenco, but as I turned the corner I realised that the music was not real. It was heavily amplified – part performed, part recorded. Yes, we could hear it more clearly in the bustle of the Sunday streets, but it was like instant coffee – it lacked depth, kick, bite. However much *duende* was created by the woman turning her proud head, stamping her petulant foot, or arching her jet-black, plucked eyebrows, it fell flat next to the buzzing boxes providing the music. I wanted to hear a guitar's strings straining and slowly going out of tune; I wanted to see the young gypsy's tattooed arm embracing his instrument with a cruel passion; I wanted to see the castanets hot with wood-splintering sparks. But instead there was a soulless, flabby accompaniment, as innocuous, as bland, as the Manchego sandwich I had just had for lunch.

PPProjection

The ability to project sound to the back of a hall above the full resonance of an orchestra without a microphone is one thing, but we must also be able to communicate with the softest whisper as well as with that thunderous roar. For a pianist, there are some technical aspects involved. For instance, we have to judge the arm-weight and timbre of an extremely soft note or chord – a gentle 'laying down' of the hand on the keys combining a caressing lift with a sinking to the bottom of the keybed. The elbow is the fulcrum – the wings to the fingers' landing wheels. It's hard to put into words, and not much easier to perfect over decades of stubborn work.

There are some more prosaic aspects to projection too. The first time we have to speak in public, at a brother's wedding perhaps, the standard advice is: don't speak too fast, pause between sentences, choose one word in a phrase to emphasise. These are all equally relevant to musical performance. A rapid passage or trill played clearly will sound faster than one that is uneven in sound and rhythm.

A real pianissimo forces the audience to listen in a much more active way than a force of sound hitting them between the eyes. The ear has to lean forward when the sound is floating gently in the air. Even our breathing has to be restrained sometimes when we are making sure to catch that delicate aural feather, and when the strings themselves seem barely to have been brushed by the cushioned felt of the piano's rising hammers.

Charismatic

Projection has as much to do with intensity of intention as with decibels. In the end it's the projection of an *idea* that is key: the force of will, the ability to compel an audience to listen. How is it that someone can enter a room and set it alight merely by her presence, without speaking a word, whereas another fails even to be noticed? Similarly, someone can walk onto a stage to perform or ascend a podium to speak and can have everyone in the house instantly bewitched with bated breath before anything has disturbed the silence. This phenomenon is often called charisma, or, more poetically perhaps, magnetism. It's an inexplicable quality but we know when someone possess it, and it can explain why certain people become famous or powerful. It has a whiff of dynamite about it, and it might well have been used more for evil ends than good in human history.

When Orson Welles makes his first appearance on the screen as Harry Lime in Carol Reed's classic movie *The Third Man*, such a moment occurs. Not a word is spoken, and his body is still, but the two glances up and down (the second staying a micro-second longer in its upward movement than the first) and the way the mouth incrementally dissolves into a smile then a half-formed word, has to qualify as one of the greatest acting moments ever captured on film. Was it a moment of thespian brilliance or was it just Welles's natural charisma? Are those flickers of rubato in Ignaz Friedman's playing of Chopin mazurkas a practised, knowing expression or a subconscious, direct line from the folk rhythms where gnarl the roots of all human musical expression? With true magnetism, the question need not be asked.

Stanley Kubrick and recording

I think I might have learned more about making records from Stanley Kubrick than from anyone else. I remember my sense of astonishment and recognition when I saw a documentary about his filming of *The Shining*. He must have thought about this movie intensely, obsessively, for at least a year before filming, absorbing its mood of frightening descent into violent madness. Then there would have been the planning, and casting, and the thousands of different details that are part of the preparation process before the day when the camera first begins to shoot. But then I saw the famous director, known for his perfectionism, making it up on the spot – changing the script, the camera angle, everything. He looked as if he was improvising, freewheeling; unsure, then suddenly more sure than he'd ever been; pausing to think, then tumbling into wildly passionate action; devouring and being devoured by this monster of a movie that sprang to life take after take, beyond all planning, beyond all vision.

This is how I want to feel when I make a recording. To have thought deeply about the music I'm about to record, but not to walk in, sit down and simply play it through, like some mock concert – one take, and maybe a few extra ones to cover the mistakes. No, even though I know the scores on the producer's desk intimately, the process of recording is a process of fascinating, invigorating discovery. This happens in the playbacks, of course – 'Did I *really* mean that left-hand line to be as prominent as that? That phrase sounds very tame as I listen, whereas it seemed exaggerated to me when I was playing. What if I continued that diminuendo into the next phrase?' – but also *as* I'm playing. To be able to throw caution, notes, taste, technique to the winds . . . knowing that nothing is lost while there's still time to do another take, and while the producer and engineer are still awake in their chairs. That's the equivalent of the danger of the live concert for me: not the once-through risk before an audience generating the excitement, but the risk of keeping sanity and soul intact as I explore every nuance the piano is capable of . . . and then to try for more.

Red-light district I: the background

Around a century ago recordings were souvenirs of concerts. A pianist would play in town and those who liked what they heard would buy a scratchy memento, waiting anxiously for the next live visit on the next tour. But since the 1950s, with the invention of the LP and the steady increase of sound quality and capacity, recordings have gradually replaced concerts as the public's first step of acquaintance with music and the artists who play it. Exact statistics are unknowable, of course, but I would guess that over 95 per cent of the music we hear today is from recordings. Since the era of the LP it has been almost unheard of for a soloist to have a major career without recordings. At the point of writing, whether we like it or not, to be a 'concert' pianist is to be a 'recording' pianist.

Making a record is not just a matter of sitting down and playing well in front of a microphone; it's a different art form, and requires a different technique. I like the comparison between cinema and the theatre: if you put a camera in front of a wonderful 'live' play it won't necessarily make a good movie; it's another way of working altogether. When I made my first record I wasn't fully aware of this and I was scared of having to do retakes. The fewer the takes, the better the pianist was the subconscious accusation underpinning, undermining each rejected attempt. But it shouldn't be like a test or an exam – or, worse, like a sports event. We can (and should) approach the diving board as many times as we like. All that matters in the end is whether the recording sounds good. I'd say the only thing that is ethically unacceptable is if it sounds better than you on your best day. Nobody cares how many times it takes a great poet to rework the lines, or a great painter to reshape the forms. The poem, the canvas . . . and the shiny silver disc *are* the artforms, not the arduous process through which they come into being.

Red-light district II: frenzy

There are three types of recording in which I've been involved: 'live' recordings from concerts, studio recordings of solo or chamber repertoire, and studio recordings of concertos with orchestras. Each of these categories is completely different and needs to be explored separately.

Let's begin with orchestras in the studio. The first thing to point out is how little time there is to make a recording with an -orchestra unless there is an unlimited budget. Normally there are two three-hour sessions out of which around 40 minutes needs to be deducted for breaks. That sounds like a lot for 30 minutes of music, but not if you include rehearsal time, listening-back time (and walking-back time to the control room) and, most difficult of all, trying to get a good sound with the engineer. I recorded the Brahms Second Concerto in the late 1980s with the BBC Symphony and Sir Andrew Davis and I can still remember that after an hour of trying microphones in every position we still did not have a sound we liked. The piano was too distant, then too close, then too dry, then too reverberant. Then the woodwinds sounded boxed in, then the strings lacked clarity. By the first break we had nothing in the can (professional-speak for a usable take), yet I had been playing this toughest of concertos for over an hour. By the time we settled on a sound I was exhausted, frustrated and anxious. Because studio sessions with orchestras are rigorously controlled by union rules the clock ticks away and nothing but a huge overtime payment can make a difference . . . and even with a large budget the orchestral players still have to agree to the overtime. And all of this is just to get the notes down, never mind with what finesse or inspiration. In the end things gelled then caught fire, but for a while we were perilously close to releasing at best a workaday recording.

How does one generate that danger, that spark of excitement, when a session is drawing to a close and everything is suggesting safety – covering a split note in the horns here or an out-of-tune phrase in the cellos there? I remember very clearly recording the 4th movement of Scharwenka's Fourth Concerto – one of the hardest pieces I've ever learned – with the City of Birmingham Symphony. We'd done a good take, perfectly releasable with a few patches here and there. The conductor, Lawrence Foster, turned to me with a smile as if to suggest that things were going well. They were, but I had a feeling they could go better. We'd played accurately and musically, but I knew there was more to be done. 'Can we do it again?' I asked. 'Of course,' said Larry and raised his baton. I pushed the tempo a few notches faster and saw some players sit forward in their chairs. It was more exciting this time, if a little less accurate. 'Let's do it again,' I said, flushed and a little frenzied. A few notches higher again. By the fourth or fifth take there was a whiff of madness in the room. I felt sick, dizzy, almost on the verge of hysteria by the end . . . but I think the movement did eventually come alive, even if I myself left the piano that evening feeling half dead.

Red-light district III: solo lows and highs

So much for the time limits, the energy limits, the union limits and how to inject adrenalin into a studio recording with an orchestra when spirits and standards are sagging. Making a solo or chamber recording in a studio . . . now this should be a doddle, shouldn't it? Sometimes with as many as three days to record one solo CD; no start or finish time except what is agreed by pianist and colleagues and producer, and a vast horizon of possibilities towards which to saunter with ease and confidence. Ah, but therein lies part of the problem: too many choices, too much freedom. Not that I would want voluntarily to make the sessions less flexible, but there's nothing like a deadline for inspiration, and lack of time constraints can allow time for neuroses to ferment.

I remember recording the Chopin ballades and scherzos for Virgin in the late 1980s. (At my request this CD was never released and I ended up re-recording these pieces for Hyperion over a decade later.) I don't entirely know why, but things just went badly from the start. The piano I'd selected a month or so earlier had totally changed character in the interim. It had been juiced up for a concerto recording and was strident and punchy whereas before it had been mellifluous and lyrical. There was no time to have the piano completely revoiced and I probably should have cancelled the sessions there and then, but we went ahead at the request of the company. In Chopin the correct piano sound is essential for the correct rubato and shaping of phrases; if the first phrase feels right you become inspired and the next phrase tends to feel even better and on and on . . . a snowball effect of inspiration and confidence. Conversely, if the sound is unsatisfactory, there is nothing you can do. Without well-judged colour and nuance, the delicate rhythmic freedom essential for Chopin sounds staged and artificial. This is one of the causes of much dull or lumpy Chopin playing.

During the first day of recording there was not *one* line of music without some jangle from the metallic instrument making me wince. By the evening I was thoroughly dissatisfied and in a thoroughly bad mood, even though we had masses of material on tape. We got the tuner to do some extensive work on the piano before the second day and then started again. It was better but somehow a mental block had set in. Everything I played sounded bad, every take seemed worse than the last, and it spiralled into an inability to play even the simplest phrase: 'Where is middle C?' In the end we had enough usable material to issue the CD, but I was unhappy with the first edit of the ballades when I heard it and asked the record company if we could scrap the whole project. They agreed, much to my relief. There are often black moments in solo recordings but this is the only occasion when I was unable to work through them.

The other side of the coin was my recording of a selection of Federico Mompou's piano music for Hyperion. I remember well the sunny sessions in St George's, Brandon Hill, as afternoon light filled this former church with a gentle glow of affirmation. Those heartwarming pieces seemed to put everyone in a good mood – even the piano was smiling – and we finished the record very quickly.

Red-light district IV: live or alive?

And so to the third category, making a recording from 'live' concerts. I've done this a number of times now: the complete Beethoven violin sonatas with Robert Mann, the Rachmaninov concertos with Andrew Litton and the Dallas Symphony, the Tchaikovsky concertos with Osmo Vänskä and the Minnesota Orchestra and the Dvořák and Schumann concertos with Andris Nelsons and the City of Birmingham Symphony. All of these involved taping the performances with patch sessions afterwards. With the orchestral recordings we always had more than one concert from which to select material – two, three or four performances of each piece.

In some ways (and for some repertoire) this is the best way to record. It enables you to utilise the natural excitement and adrenalin of a concert but to shape and refine some essential details later in the safety of studio conditions. Purists sometimes ask, 'Why don't you just release a concert unedited?' There have been some wonderful direct concert-to-disc recordings over the decades but this has almost always been decided after the event: a particularly great concert was subsequently deemed worthy of being issued. I don't think that recording in any form should ever be a stunt: 'Can we play the piece without needing retakes?' It's about getting the best final results for the sake of the music. An out-of-tune violin passage, a misplaced cymbal crash, a raucous cough, or a perky mobile-phone ring does not add quality to the experience of listening to Rachmaninov's Fourth Piano Concerto. With repeated hearing it simply becomes an annoyance . . . and it's not just a matter of damage limitation. If, in the course of three concerts, the third movement on Thursday really took wing but the second movement on Saturday had a special wistfulness about it, only a purist would demand that you kept one of the performances complete. What would probably end up happening is that you'd take Friday's more measured account of the whole piece because fewer things went wrong.

If there are details not adequately covered by any of the concerts, there are the patch sessions. How innocuous they sound, but *nothing* in my professional life has been more stressful. It could be seen as a safety net in one sense, but the tension involved is more like walking on a high wire. In Minnesota we had thirty minutes per concerto, of which ten minutes needed to be break time, all at once or in bite sizes. The stopwatch was ticking away like an unexploded bomb, and the producer, the (mostly) unflappable Andrew Keener, would bark out the bars we needed to cover in a manic sequence: 'Bar 254, second chord in winds, never together.' Osmo would quickly find the place, raise his baton, and we were off. Sometimes these inserts would be in the middle of a blizzard of an awkward passage and I would have to jump in as if onto a merry-go-round spinning at high speed. Usually we ended up covering what we needed with only seconds left. We would stagger off the stage, shell-shocked, dazed, trusting that the snippets we recorded could be stitched in seamlessly at the later editing stage.

Red-light district V:
play it again (and again), Sergei

I was fascinated to read an article in *Gramophone* magazine in which Rachmaninov compared recording and broadcasting. We know that he hated the latter and in fact refused to allow any of his concerts to be transmitted. Instead, in the middle of the concert, the radio station would make a sudden switch and play one of his records instead of the performance about to take place. There was obviously something about the immediacy of the broadcasting medium that meant he felt uneasy and out of control. This is confirmed by this fascinating article, with its strange contradictions and lopsided arguments. He says:

> Through the medium of the gramophone we can now offer the public performances closely similar to those we give on the concert platform. Our records should not disappoint the most critical listener who has heard us in the flesh; to the millions who have no opportunity of doing so, they convey a just and accurate impression of our work.

Is this really what he thinks? Surely a broadcast is closer to a performance on stage because it *is* a performance on stage. He goes on to say a little later:

When making records it is actually possible to achieve something approaching artistic perfection. If once, twice or three times I do not play as well as I can, it is possible to record and re-record, to destroy and remake until, at last, I am content with the result.

But isn't that the direct opposite of a concert performance? Although I got into trouble once from a Rachmaninov fan for suggesting that the Russian master was nervous onstage, as if this made him less of a pianistic god, Adele Marcus, who was a teaching assistant to Josef Lhévinne, one of Rachmaninov's friends and a fellow student with him in Moscow, told me that Lhévinne sometimes had to push Rachmaninov out towards the piano at Carnegie Hall from the wings because he was so petrified. If this is true, might it have been this anxiety that influenced his attitude towards recording versus broadcasting, the loss of control in the latter, a magnifying glass held up to every flaw?

His recording with Fritz Kreisler of the Grieg C minor Violin Sonata, made in Berlin in 1928, is one of the glories of musical history. But it was not made in one take, as we tend to think 78s were. Rachmaninov remembers that 'the six sides of the Grieg set we recorded no fewer than five times each. From these thirty discs we finally selected the best, destroying the remainder.' I have a feeling that had he lived into the era of the tape machine and beyond, he might well have been as demanding and fastidious as Glenn Gould, spending days and days, playing pieces again and again, honing every bar.

Red-light district VI: did I really play it like that?

If playing in front of a microphone is hard enough, listening back can be as great a challenge. Sometimes quick decisions have to be made in the sessions themselves. 'Are we covered?' is the horrible phrase for the minimum requirement. Have we actually got all the bars of the piece down in an acceptable manner? But then do I like this version or that version? The one when the phrase tails off to nothing in a perfect diminuendo but is a little too slow, or the one where the sound is more present but the rubato works well? Or should I try another take? Ah, this time there was a crack in the floorboards. *Is* that a wrong note in the thicket of Scriabin's harmonies? Yes, no, yes, no . . . the ear can be cruelly deceived when under pressure and after hours of intense work – like looking at a simple word over and over again and wondering if the spelling is correct. Or that slip in the middle of an exciting passage: 'Yes, let's leave it. I like the sense of danger.' But then later I hear it again and it no longer sounds exciting or dangerous, just wrong.

The Austrian pianist Artur Schnabel referred to the recording studio as 'the torture chamber', but the real agony comes when the first edit drops onto my doormat. No more playing is possible, but quite a lot can still be adjusted at this stage. The problem is hearing objectively. I put the CD into the player and start to listen. Every note sounds horrible. Panic sets in and my ears close. Sometimes I drive off in the car to listen to it there, the engine noise allowing me space to face the truth gradually.

When the final, finished, packaged CD arrives months later, with a serial number and a glossy booklet inside its plastic case, it seems like something outside me – distant, separate – and I rarely listen to it again.

A promiscuous weekend in Amsterdam

A few years ago I was in Amsterdam to play the Grieg Concerto with Andrew Litton and the Netherlands Philharmonic. We'd had our first rehearsal and as we'd recorded the work not long before, things were smooth and enjoyable. Then in the afternoon, as I was practising, I got a call from my manager: would I like to play the Grieg Concerto tomorrow . . . twice! There was to be another performance of the piece by Nikolai Tokarev and Roman Kofman at 2.15 p.m., also at the Concertgebouw, but this time with the Netherlands *Radio* Philharmonic. Apparently Nikolai was unwell and the orchestra was asking if I would be prepared to step in. I thought about it for a minute and then agreed it would work out as long as everyone was happy with the arrangement and that it was logistically possible.

So I ended up doing my dress rehearsal with Andrew at 11 a.m. at the Yakult Zaal; then I was whisked off to the Concertgebouw to do my dress rehearsal there with Roman at 12 noon; then I grabbed a quick bite before playing the Grieg on the stage of the Concertgebouw at 2.15 p.m. I was then whisked back to my hotel for a quick rest and shower before being whisked back to the Concertgebouw to do a final rehearsal on stage with Andrew at 6.30 p.m. before playing the Grieg again on the stage of the Concertgebouw at 8.15 p.m.

Never was a post-concert supper more welcomed or more relaxed.

Ringtone in Padua

Once I was in Padua playing a recital. All was normal – or as normal as the madness of pressing down black and white keys in profile to an audience who hit the palms of their hands together every time I stopped playing could be . . . until I finished the first movement of the Chopin B minor Sonata. I played the final two chords and brought my hands down to my lap to pause before launching into the Scherzo. A mobile phone rang – or rather *shattered* the silence. I have never heard such a racket: an explosion of acid rock that would corrode the most abused eardrums; heavy metal that would sink, even in the Dead Sea. It was not coming from the audience but from the wings. I looked round after five seconds of this aural abuse to see if anyone was there. Not a person in sight. So, as it made no sign of stopping, I left the piano, walked offstage, and began to hunt for the phone. I finally found it, still screaming its head off, in a cupboard on the wall. I pressed the red button and . . . *silenzio*. There was much laughter from the audience and applause as I returned to the piano to continue the Chopin. All was normal – or as normal as the madness of pressing down black and white keys in profile to an audience who hit the palms of their hands together every time I stopped playing could be . . . until, in my dressing room afterwards, the presenter winked at me as if to say, 'You naughty boy!' I didn't think my rubatos had been *that* outrageous in the Chopin, but you never know people's tastes.

'We were surprised at your choice of ringtone!'

It transpired that the *entire* audience had thought that the phone had been mine!

Hysterical laughter on stage

There was that memorable tour with Steven Isserlis when we lost it – on stage. Our mirth spilled out, gushed forth, totally unchecked, unstoppable, unforgettable, in full view of the audience.

Something was going on during this whole concert. We were in Newcastle, New South Wales, where my father happened to have been born – maybe his ghost was egging me on. The splendid Stuart & Sons concert grand I was playing seemed to encourage me to bring out wild inner voices, frilly petticoats of counterpoint, which the composers themselves might not have suspected could lurk under the sober dress of their work. Indeed in the Rachmaninov sonata there were a few teasing rubatos from the pianist that caused the cellist to turn around in astonishment, so far had my eyebrow of expression arched upwards. Finally, we got to the encores. The first one was my little piece 'Angelic Song', dedicated to Steven's son Gabriel. Then we did 'The Haunted House' – a dramatic monologue composed by Steven, in which he declaimed a ghost story while making all sorts of noises and sounds (some of them musical) on his Stradivarius, with me accompanying him on the Stuart. It is a wonderful piece of Gothic camp, a children's horror story that always produces laughter from the audience.

But on this occasion . . . well, we lost it. I had one line to declaim, at the end of the piece. As if playing Norma Bates in *Psycho*, I had to croak, 'My son, it's good to have you home.' I had a small white towel on the side of the piano so I decided on this occasion to balance this 'veil' on my head as I said the words. As I did so, the audience laughed even more than usual, and suddenly it hit me: I couldn't speak for laughing. Steven, of course, was facing the back of the hall, so he wasn't able to see me. When the punchline of his piece failed to be spoken by his pianist, he turned around one last time. Tears were streaming down my face and I was unable to see or play or speak. By now the audience was laughing yet more, and he, after a twitch or two of attempted self-control, started to laugh uncontrollably too. Within seconds we were both completely limp with hysteria. 'He's got another line,' he moaned at the sea of roaring faces in the auditorium. I tried again and again: 'My ssson, it's . . .' 'My son, it's good ttt . . .' Hopeless. In the end we just walked off stage, tails between our legs, faces glistening, noses dripping, eyes red.

STUDIO

The practice of practising: for professionals

Concert pianists spend much more of their lifetimes practising than they do playing concerts. It's not just that pieces need to be kept in the memory – muscle and mind – but the very act of playing the piano is physical and athletic. It involves reflex and endurance. It might be true that you never forget how to ride a bicycle, but if you and it are rusty there's not much hope of winning or even completing the Tour de France. So we need to practise. The key is how we make our time offstage best serve our briefer time onstage. A pianist who has concerts has little time to spare, so it's important that those spare hours, even minutes, be used well.

My teacher, Gordon Green, used to say, 'In practice a perfectionist, in performance a realist.' In other words, prepare assiduously, tirelessly, at home, but when onstage accept the situation at hand without wishing the piano were more in tune, the audience were more appreciative (or larger), you hadn't made a mess of that octave passage, and so on.

Being a 'realist' sounds rather prosaic when faced with bringing to poetic, passionate life the masterworks of master composers. I might put it differently from Gordon: in practice an engineer, in performance a pilot. Nuts and bolts in a plane are incomparably important, but when you sit at the cockpit of a Steinway concert grand your eyes need to look ahead not underneath.

The purpose of practising is so that we (offstage as engineers) make sure that we (onstage as pilots) are completely free to fly to the destination of our choice. That destination is one involving imagination and creativity and spirituality and danger and

ecstasy of course, not merely the A to B of playing the notes –
but without the nuts and bolts in place we shall never be airborne. The greatest interpretative vision of the final pages of
the final sonata of Beethoven will nosedive to oblivion if we
can't play an even trill.

So, moving inside the hangar, spanner at the ready, how do
we practise? There are as many answers to that question as
pieces in our repertoire, but maybe some signposts can help.

Study

Relish the task, whether beginning to learn a piece or revising
one long familiar. Decode the message behind the notation.
Map out the journey. Look for the obstacles. Know the (good)
tradition of historical evidence; distrust the (bad) tradition of
'it's always done this way'. You might be Brahms's secretary in
the practice room, but on stage you are his mouthpiece. And a
composer's message is always more than words: it's a drama in
which you and Brahms are a single character.

Slow

Slow practice can be a complete waste of time if the mind is not
working quickly. Simply to trawl through passages like a con-
tented tortoise is a waste of the felt on your piano's hammers.
Good slow practice is more like a hare pausing to survey the
scene: sharp in analysis, watching through the blades of grass,
calculating the next sprint. My favourite kind of slow practice is
the half-and-half variety. For example, in a semiquaver passage
I will play four notes at performance tempo, then four notes
exactly half the speed – then reverse the groups. It can sometimes be useful to do this with eight-note groups. It stops any
testudinal ambling, and it focuses the mind quickly from one
reflex to another. It is a hare with alert eyes.

Mind

As important as it is to have strong fingers, muscles, tendons and joints loose and lithe, we need a strong mind at the piano too. Strong in concentration, on- and offstage; ever striving for improvement but relaxed when none seems to take place; aiming the dart tirelessly at every bullseye but gentle and kind when it clatters to the floor. Muscles are effective when they are able to tense and relax at will, not just when they bulge in a ripple of aggression. This is true for the physical side of playing as well as for the mental challenges. The mind's clear vision is not a stare; it needs to be able to focus near and far with flexibility and wisdom. There is a well-worn saying: practice makes perfect. I don't believe this, at least in reference to playing the piano. Abstract 'perfection' is rarely what we seek but good practicing does make it more likely that we shall give a good performance. Its attention, its concentration, its tightening of the screws enable the concert experience to take wing in freedom.

The practice of practising: for amateurs

So much for students and professionals, what about amateur musicians? I think it's important to begin with the origin of the word 'amateur'. It comes from the Latin *amare* and it means 'to love'. An amateur is not someone who is less good than a professional but rather someone for whom love overcomes obstacles – and practising is all about overcoming obstacles. In fact, many professionals could learn a thing or two about the love for music that fills the lives of so many who have other daytime jobs. The French novelist Julien Green wrote that if students still wanted to read books after they'd completed his literature class he considered his teaching to have been a success.

If we think of practising itself from the viewpoint of love I think many things will slot into place.

But love is not quite enough, as anyone who has placed stiff hands on keys or dry lips to a mouthpiece will know. The first problem is how to maximise limited time at the end (or the beginning) of a busy day. There is no question that a lot of time is wasted when practising, particularly in music colleges. Passages are repeated over and over again with no improvement and no concentration. The hands of the clock are impatiently urged forward: 'Three hours done; oh, that's enough for today.' Nothing of the amateur about this attitude. But by the time a student has become a professional there can be surprisingly little time to practise – on the days of concerts perhaps only twenty minutes grabbed backstage in a dressing room.

What's essential is to focus on why something is not good, and in almost every case there is a clear, logical reason. There is not room here to go into every example (and every problem will have a slightly different solution) but mistakes occur for the pianist when fingers fall in the wrong place. That might seem like a banal truism but it's surprising how useful it can be to think in these terms. You want to hit that E; therefore your hand needs to be there in order to do so. Take all the time you need to get there (there's always a split second more than you think) and play it calmly, however frenetic the music might be. And however expressive the music, playing an instrument is doing something finite: a practical, physical action. The effect of that vibrato might be to create a tear in the corner of an eye, but what's actually happening on the string is a wiggle of a finger in the right place.

Perhaps the main thing that can hold an amateur back is the sheer physicality of muscle development and stamina with insufficient practice time to achieve it. To do anything technically difficult requires the body (the fingers, the lips, the arms) to be in good shape. Possessing good shoes and a good posture will help you run better, but you won't win the marathon without serious training. Some people have a natural flair at the keyboard and learn much more quickly than others, but for some people certain pieces will never be possible. It's not a bad thing to realise this and not to waste time banging through that Liszt piece, which you know in your heart is never going to be rid of the lumps and bumps. Choose repertoire sensibly . . . but do stretch yourself as well. Keep polishing your old party pieces (especially if you plan playing them at parties) but always try to learn something new. Maybe one out of five days can be for new repertoire.

Finally it's important to remember that being an amateur (a lover) should be a carefree task. Leave the ego-posturing to the professionals. Make demands on yourself, fill the time well, concentrate . . . but then enjoy. Find joy inside the music you play and inside yourself. Who knows, you might end up bringing some of that joy to your family and – one can always hope – to your neighbours.

Random practice tips

And so, here are some random practice tips for professionals and amateurs alike:

Let's (not) start at the very beginning

This is true in a multi-movement work and even within movements. I've often noticed in masterclasses how students play the exposition (the first time the themes appear) better than the recapitulation (when they return in the final section). I think this is because they always start working at the beginning, and practise that section with greater focus and energy. In Brahms's Second Concerto, for example, we can spend a good hour or two working on the first half of the first movement and then find when the second-subject material returns that we're already tired or distracted. Try sometimes starting to work from the development section onwards and see what a difference it can make.

Take a bite

It's not always necessary to practise a piece all the way through on a single day. For instance, in a big sonata it can be helpful, say, to practise the first movement on Tuesday and the rest of the piece on Thursday. Even within a work this can be useful. Let's say you're playing the Fourth Ballade of Chopin – a challenge to any pianist's hands; you might want just to practise the last three pages or so of the piece on one day. Take an hour and home in on the specific difficulties there, calmly and coolly, then put it aside and work on something else. It stops that feeling of being overwhelmed by how much needs working on. If you practise that tricky coda carefully, out of context, it should feel more secure when the footlights are at full glare and a microphone is poking its nose inside the piano.

Either side of the crack

When you reach a hurdle in a difficult piece and stumble, keep going for a few seconds. Don't stop and go back straight away, because if you do this too often you will find that the problem will have become ingrained. You will never have actually played the passage without this 'stopping and going back'. An example of this is in the final Chopin prélude. There is a descending run of chromatic double-thirds that often causes difficulties. I've heard this practised in conservatories over the years. Students reach this point, get in a tangle, stop for a second and then have another (usually more successful) go. By the time they come to play the piece in an exam or concert the mistake itself is ingrained. Not only should you keep going beyond the stumble before going back, but make sure when you do go back that you start a little earlier than the problem moment itself to cover the crack. Very often getting into a passage is more difficult than the passage itself.

Tick tock

Some people are disdainful of the metronome, as if using it means that you are somehow 'unmusical'. This is irrational as it can be a really useful tool to check tempos and to check steadiness of rhythm within those tempos, enabling us then to be free to be free. But it has a further use in practising. Josef Lhévinne used to work on certain passages or pieces at four different tempos. Let's say your performance tempo is crotchet (quarter-note) = 120. Try practising at 100, 80 and 60. You'll find that different difficulties rear their heads at the four different tempos, and that the middle two levels are often the hardest to maintain.

Be boring

Don't feel you have to perform with full emotional expression at every practice session, especially by filling the hours crashing through pieces without improvement. This is a common occurrence in conservatories – Rachmaninov concertos pounded with adolescent passion and coarse, crude effects. In the same way that an actor will go over lines backstage, sometimes it's really good just to go through the notes, *thinking* about what you want to do expressively but not fully engaging with it. This is especially valuable on the day of a concert: don't let the rehearsal use up all the energy for the performance.

Foot off the pedal

If you take your foot off the pedal when you practise, the sound instantly becomes semi-skimmed, and you'll really hear what's going on. You'll also see whether the fingering you've chosen is lazy and a fudge, or whether it will enable you to sing every line with fervour and confidence. In addition it will help you to be boring, as in the previous tip.

Close your eyes

Leopold Godowsky and Josef Lhévinne both recommended practising with eyes closed, and it's an astonishingly effective technique. It forces us to use our other senses more acutely – hearing, of course, but also to map out the geography of the keyboard (my teacher Derrick Wyndham's term). It's helpful for almost everything, but especially if you're working on a passage with jumps. If you can play that passage in Liszt's *Mephisto Waltz* no. 1 or the end of the second movement of Schumann's *Fantasie* op. 17 with your eyes closed (even if it's at the speed of a tortoise with a missing leg) it will be much easier when you open your eyes again.

Rainbow

I like to use coloured pencils to highlight particular points of interest in a score: inner voices, important notes in harmonies, shapes of phrasings, patterns in passagework, unusual pedallings, aids for memory. I find that writing in a score is an essential tool in the excavation process of learning a piece, especially when choosing fingerings.

Don't warm up

Gordon Green used to warn me against warming up before playing. He meant to alert me to the danger of having a specific routine, favourite exercises without which I didn't feel ready to begin playing the pieces I was studying. As most of the problems in playing the piano are in the head not the hands this is wise advice. Any superstition or artificial requirement we build into our psyche is dangerous because there will be a time when it can't be fulfilled. Many times I have played in a concert hall where there was no warm-up piano backstage, and I've just had to go out onto the platform cold. We need to prepare for this eventuality in our heads, and in our practice rooms.

Massage and table tops

However, following on from the previous tip, we shouldn't just start playing the cadenza of Prokofiev's Second Concerto, full-tilt, straight after breakfast. At home we can begin with physically less strenuous passages to loosen up, but what do we do when we're backstage at a concert hall with no piano on which to doodle? I've spent many hours of my life drumming my fingers on table tops – not while waiting for a barman to bring over a Martini, but nervously trying to get my fingers warm in a draughty dressing room. I don't think trying to play the patterns of an actual piece is of much help, but taking simple, Hanon-like exercises tapped out on a hard surface (I've used sinks, chairs, walls, music stands, water machines) can be a good way to prepare for playing. I would add to this stretching and massage – and not just our hands. Tightness in any part of the body can be a handicap at the keyboard. Just before a performance I like to tease out the knots in my forearms and between my thumbs and forefingers. A good way to do this is to take a non-sharp corner of a piece of furniture and gently press on the various pressure points.

Know the score

Most pianists, when learning a new concerto, begin with the two-piano reduction with the orchestral part transcribed for a second piano. Not only is this score readable and carry-able, but it enables us to run through the piece on two pianos before playing it with a full orchestra. But we need to study the original, orchestral score too – not only to learn what's really going on in the other parts, but because there are sometimes mistakes in the two-piano scores.

Waiting for my carriage

The great Hans von Bülow had a tip that I've found very useful over the years: 'Do not despise the fifteen minutes spent waiting for your carriage to arrive.' In other words, a lot can be achieved in a little time. I like to take a problem passage from a piece I'm working on and slowly, carefully, study it in those free minutes. It's related to advice from fitness gurus who tell us that even a short walk (especially up a staircase) can make a significant impact on our health.

Descaled

Many great pianists talk about the importance of practising scales. Even if we don't do it every day it's still quite good to isolate a technique like this from time to time, out of the context of the piece we're working on. For instance, if you're learning Beethoven's 'Emperor' Concerto you might want to spend some minutes just playing scales and arpeggios; there are certainly enough of them in the work itself. Or, if you're playing a piece with a difficult octave passage, practise some octaves by themselves – simple scales and arpeggios can work well.

Rhythm method

Pianists and their teachers tend either to advocate practising in rhythms with an evangelical fervour, or to maintain that it's a total waste of time. All I can say is that I have found it useful throughout my life for certain passages, if done correctly. Very rarely do I use dotted rhythms, but rather stopping on the first, second, third and fourth notes of a group. What is essential is absolute rhythmic stability. If these rhythms are done sloppily they will merely make you play more unevenly. A metronome is a good way to keep the spacing between the notes of military precision. I discussed a variant of this earlier – playing one group at one tempo and the next at exactly double or half the tempo. These 'groups' can be two, four or eight notes – or one bar, or even two bars. Again, this is useless if it's kind of a bit slower, then kind of a bit faster; we must keep the same pulse but vary the note values. You'll find that it not only helps accuracy and velocity but can aid memory too.

Arms apart

When running passages have both hands playing the same fast notes an octave apart (the third-movement coda of Tchaikovsky's First Concerto, or the fourth movement of Chopin's B flat minor Sonata), try practising them two octaves apart. It will wrong-foot you at first, but it will make the patterns more secure and will enable you to hear both voices more clearly.

Easy-peasy

Don't forget to practise the easy parts of a piece, especially to make memory secure. There's a passage in the third movement of Rachmaninov's Second Concerto, the simplest few bars in the movement, that can come apart in a performance if not worked on. For this example, memorise the first note of each of the three groups – they make up a major triad – and keep them consciously in mind.

Use the butter wrapper to grease your baking tray

As well as doing scales, arpeggios and other exercises, we should devise exercises from figuration in the pieces we are playing. Alfred Cortot's editions of Chopin reign supreme here and Godowsky's *Studies on the Chopin Études* also have superlative examples of this. Take a knotty corner (almost any piece you learn will yield such a starting point) and work it through as a finger exercise.

Listen to the other hand

When one hand has a difficult passage, focus on the easier hand. You need to have worked hard on the tricky parts, of course, but in performance this tip will often make the problem disappear.

Stop practising!

. . . when you feel any tension in the arms or hands. If you don't, you might find you have to stop playing altogether as you nurse an injury.

There's no such thing as a difficult piece

I've sometimes been asked, 'What is the hardest piece you've played?', or 'Is Scriabin's Fifth Sonata more difficult than his Fourth?', and so on. It's certainly common for audience members to marvel at notes flying over the keys in every direction ('Your hands were a blur'), but less common for someone to comment about the voicing of a soft chord, or the spinning of a singing line over a delicate counterpoint. What is difficult or easy in execution is not always what it seems to the listening eye – a torrential glissando is just about the simplest thing to do on the piano, yet it can still produce a gasp of wonder. Great performances of the Chopin études are not those when the right hand is busy with speed, but those when the left hand shapes and colours the harmony and counterpoint with infinite finesse. Although it's a frivolity to discuss whether this piece is more difficult than that piece it's of crucial importance to analyse what makes something difficult in a passage, so that we can solve the problems. Few pieces (except certain études) are 'difficult' – they merely have difficult passages in them. And even these tricky passages are not tricky in themselves. Rather they contain tricky parts, or the combination of one part with another is tricky. To keep this in mind in the practice room is an important way of ensuring the performance onstage is safe and secure.

Unfinished

When is something finished? For a painter or composer the question is very real: when do you set aside a canvas or a manuscript and feel that you've given birth at last to something separate from you, the creative umbilical cord cut, its knot tied? Adrian Searle, in an illuminating essay on the painter Peter Doig, put it this way:

> Painters are often asked how they know when a painting
> is finished, and frequently find the question puzzling and
> mysterious even to themselves. The answer may lie in the
> fact that, having in a sense painted themselves into a space,
> having invested themselves in it through all the hours of
> looking and painting, the artist must eventually find a way
> out of this mental territory. At this point the painting becomes
> other to them, resists and even reproaches and denies them.

But what about a performer? When is the piece to be played actually learned? It's a vexing question, and I often wake up in the morning with an anxious feeling about it: is that sonata I'm playing next week *really* ready? And what does 'being ready' mean? It's not just being able to play through something at the right tempo, with the right notes, without forgetting – although that's a good start. It is more like feeling that you *wear* a piece. You feel so united with it and its intricacies of text, texture and mood that it's almost as if you have actually created it. I can feel for months that a piece is not properly under my fingers in the learning stage, and it's impossible to predict when the penny will finally drop and it will be ready to go. It's one reason I try to start working on new repertoire about a year before the first performance, allowing myself months of leeway, and, more importantly, months of marinating time.

But then there is the instant decomposition – like the sound on a piano itself, which starts to disappear as soon as the note is struck. I often find that a month or so without practising a complex piece and the ability to play it begins to melt away like ice from an unplugged freezer. It is here where I really envy the painter's ability to sign a piece, frame it, and forget about it; or the sculptor who can hang a hat on the arm of a finished statue. The closest instrumentalists come to this is in recording, but then the *listener* becomes the person experiencing the artistic creation in unfinished, imperfect time: the CD is always the same, frozen in immortality; the person hearing is always changing, experiencing the music through ever-decaying mortality.

Fingering

One of the most important aspects of learning a piece, then memorising it, then playing it well, is our choice of fingering.

We have ten digits with which to play thousands of notes in countless permutations, and whether we select the fingers we will use beforehand or just wing it on the night, a choice still has to be made. This choice is crucial at times because playing a certain note with the fourth rather than the second finger can mean the difference between a passage always feeling awkward and uncomfortable, or it rippling along effortlessly. And, as Artur Schnabel pointed out, we should not just look for the easiest fingering but for the most musical fingering, one that matches the phrasing, brings out the accents or inflections or allows a singing line to float along seamlessly.

For me, making those decisions during the learning process (however many times I might change my mind – that too is part of the deal) is essential. Not only does writing in the fingerings as you learn the notes make memorising easier and playing the notes more secure, it makes the learning process a real study . . . an uncovering and polishing of musical and technical stones. Too often students learn new pieces by sloppily sight-reading them until somehow they can play them through, rather than with a rabbinical pouring over the score. Fingering for clarity, for angularity, for texture, for sound, different for soft or loud passages, different for fast or slow passages.

In the early years of a career we can be asked to step in at the last moment for a colleague who has cancelled. I remember an occasion when I was in my early twenties getting a call to play the Bartók Third with the Chicago Symphony and Esa-Pekka Salonen. There was about a day's notice and I hadn't played the piece for a couple of years. I could accept the date because the nasty, twisting passage towards the end of the third movement was fingered and thus easier to recall quickly to my motor memory. It saved me a couple of hours work when I had only twenty-four hours to pack my bags and fly across the Atlantic.

Remembering what watered our roots

I recently came across an interview with Rachmaninov from 1910 in the *Etude*, a popular American magazine published by Theodore Presser from 1883 until 1957 that covered many musical topics and included contributions from many pianists over the years.

Any thoughts about playing the piano by a pianist as great as Rachmaninov are cherishable but what struck me most in this article was his belief that young pianists should study Hanon for up to five years during their formation and that they should play scales with the metronome in their exams:

> Personally, I believe this matter of insisting upon a thorough technical knowledge is a very vital one. The mere ability to play a few pieces does not constitute musical proficiency. It is like those music boxes which possess only a few tunes. The student's technical grasp should be all embracing.

It struck me because, although many of us have spent gruelling hours in the practice studio grinding through pianistic callisthenics of this kind, most pianists, when reaching maturity and having professional careers, discount their use: 'Oh, they're all a waste of time . . . You can study technique in the context of the pieces you're practising . . . Scales, arpeggios . . . useless!' And so on. I've heard such dismissive statements countless times from colleagues, both teachers and performers.

What's curious, though, is that those doing the dismissing have often done the exercises in their early years. They say their rejection of them comes from later experience, yet who is to assess how much benefit they derived from the exercises before they decided to trash them? Who can say if those pearly passages they are able to play today were made more lustrous by a facility developed years before?

I do think there comes a time when exercises are less useful, and time can certainly be wasted for young pianists if they rattle through Hanon mindlessly for hours on end. But I remember clearly my early teachers guiding me towards Beringer, then Joseffy and Pischna, then Hanon (although to be done in keys other than C major) and later other invented exercises of their own. Gordon Green, Derrick Wyndham and Adele Marcus all had their own drills. I still use my own adapted version of the latter's exercise passed down from her own teacher, Josef Lhévinne, as well as others I have stumbled upon, fiddling on backstage pianos.

I've never doubted the importance of such workouts in the early years, provided that they are done correctly, because playing the piano is about muscles and tendons and reflexes and joints as well as emotions and intellect. Reading an endorsement from one of the greatest pianists of all time reassured me. It's important to remember our roots, and to remember what nourished them in formative times.

A good edition

'What edition should I use?' – a common question from music students to their teachers. It might seem amazing to non-musicians, but when you decide to play a Beethoven sonata it isn't just a matter of going to the library and taking BEETHOVEN SONATAS off the shelf. Different editions will not only have a different layout on the page, but often different phrasings, dynamics, pedallings, and sometimes notes – and that's just those that aim to be faithful to the composer's intention, the so-called 'urtext' editions. The situation is much better today than it was a hundred years ago. Until roughly the 1950s music publishers would seek out famous pianists as editors, and it was expected that not only their personal fingerings would be added, but that changes would be made corresponding to the way they performed the pieces on stage – sometimes simplifications, sometimes added notes for extra brilliance, always extra dynamics and phrasing. Most of these editions are now largely to be found only in second-hand shops, although there is much in the von Bülow Beethoven sonatas or the Cortot Chopin works that is still of interest.

The problems often began within the composers' lifetimes, and there is still debate as to whether the original handwritten manuscript or the first printed edition should take precedence. When there are differences between the two, was it because of the composer's change of mind at the proofreading stage, or was it an error in the printing process, or was it the editor presuming a mistake and correcting it without checking with its originator? Furthermore, are a composer's second thoughts, read through in the cold light of day, always to be preferred to the original text, written in the full heat of creation? Chopin is a particularly vexed example because changing his mind in small details seems to have been part of his unique style of extemporised decoration within carefully thought-out structures. But then we are told by contemporaries that, however beautiful we might find his ballades, the ones heard when he was improvising in the salons of Paris were even more extraordinary. Thank goodness we have four of them written down, whatever edition we end up using.

Where do you sit to play the piano?

Well, in front of the keyboard, of course. Ah, but where?

Well, mostly in the centre, which (on a piano with 88 keys) is not middle C, but middle E. We sit there because it's where the body is best balanced. The fingers are only one part of playing the piano. Wrists, arms, shoulders, back, knees, legs, feet and elbows all play a vital role, and these need to work in complete union with optimum relaxation, strength, flexibility and control.

I realised many years ago, when learning Britten's *Diversions*, that when I played something for the left hand alone I had to sit slightly to the right of centre to achieve the necessary balance. It is a lot easier to reach out for notes at arm's length than to squash the arm in the opposite direction (think a tennis backhand stroke), so by sitting to the right you add an extra octave of ease to your keyboard possibilities. This is a fairly commonly known phenomenon. As the years passed, I realised that in certain two-handed passages the centre of gravity was not actually in the centre of the keyboard either, so I started experimenting with sitting slightly to the left or right and found it a revelation. Now, in almost every piece I play, I will adjust my position many times during its course.

Here are some examples:

Sitting to the right

There are so many possibilities in so many pieces, but try two passages in Rachmaninov's Third Concerto, the opening section of the third movement and the double-note passage after figure 56. The centre of gravity in both of these sparkling virtuosic passages is far to the right of middle C, so if you're facing the C above middle C for the former and a couple of notes further towards the right for the latter you will find you have much more control, particularly of the left hand. So much for *control* of difficult passagework; what about power? Try moving to the right during the third and fourth bars after figure 75 in the same movement. Because your body will be central to the massive chords being played you can direct all of the muscle power evenly between the notes, and increase the volume by about a fifth.

Sitting to the left

This is less frequently helpful, although try the opening of Rachmaninov's Second Concerto, up to figure 3, sitting opposite the A below middle C rather than the usual E above middle C. Again, you'll have more power in a passage where it's easy to be swamped by the orchestra because you'll be centred on the notes being played. One further example is the Brahms Fourth Ballade op. 10. To achieve a perfect tonal control of the Più lento section (bars 47–73) try sitting opposite the G below middle C. I can guarantee you'll be amazed by how much easier it is to shape these soft, murmuring phrases when the right elbow is not squashed into your ribs. In fact, I decided to play the whole of this piece sitting in this position to avoid having to shift during it and breaking the mood.

Anchored in the middle

Then there are those moments when you are sitting centre keyboard yet have to move temporarily or suddenly to the right or left. Rarely does a professional pianist actually fall off the stool but the very muscles we need to keep our balance are also those needed to play that arpeggio or chord with tonal control. This is when our knees can help. If we push them up under the keyframe (right knee if leaning left, left knee if leaning right, or sometimes both knees together) they will give stability to the torso, enabling us to move freely and to use all of the relaxed weight of our shoulders and backs to depress the keys.

Romantic in soul not body:
sitting still at the piano

In an earlier world an aristocratic elegance and effortlessness at the keyboard was something to be prized. I haven't asked an ear specialist about this, but I've often wondered whether we actually hear better when our heads are still. Even animals freeze to attention, cocking their heads, when they want to hear something important. Few things are more important for the pianist on the physical level than listening to the shaping of a phrase, the filtering of a pedal effect, or the balancing of a chord.

People often have a vision of the Romantic instrumentalist as someone who moves around, as if a physical embodiment of the music's inner turbulence. Conversely, some have the belief that the cooler the body language the cooler the music making. Historically this was not the case, and artists of premium Romantic credentials were often physically the most still when they played: Horowitz, Rubinstein, Hofmann, Rachmaninov . . . and Rachmaninov's great friend and favoured interpreter, Benno Moiseiwitsch.

Depressed: the amazing world of the pedal

Anton Rubinstein (the nineteenth-century composer, teacher, pianist and, indeed, founder of Russian pianism – not Artur Rubinstein, the twentieth-century pianist) is credited with saying that the pedal is 'the soul of the piano'. It's a lovely phrase, poetic and precise at the same time. The 'soul' both as the principle of being – what makes me *me* – and also the source of meaning for that 'me', the warmth that heats the blood.

Actually, if I'm going to be a stickler for complete accuracy, Rubinstein probably should have said 'dampers' instead of 'pedal', as the latter is merely the tool to activate the former:

the sole connecting with the soul. Every note on a piano is a hammer striking strings, and every one of those strings (except the short ones in the far treble) has a damper on it. As each key is depressed a damper automatically rises to allow strings to vibrate. Then, as the note is released, the damper falls down again onto the strings to snuff out the vibration. The pedal (we always mean the right pedal when using the singular word) lifts up all of the dampers at once, making the whole instrument a box of resonance. It's the opening of the curtains on a sunny day.

Up and down are the two simple actions the pedal can make the dampers perform, but just as there are a vast variety of curtains, so there is a variety of shadings these dampers can create. For many pianists the pedal is simply on or off – a binary blindness deaf to the infinite spectrum of possible sound. We are dealing with felt not a light switch, so how much of the fuzz is resting on the strings makes a crucial difference to how much of the sound is damped. I've isolated around eight different levels at which the right pedal can be deployed – from all the way down to all the way up. To have a truly sophisticated pedal technique means that we can use any of these levels at any time and in any combination. This can happen over a dozen times in every bar. A level 5 can change to a level 4 to a level 2 to a level 7 – all in under two seconds of music played – and that music can be racing along as if behind the wheel of a sports car.

In Sviatoslav Richter's notebooks he recalls an evening of chamber music at his festival in Tours, La Grange de Meslay, when there was no pianist taking part. All the pieces were for solo violin and cello and then duos for these instruments, with Oleg Kagan and Natalia Gutman. He says that, wonderful as the concert was, he missed the sound of the piano – or rather the pedal 'which would have created an impressionistic sound'. Of course, the pedal doesn't make any sound itself (unless it has an annoying squeak – unfortunately not unknown!) but it adds life to the piano's sound. Its absence is muesli without milk . . . or, indeed, life without music.

Depressed again: the (not so) soft pedal

It's not just the right, sustaining pedal that has rich possibilities lying between the foot's first touch and the pedal's full depression. The left pedal too has a similarly wide range of uses, and also six to eight levels at which it can be deployed. Rather than controlling the dampers, this pedal controls the hammers on a grand piano. It moves them from left to right as it's depressed, and then back again as it's lifted. Because most notes on the piano are produced by three identically tuned strings, when the hammers are moved to the right they strike only two of them, resulting in a change in sound. On earlier pianos the hammers could be moved even further across to play on only one string, hence this pedal's most common name: the una corda.

The una corda is much maligned and abused, mainly by being given the inaccurate and insulting name 'soft pedal' – a gross misrepresentation of its action and sophistication. Because of this, there has arisen a sort of shame about using it, as if it might suggest that a pianist's control of quieter dynamics were inadequate. It can certainly make the sound more muffled or muted, not so much because you are playing on only two strings, but rather that you are using a different, less worn part of the felt of the hammers. Herein lies the subtlety of this pedal's six to eight possible levels: every time you press the pedal even a millimetre you are striking the strings with a totally fresh set of felts. It's almost like inserting a new action into the piano with each increment of pressure exerted by a sensitive foot. So, rather than just crudely pushing this pedal down when you want to play softly, it should be used with the utmost delicacy and refinement, and used lavishly on its different levels. It's like another tool in your kit – a different brush (or eight of them) to achieve different textures on the canvas. I remember the French pianist Vlado Perlemuter suggesting its use at the beginning of Liszt's *Mephisto Waltz* no. 1 to create an incisive but restrained tone. I didn't do this myself, but in certain other Liszt works where I want a searing cantabile, I like to take the pedal down a tiny bit to level 1 or 2, where it's then possible to sink deep into the keys but avoid a strident jangle.

Oedipus might have looked at the modern piano and wondered why, if we have only two legs, there should be three pedals. We now turn to the one in the middle, which few people use.

Seldom depressed: the middle pedal

Richard Dawkins probably has more appreciation for the benefits of frequent Holy Communion than I do for the virtues of the middle pedal. I'm a true sostenuto pedal sceptic. I worked out that I've used it fewer than fifty times in over thirty years of playing concerts and over sixty CD recordings. In fact only three pieces I've played actually *require* its use: my own transcription of Franck's Organ Chorale no. 3, my reworking of Alfred Cortot's transcription of the Toccata and Fugue in D minor by Bach, and John Corigliano's *Etude Fantasy*.

So how does it work? Well, unlike the sustaining pedal's vertical shifting of the dampers, or the una corda's horizontal shifting of the hammers, the middle pedal is either on or off. It allows the pianist to sustain specific notes (isolating the dampers for those strings in the 'up' position) while leaving the rest untouched, as if a helpful pair of extra hands were holding those keys down for us. If the other two pedals evoke the world of a master magician weaving sounds mysteriously in the air, the middle pedal is more like a confidence trickster. Indeed, it has about it something of a wide boy's boast: 'Look! No hands.'

To be fair, it has been used very effectively by modern composers, and the Corigliano piece cannot be played without it. In the last moments of its Third Etude a minor third is held in the tenor register by this pedal, followed by the right and left hands scuttling up the keyboard in a non legato, chattering flurry of thirds and fifths – a brilliant effect. But I would never use it in repertoire where it was not explicitly requested by the composer. Debussy is the clearest case for me, as he didn't compose on a piano with a middle pedal. Although some of his long-held chords vibrating underneath other textures seem tailor-made for this device (*La Cathédrale engloutie* is a good example), it always ends up sounding synthetic to me . . . like a polyester patch on a woollen suit. Not to mention its mechanical unreliability. So often it either pulls other notes along with it in a mush of unintended discord, or it fails to work at all, leaving the pianist with his pants down, high and dry, the bottom fallen out of his harmonic world.

A different depression: finger pedal

For those who thought we'd exhausted the subject of pedalling there is still the question of something we call 'finger pedal'. Not to worry, this does not involve getting down on your knees and using your hands to push down the metal levers. It merely means using the fingers to hold down notes as an equivalent of using the sustaining pedal.

Generally speaking, we hold on to a key for as long as the composer asks us, and then we release it when we move on to the next note. In fact, one of the signs that a student is progressing in the early stages of learning the piano is when such independence of the fingers is perceived, and when the digits are moving up and down with logic and litheness. When we add a skilful right-pedal technique to such clarity of fingerwork we are reaching the stage of true proficiency. However, that is not the end of the story. We want to have our cake and eat it. We want a clear melodic line, unblurred, unconfused – but we also want the harmony to blend and to provide us with the foundation of a bass line. This is the moment to use finger pedal: a deliberate holding on to notes, making it sound as if we have included them in the sustaining pedal, but actually giving that foot pedal the freedom to enhance the melody rather than just bind together the harmony. In, say, a Mozart sonata we can cling to the contours of an Alberti bass (the omnipresent zigzag accompaniment of the Classical period) keeping the harmony from sounding dry while allowing the melody to sing above, untrammelled by muddy pedalling. Indeed, in some of Chopin's works he even notates this, giving the bass line longer note values.

A skilful use of this technique requires the most sophisticated virtuosity when we begin to create not just harmonic foundations, but inner melodies – counterpoint underpinning or weaving around the principal voice, everything working together in unity but with total independence of sound and rubato. As with the use of the left and right pedals, the possibilities of finger pedal are limitless. From whole passages to a single note, it can liberate lines, clarify textures, and enable our foot pedalling to be free to support the greatest flights of sonic fancy.

Trills I: easy does it

The trill is described by the Dolmetsch Online dictionary as 'a musical ornament or embellishment consisting of a rapid alternation between two adjacent notes of a scale'. A little more surfing and you can read about a great variety of ornamentation. This is one of the few areas in music theory and practice that has become simpler over the years. Harmony, rhythm, orchestration, form and instrumental techniques have increased in complexity, but trills since the time of Beethoven have stayed as trills: take a note and wiggle up and down with the note a semitone or whole tone above it.

I don't want to talk here about the vast topic of embellishment in earlier styles but rather about the practicality of actually executing trills on the piano. The guiding principle is evenness. If a trill is even, in volume and in the rhythmic space between the notes, it will sound good. This might seem like an obvious point, but trills frequently sound lame and lumpy because one of these aspects is missing. In particular, pianists often try to play trills too quickly. A slow, even trill will sound faster in a hall than a rapid, uneven one. It is also possible for a trill to be louder if it is played more slowly: there is literally more time to address the vertical stroke of finger pressure on key.

All of these points apply too to the trill's cousin, the tremolo. One example of this is at the end of Liszt's First Concerto where there is a tremolo between both hands that should be capable of drowning out a fire bell. With a relaxed arm (and a sufficiently brilliant piano) it can be a thrilling moment. If you play this piece, try that tremolo as fast as you can; then try it again, taking it down a notch or two in speed. You'll find that it is more powerful if it's slightly slower and completely even.

Trills II: a good fingering but not with the fingers

So trills will sound good if they are even, and a well-chosen fingering is a crucial aspect of this. The Russian pianist Josef

Lhévinne had a nice saying in support of using alternate fingers (first and third; second and fourth; third and fifth): 'Neighbours don't like each other.' There is a physiological element involved here: neighbouring fingers share tendons and muscles, and so trilling with the third and fourth fingers is an inefficient employment of the hand's natural design. But the real issue is a technical one: except for short, decorative ornaments, trills are best executed on the piano with wrist rather than fingers. If you trill with the thumb and the third finger (probably the best all-round choice for a strong, even trill) then these digits should remain almost still with a low-held wrist, rocking left and right, supplying all the motion. There is tremendous power and endurance in this sort of trill.

A few summers ago I was playing the Liszt First Concerto at the outdoor Blossom Festival with the Cleveland Orchestra. The performance was but a few minutes under way when a ferocious thunderstorm swept in. Shrieks came from all over the auditorium because it sounded (and felt) as if we were in the middle of an aerial bombardment. I had reached the long trill (E and F sharp) at the top of the piano in the third cadenza passage. What to do? The conductor John Storgårds had put down his baton with a broad smile, as if to pause the performance. But I kept trilling. The storm continued to rage. Should I stop? I kept trilling as I considered the options, preferring not to stop the piece. After about a minute or possibly more the centre of the storm moved away and I was able to continue the concerto from the trill, which had kept the faith while all around had doubted.

Without a relaxed arm and a gently rotating wrist it would have been impossible to continue this embellishment for as long as I did without seizing up. Perhaps when audience members ask to see a pianist's hands they should really ask to see his or her wrists, forearms, elbows (especially), shoulders, and feet too for they all have an essential role to play when seated in front of the keyboard of a piano.

Trills III: six random tricks

1. If a trill (say, from A to B) is causing you problems, try thinking it downwards (from B to A).
2. As well as slowing down your trills to gain evenness, try measuring the shorter ones in exact numbers of notes. We sometimes think a measured trill will sound stiff, but any trill does actually have a finite number of notes. Sometimes it can be useful to decide on that number before playing.
3. Starting a trill can be tricky. Try starting the trill slightly more slowly and making an (imperceptible) accelerando.
4. Ditto with ending a trill. Sometimes we can swallow the endings of trills and create a lump. So consciously relax as the trill ends.
5. Experiment with fingerings. It can be good sometimes to start with 13231323 and then switch to 1313.
6. If you want to make a diminuendo in a strong 1313 trill, try switching to 1212. This automatically makes the rotating movement of the wrist less wide, thus automatically reducing the trill's volume.

Up to speed

I made the point earlier that there's no such thing as a difficult piece but Hummel's B minor Concerto op. 89, to take one example, raises an interesting issue. Although it is not difficult to learn the notes – the patterns are all easily memorable, and the figuration usually lies quite well under the hand – it's extremely difficult to play. This is due to a combination of the speed and digital dexterity required to play the double-notes and awkward extensions when the tempo is as fast as it should be. To play one of the harder passages at crotchet (quarter note) = 60 is, shall we say, about Grade 8; to crank it up to crotchet = 100 is not just a bit harder ('Press down the accelerator a bit more'; 'Practise for three months rather than three weeks and you'll find it falls into place'). It involves a *totally* different technique. We need to fit a whole new engine in the car. We have to lighten and clarify articulation at high speeds, to shape chordal textures, to adjust reflexes, and the key to this new technique largely rests in the way the elbow serves as a fulcrum.

Aunt Mabel chasing after her cat as it runs towards her beloved vegetable patch might hitch up her skirts and achieve quite a speed, but on an Olympic racetrack she is not going to be able to come close to a world-record holder – even if she's being chased by a tiger.

Agile wings not muscular legs

Controversies about fast tempos do not just occur in fast pieces. Chopin left us metronome markings for many of his works but some people find them too fast, especially for the 'slow' pieces. His Nocturne op. 27 no. 2 is marked dotted crotchet = 50; and the Étude op. 10 no. 3 is a similar case, marked quaver (eighth note) = 100. In both of these pieces I've not heard a single recording or performance that comes close to the tempo indicated by the composer. The étude has a lovely, romantic tune . . . so people simply play it slowly. Chopin gave us metronome markings for all his études so why is it that they're played by everyone (who can manage them) at roughly the tempos marked, except just *this* one, and the other slower Étude op. 10 no. 6? In many performances they barely reach half tempo. What makes the case of op. 10 no. 3 extra puzzling for me is that when we reach the central section (when the lovely, romantic tune is finished and it is marked poco più animato) pianists often simply double the speed. Could Chopin have been right with his original choice of tempo? I absolutely think he was, and only in Josef Hofmann's Chopin recordings (sadly he didn't record these three pieces) do you hear how these slow, but not so slow, tempos in Chopin might sound. The second movements of the latter's Chopin concerto recordings come close to the metronome markings and sound perfect to me.

I think there are two vital clues to finding a solution to this tempo conundrum: first, Chopin's style is a step forward from Hummel, not two steps backward from Rachmaninov. It is 'Classical plus' not 'Romantic minus'. Second, the bel canto, coloratura style that so influenced Chopin aims for maximum grace, poise, lightness . . . and velocity. It is the virtuosity of leggiero: agile wings, not muscular legs.

Beats and bleats

It's misleading to refer to the middle movement of sonatas or concertos as 'the slow movement'. It would be more accurate to label them *slower* movements, as, historically, they served as a contrast in pace between two livelier sections. Too often this uniform 'slow' appellation is misleading. We reach the middle movement and everything sags and comes to a halt, including our pulses. Pulse is a wonderful way to describe the rhythmic undertow in music because it's related to the very lifeblood coursing through our bodies: the heartbeat of harmony.

The second movement of Mozart's C major Concerto K. 467 is marked Andante (walking pace) and in two beats rather than in four by the composer. This makes the pulse slower as the music is faster. Here is an example of how this works. Try singing and conducting (probably best when no one is around) 'Baa Baa Black Sheep' in four and in two. In four the stress would be on the italicised words: *baa baa black sheep have* you *any wool*. See how stodgy it sounds. Now try it in two: *baa* baa *black* sheep *have* you any *wool*. Although the pulse is slower, the music flows; it has a line. The same is true in the Mozart, although many people play it too slowly. So slowly in fact that its two 'baa's barely bleat in the same breath, and it is almost impossible to hear it in two.

Tempo is one of the most subjective elements in music as it depends on acoustic, instrument, and often on context and mood. It seems that performance tempos have generally become slower over the years. When this flows from a desire to inject expression into music we love, it can be excusable – and sometimes sublime; less so when it is an artificial attempt to appear profound. Some composers have resorted to using metronomes to narrow down a performer's choice of tempo, although it is curious how our selection of the exact beats-per-minute can change from day to day. Brahms gave a few of his works metronome markings but then, disillusioned, gave up. One of the pieces to which he did give a marking though (the Second Piano Concerto) is a fascinating case. The first, second and fourth movements (unusually, this concerto has a symphonic extra one) are totally non-controversial – the marked tempos are roughly observed by everyone. The 'slower' third movement (another Andante) is almost *never* done at Brahms's suggested tempo. This example is particularly interesting because it rules out the frequent excuse that a composer's machine might have been faulty. A few notches slower could be a matter of taste or circumstance; half the speed is simply wrong.

Those who do can't necessarily teach

George Bernard Shaw famously wrote in his play *Man and Superman*: 'He who can, does; he who cannot, teaches.' This 'Maxim for Revolutionists' was meant to take the wind out of the sails of teachers, and there might be some who fit this description, although instantly I can think of those who can do both well and those who do neither well.

To invert GBS's barbed quip, there are definitely those who can do but who can't teach. Gordon Green – someone for whom teaching was a passion – felt that only those who had struggled to play the piano, who didn't find tearing through the complete Chopin études before breakfast a doddle, would be able to understand and help students. When Horowitz was asked by Gary Graffman how to play octaves, his advice was merely to practise them slowly. Either his secret was to remain secret or – more likely – Horowitz had no idea how his particular fingers, wrists and arms worked in the way they did. It was a freak of nature.

Those teachers who work mainly with pre-college students are much less famous than conservatory professors, yet they are much more important. If someone can't play by the time they're sixteen it's unlikely they will suddenly learn how to do so. Things can be improved vastly in the later teens and early twenties (and there are notable exceptions such as the late-starters Harold Bauer and Sviatoslav Richter), but good foundations are essential for good buildings, and it's those teachers hidden away in studios working long, dedicated hours who deserve much more recognition than they get. This is the time and the place when technique is being formed in subconscious reflexes, when habits good or bad are being established, when we learn how to read a score in all of its subtle detail.

In those formative years it is essential for a teacher to be strict, but as the years progress, and after the technique is well established, the teacher (like a parent) needs gradually to step back, to allow the personality and individuality of the student to flourish. By the time the pianist reaches college age it is vital that the teacher values the uniqueness of the student and allows for lots of freedom. One of the curses of the competition mentality is that it forces talented young players to present fully groomed interpretations early on. There is insufficient time for experimentation, for exploring dead ends, for making mistakes, for trying daring or outrageous options. In short, the student has to sound like a (usually boring) CD as soon as possible. Gordon Green used to say to me when I was around fifteen, 'My dear boy, forget about competitions', so convinced was he that their deadlines limited the development of the imagination. He added: 'I don't really care how you play now. It's how you will play in ten years that interests me.' He took the long view. I think he would have made a good farmer.

One of the easiest ways to tell if a conservatory teacher is good is if each one of his students sounds different. Leschetizky was a case in point. His pupils included pianists as diverse in style as Artur Schnabel, Paderewski and Ignaz Friedman (and Gordon Green's teacher Frank Merrick). In fact, good teachers should probably not even *like* everything each of their students does. The more talented the pupil, the longer the leash of freedom should be. At early pre-college level I am suspicious if there is a large divergence in the quality of students in a studio; necessary technical and musical knowledge is not being transmitted. At conservatory level I am suspicious if the quality of students in a studio is too uniform; it can suggest that grooming is taking place. A teacher at this advanced level should be a guide and a mentor . . . and, gradually, eventually, a colleague.

Masterclasses

In later life Franz Liszt spent a lot of time teaching, not so much one-to-one lessons but public sessions with students gathered around him from all over the world. The 'masterclass' is a form virtually invented by Liszt and it survives in good health up to the present day. I give them myself regularly in cities all over the world.

Not all the students who travelled to play for Liszt were equally talented and on one occasion a certain young man failed to impress him. We don't know exactly what was said, whether it was harshly critical or merely discouraging, but the man left the class and went off and killed himself. Liszt's other students didn't tell the Master about this as they knew it would cause him deep distress (he was by nature a kind and immensely generous man) but this event has stuck in my mind over the years as an example of the power our words can have on others, particularly when uttered in front of other people.

Teaching a musical instrument is a very personal, almost intimate process. Over the years many students have formed relationships with their teachers that have gone beyond the musical. On occasion this has been sordid, sometimes criminal, and at other times it has led to a stable marriage, but even in the most innocent circumstances what is being handed on from teacher to pupil is explosive. To lead someone to be more expressive in a piece seething with passion and emotion is to handle fire. Individual lessons have their own kind of danger and all of us who have private students are alert to this. Indeed music colleges now have many safeguards in place, including mandatory windows in their studios.

In a public class the vulnerability is of a different kind. To tell someone they lack musicality or emotional commitment, or to show up their inadequacies in front of colleagues is to hold a knife to skin. I've witnessed many examples of this over the years. One famous pianist was teaching a good but workmanlike student. At one point the teacher pushed the student aside, performed the passage just played by the student with scintillating bravura, stood up, looked at the audience to see the reaction, smiled and said, 'Now you try it.' The student was visibly humiliated and – more to the point – no more aware than before how to make the passage better. This was simply an example of someone in a position of power showing off. It was a form of abuse and most of us in the room felt uncomfortable.

We are parents to our students. We should have in mind only their welfare, both musical and personal – the two are joined at the hip. But then: 'The teacher's job is to make him- or herself dispensable.' A wise comment from a teacher who knew when (gently) to push the budding pianist-pupil out of the nest.

Why don't (music) students attend concerts?

Many universities and conservatories run recital series for visiting artists. Especially in America they often have a large budget and a distinguished history of presenting performers, sometimes even whole orchestras. It's a wonderful way to show that the arts matter to such institutions and that specially invited guests need not be restricted to academics coming to give a lecture.

I've done many recitals in these settings over the years but, surprisingly (shockingly), students often fail to attend. Even when free tickets are offered, when concerts take place after school hours, when students are music majors, the audience nearly always consists only of parents and grandparents. This is surely a serious abuse of academic life. Here are young people – one hopes too young to be jaded and too young to be wearied by the responsibilities of work and family – who simply haven't any interest. I really think it should be a requirement, at least for music students, to attend these concerts . . . even if just one a year? I must add that I've come across young musicians burning with enthusiasm, combing every noticeboard for student tickets, listening to everything they can find . . . but they're the exception to a disheartening rule.

I'm not advocating some tyrannical, rigid attitude towards higher education where there's no room to have fun in the way each person chooses, or to goof off, or to veg out, or to party a little bit too much. But education is a privilege, and even in living memory a majority was simply unable to afford to attend university. My own father was forced to work as soon as he left school and was able finally to get his longed-for arts degree only thirty years later from the Open University. Going to concerts was a luxury of which many could only dream, or for which they had to save up. I can't see how someone studying singing should expect a high grade if she found an episode of *The Sopranos* more alluring than a recital on campus by a great, living soprano.

College years are short, precious and expensive. The least we can expect is that those undergoing them should *want* to be educated.

What does the most talented young pianist need most?

There are hundreds of thousands of piano students all over the world. It is something of a wonder that so many young people are willing to spend so many millions of hours pressing down those 88 black and white keys. The best of them will usually move on to study at music colleges, academies, conservatories and universities. They arrive with hopes and objectives: to immerse themselves in music, to play better, to prepare for a future career, to gain performance experience, even sometimes to become rich and famous. Many will leave disappointed, and still more will leave with jobs different from what they expected at the start of their education. But what about those very few who are destined for major solo careers? Nothing is ever guaranteed, but after you have heard some musicians play only a few bars you know they have something special, which will at least give them a stab at success.

What advice would I give to the few, the most talented pianists entering music college? I would say, 'Learn concertos.' Almost every career starts and is established with concerto appearances. Even if a solo debut creates an initial stir the building up of a reputation will come with orchestras and conductors. It's partly the decline of the piano recital. I'm told that there are fewer recital series taking place as every year passes. But it's also that the opportunity to play in large halls and within earshot of important career-controlling managers will usually happen with an orchestra sitting on one's left. No unknown young pianist will get to play recitals in large halls but many have had the chance to stand in at the last minute for an indisposed artist in a concerto. Such an opportunity (at the Ravinia Festival in Chicago in 1999) launched the sky rocket that is Lang Lang. And, ironically, the career of the pianist he flew in to replace, André Watts, had burst into brilliance in a similar way in 1963 when he stood in for an ailing Glenn Gould in New York.

Because conservatory exams and auditions normally require solo repertoire students tend to crack open the scores of piano-and-orchestra works only when they have a date in the diary for which they are preparing, whether it's a concerto competition or a public performance. But by the time a career is beginning, and the contracts are being signed, and the travel agent is busy booking flights, it's almost too late – unless you learn phenomenally quickly, or drive yourself to the edge of a nervous breakdown.

Even after a concerto has been learned, it will often end up being rehearsed with too little time, with a cantankerous conductor, performed under great pressure, on an unknown, unresponsive piano, frequently with jet lag. While you're still at college, and have the time, you should prepare at least a handful of the most familiar concertos . . . and a few unfamiliar ones too. I've been asked over the years to play Saint-Saëns's Fifth at least as much as Beethoven's Fifth. My own baptism of fire, aged twenty-two, was to have to play them both in the same week and both for the first time, on one rehearsal at the Barbican Centre with the London Symphony Orchestra. I certainly felt older if not wiser the following week. And there were at least another five concertos on my piano awaiting urgent study.

Learn concertos before you have to, and learn them well. They will become part of your life as you play them with different orchestras and conductors throughout your career. And as you stand in the wings with the orchestra tuning and the lights dimming and the applause beginning they will await you at the keyboard like old, intimate friends.

Trying to practise away from the piano and trying to try to pray

In 2007 I wrote a book entitled *The Bible as Prayer: A Handbook for Lectio Divina*. It was certainly not written from a standpoint of expertise, nor really from experience, although I have spent countless hundreds of hours trying to pray, and I know that to *attempt* to pray is to pray. No, its purpose was to encourage me to keep trying to try to pray.

I'm not a naturally religious person: my default button is doubt; my factory setting is scepticism. But I am a Christian by conviction with roots deep in Judaism (which should be a given for any follower of Christ) and branches reaching out as widely as possible to the wisdom of other faiths and none. My own copy of my own book is in mint condition. I know its spine needs cracking as mine needs strengthening.

What is for sure is that I need to keep practising the piano. After a few days away from my instrument joints get stiff and reflexes lose their spring. But is it actually necessary physically to press down keys in order to get useful work done? Practising away from the piano is one of those wise habits I've always known about and believed in but almost never put into practice.

So difficult can it be when travelling to find an instrument that being able to practise effectively in an armchair in my hotel would be wonderful. No taxis to take to locked-up, badly lit backstages, or to overheated homes with moulting Persian Blues and over-attentive hostesses. I could simply open my score of Beethoven's Fourth and get started, with a cup of Darjeeling Second Flush steaming at my side.

Although trying to pray is itself prayer, I don't think that trying to practise is actually practising; to improve our piano playing is possible and there are tangible, concrete ways to achieve this. But despite numerous physical considerations when playing a musical instrument – and at times we are more like footballers than philosophers – in the end it's the brain that holds everything together. Thousands of hours in hundreds of music colleges are wasted by students mindlessly thrashing through repertoire.

The brain should always connect to the fingers at the keyboard, but the fingers themselves can sometimes choke the brain. Some pieces need space and silence to be fully deciphered, and sometimes we are less able to think about the music we are playing while we are actually playing it. Pacing, phrasing and the bigger architectural picture require a certain distance for their subtleties to be unlocked. We must touch a canvas to paint on it (all right, there are exceptions but you know what I mean) but unless we step back from it during the creative process we shall never grasp its full perspective.

My great-grand-teacher Leschetizky made the same point in an interview, 'In the matter of practice, I never urge a student to work so many hours a day. One may be enough. The musician is like a painter, who frequently spends his time in looking at the work he has done, and in thinking what he will make of it, without so much as touching the easel.'

So I write this in the spirit of my book on prayer: I want to work away from the piano, I know it's good and wise, I've done very little to put it into practice . . . so far. And I am allergic to cats.

PEOPLE AND PIECES

How much do we need to know about a composer?

If you didn't know that Beethoven was deaf, or that Rachmaninov was Russian, or that Liszt was a man of deep but sometimes conflicting religious beliefs, would it mean you couldn't play their music as well? Actually I do think that ignorance about Liszt's life and personality makes playing his music less likely to be convincing and idiomatic. But Chopin? I think it's less important to know that Chopin was Polish than to know the music of Hummel. Even if Chopin's native land lingered in his consciousness (although not in his conscience – he never made the slightest attempt to return home after his move to Paris at the age of twenty), it does not inform us how to play his two concertos with anything like the same level of acuity as knowing the Hummel concertos (and their metronome markings). I think our appreciation of Bartók's music would be impoverished if we did not know a little of the Hungarian roots of so many of the folk melodies and rhythmic patterns he uses, but if we thought Rachmaninov came from Moscow, Texas, rather than Moscow, Russia, I'm not sure it would make a *crucial* difference – even if the composer himself might have scowled with extra severity at such a thought.

How terribly British is our Elgar . . . yet his music owes far more to German influences (Brahms, Wagner, Richard Strauss) than anything growing in Queen Victoria's soil. But then again, each year on the Last Night of the BBC Proms, we hear 'Land of Hope and Glory' in the Royal *Albert* Hall – a grand memorial by the widowed monarch to her beloved husband, Prince Albert of Saxe-Coburg and Gotha. Their deeply loving and intimate relationship was conducted entirely in German for its duration. Perhaps knowing that does help us to play our Elgar better.

Elgar the Roman Catholic

When Elgar was fifteen years old, a girl called Thérèse Martin was born in northern France. By the time Elgar died she had already been canonised as St Thérèse of Lisieux, Patron of the Missions and of France, with her statue in countless churches all over the world – the fastest-growing cult in the history of Catholicism. All of this on account of *one* book, her autobiography, which has the simplest message of spiritual childhood and its resulting trust in the Fatherly care of God. That a girl, hidden away in a convent and dying aged only twenty-four, could have made such a revolutionary impact on popes, theologians and millions of other people is a clear indication to me of a deep and unquenched thirst in nineteenth-century Catholicism: a thirst for a warm, personal, simple approach to God. Although Thérèse was born and died within Elgar's lifetime, for him, it seems, her message came too late.

Elgar's own Catholicism is important to an understanding of his music. Although it wasn't, as it was for Olivier Messiaen, the principal subject matter, it did create many of the internal tensions and frictions out of which flowed a profusion of deeply personal musical ideas. Whether it's his struggle with its religious or moral teachings, or because it locked the doors that otherwise might have been opened to professional or social acceptance, Catholicism is the backdrop to every scene in Elgar's creative life.

It's easy to forget that less than thirty years before Elgar was born, the Catholic Emancipation Act of 1829 had finally allowed Catholics a degree of religious and civil freedom that they'd been denied for the best part of three centuries. Although the violence and martyrdoms of the reign of the first Elizabeth were more than two centuries in the past, there were still severe restrictions regarding worship, land ownership and employment until this change in the law. Indeed, when Elgar was born, Catholics were not able to attend Oxford or Cambridge Universities.

In Elgar's day, Catholics themselves were socially divided and religiously polarised, which made them both defensive and timid. At one end of the social scale were Irish labourers, with neither a voice in England nor a say back home. Contrast them with the few surviving Catholic aristocratic families, the recusants, hidden away on their vast country estates; all they wanted was to be left in peace. When John Henry Newman, a man at the centre of the Church of England, embraced Rome, he encouraged others who wanted to become Catholics; his conversion made Catholicism intellectually respectable to those born within its walls; and, in a wider context over the remaining decades of the century, it influenced Roman Catholic theology itself.

Elgar's religious life is easy to chart – or at least its recorded facts. It all began at St George's Catholic Church in Worcester where Elgar's father, William, was the organist. In 1848 William married Anne Greening, who, although an Anglican, used to accompany her husband to church regularly on Sundays. A few years later, she decided to convert to Catholicism herself. Elgar's father, on the other hand, remained an agnostic until his deathbed conversion. Edward was born and baptised in 1857, and later attended small Catholic schools in the area. After he left school aged fifteen he began to assist his father at St George's, arranging and writing music for the choir, and eventually taking over the post of organist. Soon afterwards he began to give violin lessons and among his pupils was Alice Roberts. When her mother died Elgar lent Alice his well-worn and annotated copy of a favourite poem: *The Dream of Gerontius* by Cardinal Newman. They soon became engaged and, in 1889, married at the London Oratory. They had a Catholic ceremony but without a Nuptial Mass as Alice was still a Protestant, but then three years later Alice was received into the Catholic Church at St George's.

So much for the record. Exploring Elgar's internal Catholic life is a different matter. In the 1890s, he was still attending Mass every Sunday, and often afternoon Benediction on the same day as well. He didn't talk very much about his personal faith or lack of it but there are a few clues in some of his letters. In 1892 he wrote a touching letter to the children of some friends during a Bavarian holiday, taking up a third of the text to enthuse about the folk-Catholicism he found there: 'No protestants . . . workmen carrying their rosaries . . . bells ringing at the elevation [in the Mass] at which people in the streets take off their hats and make the sign of the Cross . . . crucifixes on the roadsides . . . chapels to the blessed virgin . . .'

Also on vacation in the 1890s, Elgar made extensive notes in a travel book entitled *Tyrol and the Tyrolese*. The Victorian author's anti-Catholic remarks about the priesthood and the peasant people obviously offended Elgar and his annotations can be clearly seen in the copy now owned by the composer David Matthews. The words 'bigoted', 'superstition' and 'blind' are vigorously crossed out by Elgar. Next to the author's suggestion that sins of a sexual nature are thought less serious and more easily forgiven in Confession, Elgar has written, 'That is a lie!'

It's when we consider the background to his most Catholic work that the real clues begin to reveal themselves. When he decided in 1899 to set Cardinal Newman's *The Dream of Gerontius* to music, he was taking an enormous risk. It was his first major commission and his career was all set to take off. To choose this deeply Catholic text in a country where 'Papists' were still a suspicious, despised and even ridiculed minority was a provocation courting disaster. Yet he went ahead, with total disregard for any possible censure or disfavour. It's hard to believe that the words had no religious meaning for him at the time, especially as he was aware that his faith had been an impediment to his career. At the front of the score of *Gerontius* he wrote the bold letters: A.M.D.G. (*Ad Majorem Dei Gloriam*) – 'To the Greater Glory of God'. This is the motto of the Jesuit order who, by the way, ran St George's when Elgar was there. Elgar poured his soul into this work. He described it as 'the best of me' and said that he'd written out his 'insidest inside'. When his publisher August Jaeger suggested that there was too much 'Joseph and Mary' about the work, Elgar replied, 'Of course it will frighten the low-church party but the poem must on no account be touched! Sacrilege and not to be thought of . . . It's awfully curious the attitude (towards sacred things) of the narrow English mind.' For me, a narrow-minded, low-church, English teenager, fifty years after Elgar's death, *The Dream of Gerontius* was an exotic plant indeed, and it turned out to be the very first step on the road to my own conversion to Catholicism.

But only weeks after its famously disastrous premiere, Elgar wrote again to Jaeger, 'Providence denies me a decent hearing of my work: so I submit – I always said God was against art & I still believe it . . . I have allowed my heart to open once – it is now shut against every religious feeling & every soft, gentle impulse for ever.' Although this sounds more like a temper tantrum than a reasoned rebellion against belief, it does suggest that Elgar's Catholicism was more cultural than deep-rooted; also I think there's a telltale clue in his use of the word 'Providence': a strained and un-Catholic view of God as Fate rather than Father.

This crisis after *Gerontius* appears to mark the beginning of a steady walk away from the Church, and of an increasingly black, depressive mood that would overshadow his emotional life until the end. Although after reading Shaw's *Man and Superman* in 1904 he could still write, 'Bernard Shaw is hopelessly wrong, as all these fellows are, on fundamental things: – amongst others they punch Xtianity & try to make it fit their civilisation instead of making their civilisation fit It.' Nevertheless, there are revealing references that continue to pop up in letters mentioning Alice or their only daughter Carice being at church while he remained at home. For a Catholic to miss Mass on Sunday deliberately was considered a mortal sin, and to do so was a clear sign that Elgar's institutional faith was nominal.

After *Gerontius*, Elgar began work on a trilogy of oratorios based on the life of Christ and his Apostles. He did his own research, read many biblical scholars, and consulted two Anglican clergymen. Catholic biblical scholarship at the time lagged far behind and some of the volumes piled up on his desk would also have been on the Vatican's list of Forbidden Books. The first decade of the twentieth century was the high point of the modernism controversy, when a witch hunt was under way against certain theologians who had been making an attempt to reconcile aspects of modern science and philosophy with ancient doctrines. It's likely that Elgar was conscious of these issues and he might have been troubled by some of the discrepancies being uncovered in the latest research, undermining his trust in the veracity of traditional Catholic teaching. He never completed this trilogy, only *The Apostles* and *The Kingdom* were finished. *The Kingdom* caused him greater birth pangs than any other work, according to his wife. It seems that he'd simply lost interest in the subject matter – the embers of belief were glowing very faintly indeed.

Over the years, Elgar's attitude towards his Catholic faith degenerated from discomfort and indifference to fierce antipathy. On his deathbed in 1934 he refused to see a priest, and asked for his cremated remains to be scattered on a favourite river. Until 1963, cremation was forbidden for Catholics, and so in itself this request was a demonstrable turning away from the Church. In the event, Elgar did see a priest and is buried next to his wife in St Wulstun's Church, Little Malvern. The contrast with Gerontius's preparation for death, set to music thirty years earlier, is a chilling drama in itself.

In 1913 he wrote to his old friend Nicholas Kilburn that the only quotation he could find to fit his life was from the Demon's Chorus in *Gerontius*: 'The mind bold and independent, the purpose free must not think, must not hope . . .' To George Bernard Shaw, with whom he established a fond friendship, he's said to have wished that the negatives of the Commandments could be removed and inserted into the creed: I do *not* believe in God; thou *shalt* commit adultery, and so on. And, speaking of which, by the middle of the Edwardian reign, Elgar had formed a new, engrossing attachment to another Alice – Lady Alice Stuart Wortley, or 'Windflower' as he nicknamed her. This relationship almost certainly remained unconsummated but its intensity and passion was clear even to his wife. We can still hear its power today in works such as the Violin Concerto and the Second Symphony, both of which were written under the Windflower spell. Many have lost their faith when required to choose between it and something of which it disapproves.

Nevertheless his witticism regarding 'nots' in the commandments and creed are more than just a frustrated reaction to the denial of some forbidden fruit. There's an important and profound Christian reflex hidden here. Christ himself manifested a great intolerance of unnecessary rules and laws, which he described as heavy burdens on people's backs that religious leaders refused to help lift. 'The Italians make the rules; the Irish keep them' is a quip that reveals candidly the scrupulosity flowing vigorously in the bloodstream of the Northern European Catholicism of the time. This way of thinking created a religious atmosphere, a repressive and reactionary fog, with which someone of Elgar's background and generation would have been all too familiar. It gave little consolation or defence when someone was called on to face the doubts and darkness that often come in matters of faith.

To return, as I began, to St Thérèse of Lisieux. At the end of her short life, amid terrible physical suffering, she admitted that only her faith prevented her from committing suicide, and that even her belief in God was under assault. In his longer lifetime Elgar witnessed the collapse of England's empire with regret, but he didn't live long enough to benefit from the influence of both Thérèse and Cardinal Newman on the slow crumbling of the Vatican's outer shell, and the subsequent revealing of a more gentle, consoling heart within – a Father not Fate, with all the tied 'knots' of alienation lovingly loosed.

Tchaikovsky didn't commit suicide

Tchaikovsky didn't kill himself. At least, there is no evidence that he did, and many reasons why he might not have. The Third Piano Concerto op. 75 is an exhibit I would definitely bring along to the trial – not as a verdict-clincher, perhaps, but something to help scotch the rumour that surfaced in the months following the composer's death and that entered the textbooks by the early twentieth century.

This concerto was meant to be his Sixth Symphony, but a more famous and, it has to be said, a more wonderful piece pushed it out of the way. After he had finished writing the *Pathétique* Symphony he returned to his abandoned E flat major sketches and began to recast them as a piano concerto. Only one movement was actually finished before his death, and, unlike so much of Tchaikovsky's music, it has a mainly cheerful spirit, with distinct Gallic echoes of Saint-Saëns and the most toe-tapping trepak I know. Only in the enormous cadenza does the heart really begin to beat faster, but that is more from the wild flurries of notes flying over the keyboard than from darker clouds of passion.

Tchaikovsky's physician, Vasily Bertenson, who diagnosed his fatal illness, later wrote of him, 'It is difficult to imagine a purer optimist. His bright vivacity, his love of life and of every living thing, his faith in the triumph of good and in people . . . never left him.' I believe that the trial of Oscar Wilde, which was a contemporary event, and the wild hysteria it unleashed in the English-speaking world against homosexuality, had a lot to do with this verdict of suicide. It was a bit of scurrilous gossip that turned into a rumour and eventually became an assumed biographical fact. The self-loathing homosexual who took his own life fitted the post-mortem bill, explaining and excusing Tchaikovsky's sexuality but ultimately damaging the way we think of him – as both man and musician. The Sixth Symphony is certainly a dark, tragic work and we could choose to regard it as the most beautiful suicide note ever written; but that scenario becomes less convincing when we hear what he wrote next: the jolly, rambunctious gaiety of the Third Piano Concerto.

Tchaikovsky's First Piano Concerto

Tchaikovsky's First Piano Concerto. Every conservatory practice room, every teacher's studio, every competition's final round rings with those wretched opening D flat major chords. I avoided the work as a student and for years afterwards, despite being offered performances, and I was quite content for it to be the missing piece on my repertoire list. But then one day I was teaching it in a masterclass and it began to reveal itself. I began to see the particular conflicts within: the innocence of lost childhood singing poignantly alongside a searingly emotional adult world; the Classicism of the composer who admired Mozart above all, combined with the Romanticism of the composer whose heart and sleeve were bigger than all others. It seemed a work alive and on fire – inspired in every bar. Ideas about how I might play it started teeming in my mind and I realised that I *really* wanted to learn it.

What is it like to revisit a work like this with only hand baggage? To hear the piece that founded a style and forget the pieces that followed in its train? (It was the first time in musical history that symphonic argument and self-conscious virtuoso display would unite in a concerto.) The problem with well-known pieces is that we think we know them, and there are few pieces more 'set in their ways' than Tchaikovsky's First. But what if its famous opening chords were originally not punched-out fists of notes strutting confidently up the keyboard, but instead, sprigs of spread, harp-like arpeggios accompanying a slow waltz – one in a bar? (This is indeed what the original version of the score shows.) And what if the second movement's opening theme is not a tragic romance but instead a little girl's song on Christmas morning, all winter dreams, marked Andantino semplice ('faster than walking', 'simply')? And what if the whole piece is not the product of a self-hating neurotic who wallowed in his suffering until he ended it all by his own hand, but rather by a man beloved of children, hard-working, generous, humorous and full of sheer good fun? Listen to the last movement of the Second Piano Concerto for evidence of that!

'It's a complete mess, but come in. You're welcome.' Not his craftsmanship, of course (not for nothing was Mozart his favourite composer); but the emotional chaos and naked vulnerability of Tchaikovsky's life is channelled through, wrestled with and poured out in his music with such disarming honesty that it invites the listener into a unique intimacy. We can refuse to enter his world, and many do, but once inside, his mess becomes ours. In the sparkle of the *Nutcracker*'s naivety or in the tug of despair in the Sixth Symphony we see *our* lost childhood, *our* grown-up pain; and we find we have a new friend who understands this and gives melodious voice to the turbulence within.

Tchaikovsky's Second Piano Concerto: why I changed the second movement

On my recording of the complete Tchaikovsky concertante works there are three different versions of the slow movement of the Second Concerto. In the context of the entire piece we played the original version – not a note changed or cut; but, as an appendix, we offered two solutions to the problem of this movement – one contemporary with the composer, the other contemporary with the pianist.

At early performances of this concerto criticisms were raised about two issues: its length, and the lack of prominence of the solo piano part in the second movement. It seems from Tchaikovsky's letters that he acknowledged these problems in the piece, and he suggested some cuts himself as well as handing over the score to his friend and pupil Alexander Siloti for further amendments. Siloti incorporated the composer's first-movement cut (in the orchestral tutti of the development section) but when it came to the second movement, instead of some judicious tweaking here and there, he rewrote it entirely, slashing it to bits, reducing its length by 50 per cent and, as a result, changing a serious, deeply expressive movement into a lightweight intermezzo. Tchaikovsky was horrified when he saw what Siloti had done, and absolutely refused to accept his changes. There are at least three letters in which he makes this clear in the strongest terms, yet this version was not only published after the composer's death, but it became the only version heard for fifty years or more. (And thus became the version choreographed by George Balanchine.) Although I would never dream of playing it in the context of a performance of the piece, I thought it would be interesting to include it on my recording as a historical document.

Nevertheless, when I first played this piece in concert – in the original version – I was struck by a problem in this second movement: the music is so glorious, and I couldn't understand why it just didn't seem to 'work' as a structure. I didn't think that it needed cutting, as early critics had suggested, but I did feel that the solo instruments were out of balance. It was wonderful to hear the solo violin and cello declaim the theme at the start of the movement (especially after the first movement's extraordinary, super-virtuosic, turbo-charged pianism). The changes of character were perfectly judged: first solo violin, then solo cello with violin accompaniment, and finally the piano. Then follows the dramatic B-section that Siloti cut – full of turbulence, with brilliant cadenzas for solo violin and cello. Finally, when things have calmed down, the three solo instruments play the opening thematic material, united as an equal trio for the first time in the piece. So far, so good.

But then Tchaikovsky suggests a cut – at the point when the piano stops and the solo violin and cello continue and develop up to a passionate climax. It is one of the most inspired moments in the whole work (even Siloti kept this passage), but there is a problem with it, as Tchaikovsky obviously realised if he suggested removing it. The issue, though, is not its length but that it begins as an exact repeat of the opening section, a jarring reprise after the three instruments have already been playing together with equal prominence. It's a little as if the pianist were suddenly unwelcome in the room at the party, and is sent out to help with the dishes at the very point when the best bottle of claret is about to be opened. I realised that if the music here is played by the piano instead, leading naturally into the original piano cadenza, it would give a symmetry to the whole movement, lending a psychological cohesion, and circumventing the need to remove any music.

Tchaikovsky's Concert Fantasia

The wonderful, neglected, elegant, exuberant Concert Fantasy or Fantasia. Actually I debated whether it should really be listed in French on my recording as it is in the original Russian edition: *Fantaisie de Concert* (its form taking precedence over its function), especially as 'fantasy' in the title is about more than the structural shape of its musical journey. My computer's built-in dictionary suggests the following definition for the word: 'The faculty or activity of imagining things, especially things that are impossible . . .' – yes, the writer of those words *had* seen the first-movement cadenza of the piece in question. There is some astonishing virtuosity in the *Fantaisie de Concert*, but there is also great humour – in particular, two crazy moments.

In the second movement ('Contrasts'), after the soulful solo cello and piano melody and its orchestral development, in fact at the very point of climax, a tambourine enters, shaking and dancing with syncopated thrusts. I don't know of a more astonishing moment in any piano and orchestra piece than this. It is silenced for a couple of bars with more orchestral dolour, but then it re-enters and remains as a flamboyant jester until the end of the piece. Perhaps it is meant to evoke sleighbells on a bitter, Russian winter's morn?

But it's not the only mad moment in this 'fantastic' work. After the opening few minutes of the whole piece, with the flutes of champagne, the chiming bells, and the modal, singing melodies, there is a pause. Then the piano enters alone, ruminating on a new theme based on a descending triad. This turns out to be the beginning of a cadenza of almost ludicrous length – totally out of proportion and beyond any expectation the opening of the work might have suggested. The pianist doesn't even have the courtesy to comment on the material the orchestra has thus far supplied, but rather sweeps all aside and simply shows off for close to ten minutes. After the keyboard has been left in tatters, and after a winding-down conclusion of slightly fake profundity (the pianist playing more and more slowly, until grinding to a complete halt), the orchestra simply starts the piece all over again from the beginning, as if shrugging its shoulders and getting on with business as usual: '*Well*, I don't know what *that* was about, but we have a concert to play, so let's now get back to the task in hand.' Humorous, but also open-hearted: an intimate glimpse of Tchaikovsky the man – with a great big smile on his face.

Artificial gushing tunes

The 1954 *Grove's Dictionary of Music and Musicians* infamously evaluated Rachmaninov's music as 'monotonous in texture [with] artificial and gushing tunes', the popular success of which was 'not likely to last'. This is somehow beyond offence today, so off the mark is its prediction, so dated its taste. On just about every day of the year Rachmaninov's music is heard and applauded across the world, and his concertos will be performed as long as there are pianos made and pianists to play them.

His four concertos are like markers throughout Rachmaninov's life, covering his entire creative career. But the numbering of them is not quite so straightforward. There *is* a Piano Concerto in F sharp minor by Rachmaninov – no. 1, op. 1 – written in 1891 when he was eighteen. This youthful work is recognisably by the Russian composer with his distinctive voice (that melancholy with the samovar just a little hotter than expected), but the writing – orchestrally, pianistically and structurally – is ungainly and awkwardly tailored. Despite the heart-on-sleeve appeal of its voluptuous melodies, the shoulders are too square, the seams too visible. By 1917 Rachmaninov had published 38 other major works and, as a mature, world-famous composer, pianist and conductor, he decided to revisit this early piece. By the time he had finished, a whole new creation was revealed, keeping all the vigour of its youthful origins but tightened with the rigour of the experienced composer. The airship had become a sleek jet and this airborne work is, in fact, really his fourth piano concerto, written down on the page eight years after he had completed his Third. (He tinkered with it again two years later just to adjust a few small details – a stitch here and there.) Rachmaninov was proud and fond of the revised First Concerto, and he asked two of his closest pianist friends, Vladimir Horowitz and Gitta Gradova, to play it. They both promised to do so, but neither did. I first learned the piece as an understudy for Gradova, who was due to perform it with the Chicago Symphony and James Levine at the 1985 Ravinia Festival. She was totally committed to fulfilling her promise to Rachmaninov but, sadly, she died before she could and I played it instead.

The Second Concerto (1901) was the first to be written in its present form, and the one piece of the five piano and orchestral works for which there has never been any suggestion of revisions or cuts. It's his first great work, his most popular, most often performed and, arguably, the most perfect structurally. It sounds as if it wrote itself, so naturally does the music flow; yet, it appears to have caused the composer the most difficulty in creation. Rachmaninov had writer's block, and it is claimed that the hypnotic ministrations of Dr Nikolai Dahl (the work's dedicatee) got the composer's juices flowing again. However, Rachmaninov's grandson told me that this was not the case. His grandfather was in love with the psychiatrist's daughter; hence the visits to the doctor's house – the source of this alternative story apparently being the composer's wife. No proof, but no matter. The Second Concerto is both an open floodgate of inspiration, and a work of supreme romantic intensity. It was written in Russia at a time when Rachmaninov thought of himself principally as a composer rather than a pianist, and the solo writing is perhaps the most awkward and least natural of the five works, with thick orchestral textures always threatening to cover the piano part.

The Third Concerto (1909), however, was expressly composed for his first US tour as a pianist, and it appears that he learned it on the high seas during his voyage to New York. The piece was dedicated to the great pianist Josef Hofmann but was never played by him – possibly because of his famously small hands, but more likely because it was such a lot of work to learn. It is the most overtly virtuosic and highly strung of the five works, a veritable encyclopedia of pianistic difficulties. But it is virtuosity in the truest sense: not merely fast fingers, but an entire world of sound, nuance, pedalling, texture, rubato and dynamic control. It is these qualities that make the Third Concerto such a show-stopper in the right hands. It's also the piece in which Rachmaninov most skilfully used compositional techniques of thematic transformation. Many of these are hidden away, perhaps most wittily in the whirling dance that ends the second movement where the simple, melancholy opening theme of the whole concerto is metamorphosed into a ballroom encounter of the most sophisticated glitter.

By the time he wrote the Fourth Concerto (1926, revised in 1941) Rachmaninov had left Russia for good and had ceased to compose about ten years earlier. He was busy playing concerts and adapting to life in the West, a West that itself was changing beyond all recognition in those battered years after the First World War and the revolution that had chased the composer away from the land of his birth. Everything was shifting, nothing (social, political or musical) was certain and the Fourth Concerto is Rachmaninov's reaction to such change; it was both his attempt to keep up with fashion, as well as expressing a profound discomfort at the disappearance of a world he loved. With its fragmentation, restless melancholy and profound dis-ease, the Fourth Concerto is a musical *Waste Land*, an evocation of alienation equivalent in some ways to T. S. Eliot's poem published four years earlier. Whereas the nostalgia of the Second Concerto is heart-warming and affectionate, in the Fourth it is heart-wrenching and painful: a view of the lonely, exiled composer backstage under the harsh lights of his dressing room, rather than bathed in the footlights of the auditorium. It is the most 'modern-sounding' of his works, the least played, the least known, the least loved – except for a few who, like me, love it the most. The final 1941 version, tight as a drum, is a unique, original, twentieth-century masterpiece.

One post-war musical response to overripe romanticism and the disturbance of social change was neoclassicism – a spring-cleaning of harmony and form, with bright colours, sleek shapes and crisply defined rhythms. Stravinsky, Prokofiev,

Hindemith, Ravel, Busoni and Strauss among others all experimented with this new aesthetic, and the *Rhapsody on a Theme of Paganini* (1934) is the closest Rachmaninov came to writing his own neoclassical work. The lean orchestration and piano writing were a new departure for him. Only the eighteenth variation, one of the greatest glories of thematic transformation, is cut from the velvet plush of his earlier style (and was apparently languishing in a sketchbook for a number of years). The *Rhapsody* is perhaps the most American of all Rachmaninov's works, not just because of the crooning lyricism of variation 18, or the snappy, big-band moment in variation 10 (jazz accents and stresses clearly indicated in the score), but because of its overriding optimism. The *Dies irae* plainchant serves as a sombre counter-melody to Paganini's spiky theme but it never seems to be *that* serious in its 'Day of Doom' predictions. Indeed only a year before its composition Prohibition had been lifted, and might there be the hint of a dry (vodka) Martini in the lean sparkle of the piano's figuration, not to mention in variation 15 a tribute to Art Tatum, whom the composer admired?

Authenticity playing Rachmaninov

One of the first LPs I was given as a small child starting to learn the piano was a mixed recital including Rachmaninov's miraculous 1921 recording of his transcription of Fritz Kreisler's *Liebesleid*. From that moment a door opened for me into a pianistic world where I immediately felt at home. A few years later I was given his recordings of his concertos, long before I heard anyone else play them, and I was genuinely puzzled when I did eventually hear some modern performances. Where was the characteristic rubato of the composer's playing? Where were the flexible, fluent tempos, always pushing forward with fervour? Where were the teasing, shaded inner voices forming chromatically shifting harmonic counterpoint to the melody? And what about the portamento slides in the strings? It was like eating a traditional dish far from home and missing the correct ingredients. What is a pesto sauce without garlic? What is sushi with brown rice?

Concern with correct performance practice does not just apply to the Classical and Baroque periods; it has to do with the very dialect of musical language itself. To take too slow a tempo, with numerous ritardandos, for the first subject of the first movement of Rachmaninov's Second Concerto means that one of the longest melodies in the repertoire becomes fragmented and earthbound, robbing the second subject when it arrives of its natural place of repose and sentiment. To ignore the composer's vivacissimo marking for the 'big tune' at the end of the Third Concerto changes a climactic peak of ecstatic energy into an over-long section sounding heavy and emotionally sated. (His clear desire for this pacing is seen not only in the score and in his own recording but in the 1941 performance by Horowitz, a pianist whom the composer considered peerless in this piece.) To fail to capture the true improvisatory style of the solo melodic passages, with their agogic accents and subtle balance between ardour and languour, is to fail to communicate the message itself. And if we are concerned, as we should be, with dots and accents in Schubert, why should we not have equal interest in some of Rachmaninov's characteristic markings: his tenuto lines indicating a certain kind of lingering, or many of the slurs in the strings suggesting a gentle slide?

It would be of no service to the music and of little artistic interest to try simply to copy the composer's recorded performances. What is important is to understand and to become fluent in the pianistic language of that time – both of Rachmaninov and of his contemporaries who, though unique individuals, shared many common 'turns of phrase'; then we can feel free to speak or sing our own personal words with an authentic vocabulary and intonation.

Recording Rachmaninov

'Stephen, how about recording all of the Rachmaninov concertos?'

'Great!'

'In Dallas?'

'Great!'

'In "live" performances?'

'Great!'

'In one three-week period?'

'*What!* I need to think about this.'

But my manager caught me on a clear, sunny day when I'd slept well. I phoned back fifteen minutes later and said, 'Yes, let's do it!'

It was over two years from the time of that discussion to the recording itself and on days when I hadn't slept well, or the weather wasn't clear and sunny, many questions would haunt me. How would I have all the pieces ready at the same time? Would I play too inaccurately because of nerves? Would I play over-carefully because of nerves? Would I play both inaccurately *and* over-carefully? How could I achieve a sense of freedom and abandon with microphones pointing inside the piano and throughout the orchestra like so many shotgun barrels? How could I have the necessary romantic spontaneity when I knew that every musical breath would be frozen onto the face of a compact disc, clenched in the teeth of its jewel case?

I had played all the Rachmaninov concertos before and had always wanted to record them, as much as I did anything else in the repertoire. As I digested the idea of a 'live' recording, I became more and more excited and enthusiastic, despite the practical worries. These pieces are 'live' works written for a 'live' audience, the pianist's final bars of interlocking chords demanding applause, the songful melodies lodging as a lump in every throat.

As the contract was drawn up it was decided to record the *Rhapsody on a Theme of Paganini* on a separate occasion, after a concert and in the same hall but in a studio session. This was done ten months before the main three-week period and it turned out to be a good way to get into the swing of things. I was able to try the resident New York Steinway, which turned out to be perfect for the repertoire. I could sample the astonishing Presidential Suite at a nearby hotel, noting that it had a baby grand piano in its over-sized living room. I could hear how the piano and orchestra sounded on tape, meet the wonderful recording engineer, Jeff Mee, see where the control room was situated, see where the coffee machine was situated . . . generally have a clear picture in my mind to carry around over the following months as the demanding three-week period drew near. Over and above these thoughts was my delight at being able to work with two dear Andrews: producer Keener, and conductor Litton.

I wanted this music to sound authentic. With Andrew Litton I found a conductor who felt exactly the same way and had spent years in Dallas addressing these issues with the support of the concertmaster, Emmanuel Borok – a violinist whose understanding of Romantic style went from his bow and fingerboard deep into the entire string section. I was utterly thrilled with the sound that surrounded me on stage during the first week of concerts.

But the recording began badly. My first evening in Dallas was spent with some of the major donors. I was to talk to them onstage about how I choose a piano for a recording and to demonstrate the DSO's two Steinways, a Hamburg and an American. I knew the latter from recording the *Rhapsody* the year before and so I sat down to show the audience what I liked about its power and fabulously mouldable cantabile sound. Except that now it sounded terrible. It had become soggy, dull and uneven. I began to panic. The Hamburg piano was beautiful, but too Classical in touch and nuance for Rachmaninov and there was no time to find another instrument before the rehearsal the following afternoon. I got on the phone immediately to the piano technician, James Williams, to alert him and it turned out he had not seen the piano for two months. I was furious but took a deep breath and trusted the success of the whole recording into his skilful hands. After eight hours of work the instrument was coming back to life and by the second rehearsal it sounded like the piano I had loved before.

The first week was four performances of the Second Concerto with an 80-minute patch session just half an hour after the final concert; the second week was the First and Fourth Concertos in three performances with a slightly longer patch session on a separate day; and the final week was the same as the first but with the Third Concerto. We would convene the mornings following the concerts and listen to the tape, noting things we liked and didn't like from the performances. Four concerts sounds like a lot of time to 'get it right', but when you add mobile phones, beepers, raucous coughs, a thunderstorm with lightning that could be heard as clicks on the tape, noisy page turns from the orchestra, a snoring audience member, and the inevitable wrong notes and ensemble issues, it doesn't seem that much. And the patch sessions, rigorously controlled by union rules of starting, finishing and taking breaks, seemed desperately short – good only for emergency repairs. Oh, and did I mention the fire alarm . . . ?

The recording almost ended badly too. When I first arrived and met with Andrew Litton he told me that the Third Concerto would be the easiest of the four to put together as they had played it dozens of times and knew it very well. In fact it turned out to be the most problematic as we had very different ideas about certain musical issues and held those ideas strongly. Swords clashed and sparks flew but, in retrospect, I think this was good because a lot of energy was generated for this most energetic of pieces. And we remained the best of friends throughout, helped, of course, by succulent Texas steaks and some fine red wine from the State where Rachmaninov chose to make his final home.

The other Rach Three

The so-called 'Rach Three' is one of the most famous works in the repertoire, a fascinating and intricately lush forest of notes and perhaps the pinnacle of the Romantic piano concerto genre. But there is another, lesser-known Rach Three, his symphony, written almost thirty years after the concerto. It is the only symphony Rachmaninov recorded himself and it is a performance that shows him as an indisputably great conductor. All the late Rachmaninov works seem to me to be infused with a deep sadness as he returned to composition after a ten-year hiatus. Between his op. 39 (Études-tableaux) and his op. 40 (Fourth Piano Concerto) the world had seen the First World War, the Russian Revolution, the changing role of women, jazz, and countless other social, political and musical changes. No longer in the role of a publicly melancholy Russian Romantic, the composer is revealed in the last works in a private world of raw anguish and bewilderment, coming to terms with a new life in the New World.

The Third Symphony and the Fourth Concerto are full of tears. They seem to me a bit like a grandfather unable to understand the enthusiasms of his adored grandchildren yet trying desperately to do so. There are shadows of every movie not made, every tired, retired actress who was never a star, every thwarted opportunity in life or love, wrinkled faces dry of weeping, boxes of fading photographs, unrecorded interviews of unspoken memories. Above all, an instinctive sense that no one would understand, and if they did, they would care only a little. A return home with so much to say but no energy or opportunity to say it.

This sadness is seen in a letter Rachmaninov wrote to a friend in 1937 about his Third Symphony:

> It was played in New York, Philadelphia, Chicago, etc.
> At the first two performances I was present. It was played wonderfully. Its reception by both the public and critics was sour. One review sticks painfully in my mind: that I didn't have a Third Symphony in me any more. Personally, I am firmly convinced that this is a good work. But . . . sometimes composers are mistaken too! Be that as it may, I am holding to my opinion so far.

Eighty years after the piece was written and premiered I think he would be happy and content to know how much he, his music, and this piece are loved.

How Beethoven redesigned the cadenza

When I was in the process of playing and recording all five Beethoven concertos it struck me that there is an interesting development from one to the next in the way the composer treats the cadenza.

The cadenza developed in the eighteenth century from the

custom of delaying and decorating the final cadence (hence the name) just before the end of a movement – a dramatic, penultimate pause ruminating in freedom beyond the constraints of the Classical form's structure. In Mozart one is expected to play for about two to three minutes using themes from the movement along with stock patterns of arpeggios and other figuration and finally rounding everything off with a trill. Often in the score only this final trill is indicated, an unchangeable 'happily ever after' convention of the time. The custom was for the performer to improvise something on the spur of the moment – Robert Levin is a rare case of someone who brilliantly and audaciously continues this skill today. But in the nineteenth century it became more common to play either the cadenzas Mozart wrote as examples for his students or to play one written down, by oneself or by another.

Beethoven's first two concertos were published without cadenzas and only later did he write some – indeed two completed ones for the First Concerto (one elegant and economical, the other an insanely extravagant example of how he might have sounded when improvising). For the Second Concerto he wrote a cadenza many years after writing the actual work, on the cusp of his late period. It sounds in places as if some rejected sketches for the second movement of his Sonata op. 101 had been muddled around on his desk. I've never liked it, not because it's out of style (which it is) but because it seems to me to lack coherence. It's ungainly, awkward to play and roughly constructed. Also, it doesn't sound improvised. So I decided to write my own. At least it's authentic to do so, even if what I've written is not.

In the first movement cadenzas of Beethoven's Third and Fourth Concertos we see the beginning of the Romantic development of the idea: the cadenza as a long stretch of music that is the artistic climax of the whole work, often containing its most inspired musical ideas. This became the norm later in the concertos of Schumann, Tchaikovsky (First and Second), Grieg, Rachmaninov (First) and Prokofiev (Second) among many others. Although pianists have written their own cadenzas for Beethoven's Third and Fourth Concertos, and he would have expected as much, somehow the best bits are missing if the composer's own cadenzas are missing.

When we reach the Fifth ('Emperor') Concerto a further development has taken place. Now the cadenza is at the very beginning. Three stock-in-trade chords (I–IV–V^7) are the punctuation for exuberant pianistic decoration that covers the entire keyboard. Then, where we might expect a conventional cadenza towards the end of the first movement, Beethoven expressly comments in the score: '*Non si fa una cadenza, ma s'attacca subito il seguente*'; 'Do not play a cadenza, but instead proceed immediately to the following.' The rules have changed – and not for the first time from the hands of this mighty iconoclast.

Beethoven, in redesigning the piano concerto cadenza, prepared the ground for the whole Romantic period. From this point on, cadenzas would either be present as an unchangeable, fully composed climax, employing all the composer's skills, or absent because of a greater overriding symphonic design.

Brahms First or Second?

The Brahms piano concertos are two of the greatest pillars of the Romantic repertoire. The First is like a symphony where piano and orchestra seem involved at times in a titanic struggle, themes hurled across the stage with dramatic rhetoric; the Second is more like a massive chamber work, where the musical ideas are an exchange rather than a confrontation. If the First is more about proclamation, the Second is perhaps more about reception – a speaker versus a listener. The way each piece opens tells this story in a few seconds: the First with its ferocious drum roll, a clap of thunder pinning the audience back in its seats; the Second with a gentle horn solo inviting that same audience to lean forward in dialogue.

G. K. Chesterton, in a typical bon mot, wrote: '*Bleak House* is not certainly Dickens's best book; but perhaps it is his best novel.' If I could borrow and paraphrase that paradox I might say that of the two Brahms piano concertos the Second is the *better* piece, but the First is the *greater* piece. I think the Second is better constructed, better orchestrated; themes are better developed; harmonies are better judged; textures are better balanced – but for me the First has a greater burst of pure, utter, natural genius. Its flame flares with such intensity, and with such promise of more to come (he was only twenty-five when he wrote it), that I find myself overwhelmed by it in a way I'm not by the Second, written twenty-two years later.

That is until I recorded and played them both in the same concert in Salzburg. The First Concerto is work enough for one evening (or morning on that particular occasion) but when the interval arrived, instead of the usual backstage process of winding down I had to crank up for an even bigger piece and challenge. Returning to the piano on the Grosse Festspielhaus's stage, I was physically warmed up but emotionally spent and drained, sated by the richness of the first half's feast. But then the horn solo sang from the back of the stage and I replied with that gentle, lapping, ascending arpeggio (has a more intimate moment of chamber music even been woven into a piano concerto?) and instantly I was refreshed by this most conciliatory of musical exchanges, Brahms at the height of his confident maturity. As the orchestra took over from me after my first cadenza with their ringing tutti (only one forte not two) I was completely revitalised, as if I had received a shot in the arm – music's second wind, the eagle's strength-renewed wings.

Brahms's final stroke of genius, after the ravishing slow movement where lyrical song-like sections frame a turbulent central climax more anxious than tragic, is the Allegretto grazioso finale. Many have suggested that this understated, joyful movement lets the work down and is a misjudged anticlimax. I think the only misjudgement is when performers ignore Brahms's flowing metronome marking in the Andante and create a heavy-handed movement that makes the work's overall structure lopsided. The graceful last movement, from its opening when the melody shyly sidles in on the subdominant through its later *à la hongroise* moments to the finale tarantella, is one of Brahms's greatest compositional triumphs.

For all the grandeur and excitement of the First Concerto's youthful flare, the Second's older vintage seemed wiser, more fascinatingly complex as I revisited and rerecorded both pieces in the same concert. Its musical arguments seemed more nuanced, more open to exploration, more a search for common ground where, as in life, the sun can shine brightest . . . and warmest. Indeed, its multifaceted subtlety reminded me of reading one of those great, rich, life-enhancing Dickensian novels.

Dvořák's Concerto for Ten Thumbs

I was chatting to a musician friend, Nicholas Ashton, a few years ago and he asked me what repertoire I was learning at the time.

'The Dvořák Piano Concerto,' I replied.

'Ah . . .' The warmth of affection in his voice could be heard through my iPhone. 'That's probably my favourite piano concerto.'

Then a year or two later Sir András Schiff asked me the same thing at a party. His eyes lit up when I mentioned the Dvořák Piano Concerto and he responded by sending me a beautiful, hardbound facsimile of the autograph a few days later with a kind note: 'This wonderful work still needs our help until it's properly appreciated by musicians and the public as well.'

But then there are those, famous and distinguished conductors among them, who have told me they hate this piece and would never want to perform it. 'Oh, I did it once. A few nice moments but not one of his best efforts.' 'Just proves that Dvořák wrote some duds.' How can a piece like this provoke such diverse, extreme reactions from fine musicians? Why is the Dvořák Piano Concerto a relative rarity in concert programmes? Why is it almost never heard in the halls of music colleges? Why do many musicians not even realise that Dvořák wrote a piano concerto? I don't think it needs any apologies but it does need apologists committed to introducing this neglected but glorious, lyrical work to those who don't know it.

There are a number of reasons perhaps why it is not central to every pianist's repertoire. First, it's really, *really* hard to play . . . and it doesn't sound like it (not a performer's choice combination). Sviatoslav Richter wrote of the two months it took him to learn Bartók Second and the two years of work for the Dvořák. It's truly like a concerto for ten thumbs because the composer, who was not a pianist, seems to have had little idea where fingers comfortably or effectively sit on the keyboard. Whereas Liszt flies along the track marks as if in a sophisticated sled, Dvořák's wheels are forever getting stuck in a rut. I'm speaking physically not musically, of course.

Then there's the published score. Until very recently the only printed materials available came with two versions of the piano part, one by the composer and one by the Czech pianist and teacher Vilém Kurz. This latter version, from 1919, was the version played most (when the piece was played at all) until well after the Second World War. Recognising the fiendish and ungainly nature of the original piano-writing Kurz, rather than making a few judicious adjustments here and there, decided to try to make a Lisztian sled out of a Dvořákian cart. Unsurprisingly, it didn't work. It feels a little as if Dvořák has found himself in his farm boots at a society ball. The 'glamour' of Kurz's version sounds fake and misjudged, a rococo fireplace set into the rustic walls of a country cottage.

And then there's the famous recording, the one most people hear first, by Sviatoslav Richter and Carlos Kleiber – the dream team of the most famous pianist and conductor of their generation. Incomparable, legendary artists but, to quote Richter from his diaries, 'It's not a good recording I'm afraid because the atmosphere wasn't good . . . I wasn't on form and neither was Kleiber . . . lots of shortcomings – and not only in the piano part . . . Carlos kept splitting hairs and I myself was very tense. Hence the absence of the charm and simplicity so characteristic of Dvořák.' A refreshingly honest assessment! That recording has been frustrating for me because when the Dvořák Piano Concerto has come up in conversation with orchestral managers or conductors the exchange often goes something like this.

'Yes, I listened to that piece once and didn't like it. I don't know what you see in it.'

'Which recording have you heard?'

'The Richter one with Kleiber.'

Some pieces sound like great pieces, even in poor or uncommitted performances, but not the Dvořák Piano Concerto. It needs the help of an affectionate heart directing the pianist's fingers and the conductor's baton. In fact, I think the pianist needs to be able to say, along with my friend, Nicholas, at least during the concert itself, 'This is probably my favourite piano concerto.'

Schubert's hurdy-gurdy man

The pathos of the final song in Schubert's late cycle *Winterreise* is almost unbearable. It's as if the composer, having taken us on this bleak journey, leaves us alone at the end of it, pointing us in the direction of a man who symbolises total disintegration. Life ends not with a sacrifice but with a slinking away, like the mangy dog in the poem.

There's a performance of it by the Irish singer Harry Plunket Greene, readily accessible on the internet, which is in its own way as remarkable as the song itself. It is sung in English and with a disarming lack of vocal sophistication. We sense that all artifice has been stripped away. We hear a singer past his prime, even with a strain in his voice; it is as if he has become the song – an old man, whose vocal 'plate' is empty, conveying the hopelessness evoked by the composer. When a singer, whose instrument is his body, faces the end of a career journey, it is an existential termination. The body itself has broken down; the vocal cords are shot.

Schubert was not a sophisticated man, he was not an intellectual; but through a kind of inexplicable genius his scratching, blotching pen acted as a conduit for music of the most intense beauty and human expressiveness, without ever being calculating or self-conscious. This song was probably composed as quickly as it would take someone to write out a fair copy of the score, like water flowing out of a tap. The problem is, as the years pass and as our reverence for such a master and his masterpieces increases, we coddle and maul and groom and practise and fuss and worry and obsess . . . until we've covered over the wound of such a song with scented bandages. We want to be admired as lieder singers and pianists; we use the song as a vehicle for our own vanity; we want the world to recognise our sensitivity; we approach the hurdy-gurdy man with a coin in our hands but with a camera at our backs.

The final irony in this final song is that the Leiermann is . . . a musician. A spent, ignored, failed musician. In the crack of Plunket Greene's tired voice we hear the song acted out; we pass the lonely man; we cannot, despite the song's question, 'with him go'. We can perform the other twenty-three songs as if on stage, but for this last one the make-up must be removed. We are alone, in the dressing room, head in hands, the janitor outside, about to lock up for the night.

Schubert and Simone Weil: a note for a CD

To listen to someone is to put oneself in his place as he speaks. To put oneself in the place of someone whose soul is corroded by affliction (*malheur*), or in near danger of it, is to annihilate oneself.

Those who are unhappy need nothing in the world but people able to give them their attention . . . nearly all those who think they have this capacity do not possess it. Warmth of heart, impulsiveness, compassion, are not enough.

Simone Weil

Franz Schubert, in his late piano sonatas, is revealed more as a listener than a speaker, the 'heavenly length' being that open-ended time it takes for a person to respond to the suffering of another. The composer and performer thus enter into an intimate communion of hearts, and the audience can only ever be eavesdroppers. There is a contrast here with Beethoven, the declamatory prophet, whose individualism tends to manifest a will to power, to overcome; Schubert's individualism is more a withdrawal into solitude, and a sense of being overpowered and overcome.

Both composers reached full maturity only to discover that they had serious, debilitating physical ailments, one a loss of hearing and the other syphilis. There is something curiously enlightening in the nature of these afflictions, which almost becomes manifest in their musical personalities. Deafness is like a brick wall to be confronted, it is tangible and local; whereas syphilis is more like an ocean to be waded into, uncertain, intangible, its horror creeping up on a victim unawares.

There is not true affliction without social degradation or the fear of it in some form.

Simone Weil

The Sonata in A minor, D. 784 (1823), and the Sonata in B flat major, D. 960 (1828), are the first and last of Schubert's mature works in this form. The former was almost certainly written at the time that Schubert first learned of the seriousness of his illness. The chilling desolation of its first movement's first subject seems to be a direct response to that tragic news, the 'strong–weak' appoggiatura in bar 2 sighing wearily or angrily throughout the entire movement in both melody and accompaniment. However, as in so much of Schubert's work, it is the moments of major tonality that seem the saddest. Perhaps only Mozart equals Schubert in this ability to transform the sunshine of a major key into a mood of heartbreak and pain.

The second movement is strangely unsettling for three reasons: because of the almost enforced normality of its theme after the bittersweet bleakness of the first movement; because this theme is doubled in the tenor voice, a claustrophobic companion seeming to drag it down; and because of the constant, murmuring interjections (*ppp*) between the theme's statements. The helter-skelter finale introduces a note of panic, as triplets trip over themselves in their scurrying counterpoint. Here, as in the first movement, the glorious second subject, in the major, seems unsure whether to laugh or cry, calling to mind Rückert's poem 'Lachen und Weinen', which Schubert set the same year.

> Beauty captivates the flesh, seeking permission to pass directly to the soul. Beauty is a fruit which we contemplate without trying to grasp it.
>
> Simone Weil

The opening movement of the Sonata in B flat major goes beyond analysis. It is one of those occasions when the pen has to be set down on the desk, the body rested against the back of a chair, and a listener's whole being surrendered to enter another sphere. Here there is neither the superficial gloss of refinement nor the mawkish self-consciousness of profundity; rather Schubert's miraculous ability to bare his soul without a trace of narcissism – a combined result of his humility and universality, and an exquisite unawareness of both.

> Art is waiting: inspiration is waiting. Humility is a particular relation of the soul to time. It is an acceptance of waiting.
>
> Simone Weil

This movement's nine first-time bars (117–25) have been the subject of a certain controversy for two reasons: first, because of their strange, dislocated character; and second, because they force the pianist to repeat the movement's exposition. Hence they have often been omitted. I feel that they are important, not only because the same genius who wrote the rest of the work also wrote these bars, but also because their radical nature should alert us to a hidden message beyond the obvious. This weird, stuttering, hesitating passage has an important psychological significance in the structure of the movement: it emphasises the fact that even in the most lyrical moments there lies disquiet; it contains the only example of the shuddering bass trill played *ff* – a terrifying glance of 'recognition'; it is a premonition of drama to come in the development section, and it enables both the return of the opening bars and the C sharp minor second-time bar to have a greater, magical effect. The other objection – that repeats for Schubert were a convention he was unable to shake off, and that to hear the exposition once is enough – doesn't convince me. These nine bars are as far from convention as is possible, and a repeat is never a duplicate. It is ultimately a matter of patience – with the music, with oneself – of allowing something time to unfold and to grow.

Affliction is by its nature 'lost for words'. The afflicted silently implore to be given the words to express themselves.

Simone Weil

With the second movement a new dimension of isolation and alienation seems to be introduced, which is underlined by a contrast and separation of texture. The right hand's sorrowing song of lament seems in another world from the left hand's detached, almost oblivious accompaniment, a shadow of dance making the poignant melody even more heart-rending. The contrast here is not opposition but incomprehension. Again the paradox of Schubert's tonality: the central section, in sunny A major, should be consoling, but there is no music more anxious or troubled, a desperate attempt to remain cheerful amid over-whelming sorrow.

The third movement's marking con delicatezza seems to refer more to a fragility of emotion than just a delicacy of touch; and the finale's extraordinary subtlety of major/minor nuance, with its alternating use of playful and tender articulation, displays Schubert's ability to prise open the most resolutely locked human feelings, and to touch the most hidden nerves.

Simone Weil (1909–1943). 'A woman of genius' (T. S. Eliot). 'The only great spirit of our times' (Albert Camus). Apart from wearing unprepossessing spectacles and dying tragically young in her early thirties, Weil had little obviously in common with Schubert: she was French, Jewish, an intellectual, a political activist, and a social critic. But her writings on affliction, attention and beauty, and her stand as an 'outsider' seem to me to give her a hidden connection with Schubert across the century and beyond the confines of their different artistic disciplines.

> Poetry: impossible pain and joy . . . A joy which through its unmixed purity hurts, a pain which through its unmixed purity brings peace.
>
> Simone Weil

The shifting sandals of York Bowen: a note for a CD

As the twentieth century, which tended to live for tomorrow, is now an unquestionable yesterday, its fiercest modernism seeming almost old-fashioned, the three-day shadow of its angry young men a whiter shade of grey, it is time to re-examine a figure such as York Bowen. He is one of those artists who begin writing in the style of their time, and, feeling comfortable and inspired in that style, are reluctant to change. If you can mine a piece of ground for only a short time you will never get very deep. Bowen was a composer who loved the ground he dug, and found a lifetime of contentment in sifting through its contents.

I first came across his name as the Associated Board editor of the Mozart piano sonatas, and I also had a copy of his Twelve Studies op. 46, which had been given to me along with the other musty contents of a deceased lady's piano bench. Years later, I heard a wonderful performance by Philip Fowke of the Second Suite op. 30 on the radio. The composer's name lodged in my memory. Then I read the composer and critic Sorabji's chapter on Bowen in his book *Mi contra Fa* and came across the following description of the 24 Preludes op. 102:

In this work [is] the finest English piano music written in our time . . . With York Bowen we are in the great tradition of piano writing, the tradition to which, for all their individual and idiosyncratic differences, men such as Ravel, Rachmaninov and Medtner belong. York Bowen is master of every kind of piano writing, which, great artist that he is, he uses not to the ends of trumpery and empty virtuoso *affichage*, but to the purposes of the powerful brilliant glowing and rich expression of a very individual beautiful and interesting musical thought.

Inexhaustible pianistic invention, endlessly fascinating and imaginative harmonic subtlety and *raffinement*, a musical substance elevated and distinguished, a perfection and finely poised judgement, combined to produce an aesthetic experience as rare and delightful as it was exciting . . . York Bowen is, at the present time, the one English composer whose work can justly be said to be that of a great Master of the instrument, as Rachmaninov was or as Medtner is.

This audaciously enthusiastic opinion certainly piqued my interest in this neglected Englishman, and I resolved to explore all the music of his I could find.

I immediately discovered in Bowen a pianistic craftsman of the highest quality – piano writing so elegant and refined that it seemed to slip around the hand like an old lambskin glove, the curling counterpoint almost nestling between the fingers rather than lying under the hand. Here was a contrapuntal tailor whose voice leading, always met gracefully and inconspicuously at the seams.

His harmonic language was endlessly inventive too; rich enough for the sweetest tooth, but with enough subtlety to satisfy the more sophisticated palate. A particular characteristic of Bowen's music is a love (in the less good pieces, perhaps an obsession) for a melodic idea repeated with changing harmony – like 'shifting sandals' that walk the same path but by a different route. A melody will appear and, like a man trying on a handful of ties, Bowen lays many different fingers of harmonic colour over the melody's crisp, white cotton.

Edwin Yorke Bowen (the 'Edwin' and the 'e' of Yorke were later dropped) was born on 22 February 1884 in Crouch Hill, London. His mother was a musician and his father a founder partner in Bowen & McKechnie, whisky distillers. After early studies at the Blackheath Conservatoire with Alfred Izard, in 1898 the boy won the Erard Scholarship of the Royal Academy, where he became a student of the famous pedagogue Tobias Matthay (whose other students included Myra Hess, Moura Lympany and Eileen Joyce). He won a string of prizes and scholarships during his time there in both piano and composition and, in 1905, at the age of twenty-one, he completed his studies. Prior to this, there had already been many London performances of his works, including his First Symphony, and a symphonic tone poem *The Lament of Tasso*, both given at the Queen's Hall, the latter in a Promenade Concert conducted by Henry Wood. During the next ten years he appeared all over Britain and in Germany playing his own compositions as recitalist, and with such partners as Fritz Kreisler, Lionel Tertis, Joseph Szigeti, Hans Richter and Landon Ronald. Three piano concertos and two symphonies were performed in this period, all with the finest orchestras at the large London halls, and in 1908 Tertis premiered his Viola Concerto at a Philharmonic Society concert conducted by Landon Ronald. It was probably at this time that Saint-Saëns described Bowen as 'the most remarkable of the young British composers'.

Although the performances continued after the First World War (he was in the Scots Guards and invalided home from France in 1916) the momentum had been lost and, from his early successes, it is hard to explain fully Bowen's eventual slide into obscurity. Changing fashions, a splintered, post-war world and the composer's modest nature could all have played a part in Bowen's relegation to the sidelines of musical life. The strangely 'English' suspicion of the home-grown professional musician and the whiff of vulgarity that the post-Victorians found in a stiff collar moistened by the sweat of enthusiasm could also have contributed to the neglect. He continued writing music that increased in inspiration and craft in the post-war years, and artists such as Beatrice Harrison, Aubrey and Dennis Brain, Leon Goossens, and Carl Dolmetsch performed his works, but teaching (fifty years at his alma mater, the Royal Academy of Music) and examining (for the Associated Board) took up most of his time. Although he played quite frequently (most notably some fairly regular Wigmore Hall recitals) and a number of his works were included in the Proms (his Second and Fourth Piano Concertos with Adrian Boult conducting), the years passed and the invitations to compose or perform became less and less frequent.

Sorabji, Clinton Gray-Fisk and Jonathan Frank were three prominent critics who constantly championed his cause in these years, puzzling in print why he was so inexplicably neglected. By the time of his death on 23 November 1961 he was a name from the past, and an obituary in *The Times*, under the heading, 'Mr York Bowen, Composer of Romantic Lyricism', was inaccurate and condescending. In reply, Jonathan Frank wrote an article for *Musical Opinion* on Bowen, and made this observation: 'The greatest music of York Bowen is written with a conviction, mastery, and individuality that make considerations of 'modern' or 'old-fashioned' completely immaterial.'

The 24 Preludes op. 102 in all the major and minor keys, referred to with such ecstatic praise by Sorabji, quoted above, were written in 1938 and published in 1950 with a dedication to that admiring critic. They follow the key scheme used by Bach in *Das wohltemperierte Klavier* and encompass a vast range of moods: from the first in C major, a soaringly romantic piece full of ardour, to the mysterious humour of the E minor will-o'-the-wisp; from the dramatic intensity of the Scriabinesque G sharp minor, an astonishing tour de force of virtuosity, to the tenderly lilting lyricism of the D minor; and from the whiplash of the furioso B flat minor to its musing major counterpart.

The Ballade no. 2 in A minor op. 87 is one of the more 'English-sounding' works on the record. The siciliano rhythm of the opening theme, with its gently haunting chromaticism, recurs throughout this sonata-form piece. Although the title is an obvious tribute to Chopin, in Bowen's work the climax occurs in the centre of the piece, and the coda explores the earlier material as if in a dream, winding down in a trance of improvisation.

The Sonata in F minor op. 72 is one of Bowen's finest works (he wrote six piano sonatas of which this is the fifth) and it was written in 1923. The material is inspired and memorable, and its tightly argued development dismisses any suspicion that Bowen is merely a lightweight miniaturist. Of particular note is the opening triadic fanfare motive, a most arresting flourish, which is transformed into the lyrical second subject of the first movement (I'm not aware of a similar device in any other composer – introduction becomes second theme). This motive returns at the end of the third movement, firstly as a misty memory, and then, on the last page, as a triumphant paean before the final tumultuous octave passage. And, in case we miss it, the very last bar of the piece reproduces again, in four ferocious F minor chords, the rhythm of this fanfare.

The Berceuse op. 83 was published in 1928 and its title again comes from Chopin. Although it is of encore length, it seems to inhabit an unusually private world: reflective, restrained and intimate. Its harmonic world is rich and chromatic, but nevertheless cool and distant. It is dedicated to Bowen's only son, Philip.

The Moto Perpetuo (*Suite Mignonne* op. 39), from 1915, is very much the encore piece, a vivaciously virtuosic note-spinner, reminding us of so many salon pieces from the period. Bowen wrote five 'Suites', collections of three to seven small pieces of a generally light mood.

The Toccata op. 155 was written in 1957 when the composer was seventy-three years old. It is truly astonishing that a man of his age could conceive a work of such manic energy and brilliance, let alone play it, as he did at the Wigmore Hall in 1958.

Although his subsequent recording of it (on Lyrita in 1960) sounds rather laboured and tired, the piece itself has a vision and a dazzling display of pyrotechnics that is truly invigorating and an eloquent witness to the composer's undaunted perseverance in the face of discouragement and lack of recognition. In recent years it has become a favourite student showpiece and I was told that, at one point, six Juilliard students were learning it.

The Romance no. 1 op. 35 and the Romance no. 2 op. 45 were written in 1913 and 1917 respectively, and were both dedicated to his wife, the singer Sylvia Dalton. They are in an ABA form, and are full of the characteristic Bowen harmonic puns and twists supporting the loveliest melodies. They both shine with a most touching sentiment and warmth, the first exploring a more level plain, the second reaching a passionate central climax reminiscent of *Tristan*.

Mompou and the music of evaporation: a note for a CD

yet in sooth
I cannot of that music rightly say
Whether I hear, or touch, or taste the tones.
John Henry Newman: *The Dream of Gerontius*

Hush!
if we
make but a sound
time
will begin again
Paul Claudel: *Cent phrases pour éventails*

The music of Federico Mompou is the music of evaporation. The printed page seems to have faded, as if the bar lines, time signatures, key signatures, and even the notes themselves have disappeared over a timeless number of years. There is no development of material, little counterpoint, no drama nor climaxes to speak of; and this simplicity of expression – elusive, evasive and shy – is strangely disarming. There is nowhere for the sophisticate to hide with Mompou. We are in a glasshouse, and the resulting transparency is unnerving, for it creates a reflection in which our face and soul can be seen.

When asked once how to play his music, the composer replied, 'It's all so free.' Indeed it is, but not just free from rhythmic constraints and structural rules; it is free from affectation, posing, fashions and fads, and has the ecstatic liberty of childhood. 'Unless you become like children you will never enter the kingdom of heaven' (Matthew 18:3); and without a spirit of childhood in the listener Mompou's 'kingdom' is closed and some of his music can seem almost infantile. Such is the innocence of Mompou's world that Wilfrid Mellers (in his book on the composer, *Le Jardin retrouvé*) has compared it to a return to Paradise before the Fall. The composer himself called his style '*primitivista*', referring to its lack of bar lines and key signatures, yet it entirely lacks the pulsating passion we tend to associate with the label 'primitive' – the leering masks, the gyrating dances and indeed the mesmeric music of primeval cultures. Where these have tended to see life beginning after some initiation ceremony – a coming of age – in Mompou we see rather a wisdom in childhood itself that should be cherished and protected. The composer's muse begins and ends with innocence as a search for air beyond the smoke of experience.

There are numerous influences discernible in Mompou's music – Chopin, Debussy, Ravel and Scriabin, plainsong, folk music and jazz (its harmonies rather than its rhythms) – and he was accepted by his contemporaries in Paris, Les Six, as a sort of honorary member (making an unofficial baker's half-dozen). But his principal and fundamental stylistic ancestor, along with a whole generation of French composers, was the eccentric iconoclast Erik Satie. However, in spite of Mompou's enormous debt to Satie in so many formal and musical ways, the two composers are poles apart in their personalities and spiritual vision. Where Satie used *naïveté* or childishness to mock the pretensions and pomposity of adulthood, Mompou rather took the insights of maturity to rediscover the magic of childhood. Satie's smile has a knowing look, his eyes narrowing into cynicism; Mompou's eyes are wide open, sparkling like a child's, and his smile has all the surprise and enthralment of Creation itself.

This sense of wonder is crucial to an understanding of Mompou's style. (The philosopher Gabriel Marcel has written of 'wonder as the beginning of all philosophy'.) It is as if he manages to capture the very perfume of a chord, for he is there early in the morning when the first bud opens. His reverence for harmony comes from the humble realisation that its beauty exists outside his decision to include it. Where Satie's world tends towards a whimsical and sad isolation, Mompou is content to be alone precisely because of his absence of self-regard. His humility, paradoxically, enables him to write with a supreme confidence and assurance.

While it would be impossible to claim that Mompou was one of the 'great' composers, it is equally impossible to classify him as second-rate; his voice is too distinct, his output too fastidious, his artistic intentions too perfectly achieved. Second rank is for those who aim for certain heights and fail to achieve them. In the light of Artur Schnabel's quaint yet charming generalisation, 'Mozart is a garden; Schubert is a forest – in sunlight and shadow; Beethoven is a mountain range', perhaps Mompou is a window box. He is inside the room looking out, with the glass partly clear and partly stained. Indeed there is always an element of distance in Mompou between subject and object. The children's games, the singing and dancing are seen and heard from the next street.

> Events are the froth of things, but my real interest
> is the sea.
>
> Paul Valéry

Federico Mompou was born in Barcelona on 16 April 1893. His mother was French and his father Catalan, and he began musical studies as a child at the Liceo Conservatory in his native city. In 1911 he travelled to Paris to study piano with Isidore Philipp and Ferdinand Motte-Lacroix, and composition with Marcel Samuel-Rousseau. At the outbreak of the First World War he returned to Barcelona for a period of seven years and began composing in earnest. In 1921 he moved back to Paris, living there until his return to Barcelona in 1941, where he remained until his death in June 1987.

In interviews published in Roger Prevel's book, *La Musique et Federico Mompou* (Geneva: Ariana, 1976), the composer revealed some fascinating aspects of his character, which give us a glimpse into his personality more than any commentary could:

What are your preferred places or cities?
The solitude of all large towns. Barcelona and Paris where my dearest memories are preserved.

What are your favourite pastimes?
Contemplation. Meditation. The cinema.

What is your main defect?
Probably the one I'm unaware of . . . I would say that I
have too little sensitivity for the physical sufferings of others
. . . On the other hand I share to excess in the spiritual
sufferings of others.

Which qualities do you prefer in a person?
Naturalness, sincerity, authenticity.

Which are your favourite composers?
Almost all, with the exception of Haydn, Mozart and
Beethoven.

Which discs would you take to a desert island?
Works of Chopin, of Scriabin. Some songs of Schubert,
Schumann, Fauré and Poulenc.

Which paintings?
El Greco, Vermeer.

Mompou also talks of a growing appreciation for certain composers he did not like at first: later Stravinsky, Prokofiev, Bartók,
Berg and Webern (although he made the point that he considered
the dogmas of the twelve-note system as such to be a useless hin-
drance to creative freedom). He did, however, have an interest
in electronic music, which is perhaps surprising in the composer
who, earlier in this interview, had declared, 'Without my piano
I can do nothing. I absolutely need contact with its ivory keys.'
This bond with the piano is significant, for Mompou was a great
pianist (he was a virtuoso of tonal colour and rubato) and when
we play his piano music we have to have this same affection for
the instrument, grasping the chords, firmly or caressingly, as if
we are taking the hands of a dear friend in a warm embrace.

It is difficult, and doubly redundant, to discuss the individual pieces of Mompou in great detail. The notes are too simple and the soul too complex for conventional analysis. The musical notes are few because the chaff has blown away. It is precisely in the mist beyond the boundary of perception that we begin to see the invisible, to hear the inaudible. With the gentle guidance of the composer we can touch this enchanted world, but we cannot grasp it.

My recording focuses on the four sets of pieces written between 1917 and 1923 and explores the obscure and mystical world at the centre of Mompou's output and language. The 'sandwich' sequence is not so much designed to present a varied selection of the composer's music as to give these mysterious works space to breathe, to 'exist'. The six *Canciones y Danzas* and six preludes are pieces of a more obvious expressiveness and melodic design and act like frames around the other works, highlighting their bizarre character, and allowing the aural palate to stay clean and receptive. I included the later cycle *Paisajes* (composed between 1942 and 1960) as it inhabits the same world and is a bridge between the early sets and the *Musica callada* ('Music of Silence') cycle, his major piano work in four books written between 1959 and 1967.

Mompou wrote thirteen *Canciones y Danzas* for piano between 1921 and 1979 (plus one for guitar in 1972) and they are a richly varied collection. He described the idea behind this form as 'a contrast between lyricism and rhythm, to avoid a collection of songs and another of dances, and also due to a natural logical coincidence with a form adopted by many composers'. He goes on to cite Liszt and Bartók in their rhapsodies, although Mompou's 'gypsies' have considerably less of a swagger. These songs come from a more refined voice, and the dance steps are graceful and poised. In fact Wilfrid Mellers insightfully points out a certain affinity with Chopin's mazurkas, not least in the wistful nostalgia for home that both composers felt living as exiles in Paris.

The eleven Preludes were written between 1927 and 1960 and typically show the sweeter side of Mompou's harmonic language. Notable among them are no. 1, originally entitled by the composer 'A window with light' and marked in the score '*Dans le style romance*', and no. 6, for the left hand alone and one of the composer's most unique and profound pieces – tender and private, passionate yet chaste.

Cants màgics (1917) was Mompou's first published work and is dedicated '*À mon cher maître F. Motte-Lacroix*'. These are 'songs' in the loosest, or perhaps 'most primitive', sense of the word ('incantations', Mellers calls them, describing the vocal lines as 'pre-melodic'), and the marking '*Obscur*' at the top of no. 2 has surely never seemed more apt. These spells frighten us not through their malevolence, but because we are transported to an unknown, prehistoric world. Here is Mompou's most deliberate rejection of the cerebral complexity in much artistic thought of the period.

Charmes (1920/21) continues in the musical dialect of *Cants màgics* but now strange signposts head each piece to illuminate our path of perception – although these mottos are more like the light of flickering candles in their obscurity. They are literally 'spells', which are conjured up for specific purposes: 'to alleviate suffering' . . . 'to penetrate the soul' . . . 'to inspire love' . . . 'to effect a cure' . . . 'to evoke an image of the past' . . . 'to call up joy'. According to Antonio Inglesias, the composer had not yet met the poet Paul Valéry and did not know his poems of the same name, although these latter were published around the same time.

Trois Variations (1921), in spite of the abstract-sounding title, belongs to the same family as the other cycles. After a 'one-finger' theme there follow three contrasting variations – 'The Soldiers', 'Courtesy' and 'Nocturne' – which are like a mini-ature anthology of the three musical styles of Mompou: the first is in his typical naive, primitive style, with its echoes of Satie – these are children dressed as soldiers, not fighting men; the second is a suavely seductive waltz, which folds the theme in a succulently rich harmonic sauce – a reminder, perhaps, that Poulenc was a neighbour in Paris; and the third variation (originally called 'The Toad' and later 'The Frog' for some unknown reason) is akin to the mystical pieces, with its gentle, undulating accompaniment weaving a magic carpet of sound beneath the trance-transformed theme.

In the two *Dialogues* (1923) the keyboard textures are more complex and decorative, and the mood is a little less solitary and interior – there is an attempt at conversation, if only with oneself. The score is filled with Satiesque asides: '*expliquez . . . questionnez . . . répondez plus suppliant . . . hésitez*' and even, in the second piece, '*donnez des excuses*'. The *Dialogues* are rather atypical of Mompou's style in their keyboard writing and in the slightly self-conscious wit of the score's extra-musical indica-tions. But they come at a point of transition for the composer, the end of an eremitic path, which, some twenty years later, he would return to with the composition of *Paisajes*, written for the pianist Carmen Bravo, whom he had recently met and who was to become his wife.

The first two pieces of *Paisajes* ('Landscapes') were composed in 1942 and 1947 respectively and they are among the most visionary and distilled of Mompou's entire output; the third piece was a later addition in 1960. 'The Fountain and the Bell' was written when Mompou had just returned to Barcelona after a twenty-year exile and it was inspired by a courtyard in the Gothic quarter of the city near the cathedral. However, this piece is not concerned with prosaic description as such – there are no water effects and only a solitary, muffled bell. Rather his interest is with the essence of fountains and bells: in philosophical terms, the substance not the accidents. Similarly in 'The Lake' (inspired by Barcelona's Montjuic Park) he is removed from the 'blueness', 'wetness', 'stillness' or 'storminess' of the object; rather it is its 'waterness' that interests him. A bell is not so much one metal dome, ringing with vibration, but rather every bell ever rung – wedding, funeral, sanctuary or cow – with all their smiles and tears. Furthermore, it is that sense of distance again, of memory; we look past the lake, and it is the breath of the wind that has carried the bell to our ears. Bells are one of the principal 'presences' in Mompou's music (his grandfather had a bell foundry, which the composer must have frequented as a young boy); yet they are not so much a call to prayer, as a prayer itself, an abstract orison celebrating a sacredness in the very quiver of the metal.

The third piece in the set, 'Carts of Galicia', is contemporary with the first book of *Musica callada* and is almost atonal in its syncopated chord-clusters accompanying a twisted melody played '*très lointain*'. It is an experimental piece, a prototype for Mompou's late style, and although his journey in search of a purer language might seem rather strained here (we are far from the unaffected lyricism of the *Canciones y Danzas*), there remains an integrity and a powerful sense of striving, of refining, which calls to mind a poem of St John of the Cross whose writings were the inspiration for the *Musica callada* cycle:

> Cuanto mas alto se sube,
> Tanto menos se entendia,
> Que es la tenebrosa nube
> Que a noche esclarecia;
> Por eso quien la sabia
> Queda siempre no sabiendo
> Toda ciencia trascendiendo

> The higher he rises
> The less he understands
> Because dark is the cloud
> Which illumines the night;
> That's why he who knows
> Remains always unknowing
> Transcending all knowledge

Stanzas concerning an ecstasy experienced in high contemplation,
St John of the Cross

I don't love Bach

During a long summer drive a few years ago, with the car radio as companion along the country lanes, some wonderful Schumann songs unexpectedly came flooding out of the speakers. After thinking how beautiful they were I was struck for some reason with the thought that I don't actually *love* Schumann. I love his best works, and there are plenty of them to choose from, but I don't like his less inspired pieces and I think that is the requirement for loving a composer as separate from loving his or her music. It may seem abstruse to draw this distinction but it's not even about their personalities, in the way that some dislike Wagner because he was such a dislikeable man. It's deeper than that.

It's time to come clean with an extreme personal example: I recognise with crystal clarity that Bach is a greater composer than Mompou, in the way that Rembrandt is a better painter than Rockwell. To put the two composers on the same level would be risible, and the Spaniard would be the first to be nonplussed with embarrassed laughter. Yet, I don't get Bach, even while I understand his towering genius . . . but I do get Mompou. Perhaps it's like friendship, we just *like* certain people and not others; we resonate with certain composers; we are touched by the cracks between their notes; their music has a 'smell' that seduces us, leading us willingly into submission beyond analysis or logic.

A composer we love is one where we treasure even the dross, even as we recognise that it is dross. Tchaikovsky is one such composer for me. Maybe it's the lack of dross in Bach that prevents me from feeling completely at home with him. Or the lack of mess. Or the lack of irresolution. Or the lack of self-doubt – although maybe I'm wrong about that.

I don't hate Bach

The only way to avoid being misunderstood in print is to avoid writing anything at all. Soon after a version of the previous reflection appeared in print, with its aim to address a very specific point about whether or not a composer enters the bloodstream despite one's recognition of their genius, a friend from America emailed me to say that he'd heard an announcer on one of the major radio stations there say, 'Now we're going to hear some music by the composer Stephen Hough hates' – a loose equivalent of Hitler's well-known, lifelong obsession with building synagogues. (Actually I can't think of any composer I hate, although there are some whose music I do not choose to listen to.)

Then in Ian Bostridge's book *A Singer's Notebook* I was chided for my apostasy because I do not find Bach 'irreducible and indispensable'. I am 'the inevitable exception that proves the rule', he wrote. It would of course be ludicrous to call Bach 'dispensable', and my example comparing Bach to Mompou, also quoted by Ian, was hyperbolic and related to the way the few lines of a perfectly executed crayon sketch might touch our hearts more than Rembrandt's *Night Watch*, but the issue I'm referring to here is something hidden, which shares emotional space in that same part of our souls as our consciences. It's not open to argument or discussion because it is basically irrational – in the best, most imaginative, most creative, most ecstatic meaning of that term. I do not need convincing; I need seducing.

Liszt I: the man who invented concert life as we know it

That it's over two hundred years since the birth of Franz Liszt seems like a misprint when you consider how his influence on the musical life of the twentieth century was as great as on the nineteenth. The man who was born within an echo of the harpsichord was the most important inspiration and influence on the creation and development of the modern piano. The man who grew up in a world where pianists played perhaps just one item on mixed concert programmes ended up inventing the piano recital (his word) – pianist as star, at the centre of the stage for a whole evening, in profile to a concentrated, adoring audience.

One of the greatest composer–pianists, he was the man who habitually programmed music by other composers in his concerts. We tend to forget that as a general rule in earlier times composers either played their own music or it was not performed, and Liszt's generosity to his colleagues has scarcely been equalled and never surpassed. Liszt was the man who pretty much created the idea of the masterclass – piano teacher as guru in a format attracting students from all over the world to travel to the heady, cigar-saturated rooms of Weimar and learn as much from absorbing the atmosphere as from memorising the formulae.

He was a pioneer of the role of conductor as performer. Until Liszt (and later his son-in-law, Hans von Bülow), conductors generally raised a baton only for their own compositions, and they were seen as facilitators of ensemble more than as inspirers of a unified musical vision. And then there is the custom of playing from memory. Before Liszt, putting aside the score was considered to be a lack of seriousness, as if the performer were merely improvising; after Liszt, it became a fixed custom. Indeed, Liszt's direct influence on over a century of concert life is hard to overestimate . . . and that's before we've considered his importance as a composer.

Liszt II: the man who invented modern music

Liszt onstage, with dazzling fingers on the keyboard causing dazzling jewels to heave on bosoms in the audience, is the predominant image we have of this larger-than-life musician. But when he moved to Weimar in semi-retirement in his mid-thirties he began a far more profound and significant process of invention than pianistic acrobatics in fashionable salons.

The influences that shape new musical trends are diffuse, complex and impossible to codify, but if one person can be credited as being the fountainhead of modern music it is Franz Liszt . . . in three, totally different, stylistic directions. Whether we like his own compositions or not, we cannot avoid contact with Liszt if we have contact with music from the late nineteenth or twentieth centuries.

First, the heady combination of *bel canto* with chromaticism, a Lisztian fingerprint formed early in his life, was a major influence on Wagner and Wagner's progeny. It has been claimed that Liszt invented the 'Tristan chord'. Even if such a 'patent' is open to discussion, the febrile harmonic instability of *Tristan und Isolde* is heard in Liszt before it is heard in his son-in-law. On rare occasions of collegial generosity Wagner even admitted this debt.

A clearer and more direct path of influence can be seen in the stark rhythmic primitivism of some of Liszt's late piano pieces – *Csárdás macabre* (1881/2) is one notable example. The percussive atonality of these astonishing experiments, with their new colours and textures, is heard clearly in his compatriots Béla Bartók and Zoltán Kodály, and it opened the door for a whole century of piano music.

Throughout his creative life Liszt used impressionistic titles for his works – lakes, mountains, snow, forests abound. But not titles alone. A work such as *Les Jeux d'eaux à la Villa d'Este* (1877) from the third book of *Années de pèlerinage* shares both title and texture with Ravel; and two generations later Olivier Messiaen adopted Liszt's use of the key of F sharp major in a piece such as *Bénédiction de Dieu dans la solitude* as a symbol of spiritual contemplation in his own piano and organ music.

Liszt III: the man who broke pianos

Apart from Liszt's influence on concert life and the music we hear there, his inventive prowess at the keyboard actually changed the way we play the instrument, and forced piano makers to keep up to speed too.

It's no good learning how to execute octaves and chords with power and velocity if the action of the instrument itself jams up or breaks down. Beethoven's piano famously spewed broken strings out of its case in his more ferocious moments, but Liszt apparently broke the cases themselves. After one of his opera paraphrases the heaving, trembling instrument would be at his feet, utterly spent, and a new one would have to be carried out onto the stage from the wings. Those early, wooden- framed pianos simply could not cope with playing that now flowed in energy and force from shoulder and back, rather than merely with the earlier finger, wrist and forearm technique of a Hummel or a Czerny.

This is not to extol the virtues of banging, or to undermine the skill and subtlety of the earlier players, it is simply that Liszt discovered (uncovered) the full potential of a developing instrument, which was eventually to become a one-man orchestra. To provide more power the frames of the instruments needed to be stronger to support the increased tension of the strings and the force with which the hammers would strike them, and piano makers vied with one another to gain the endorsement of Liszt, the greatest pianist of the era. Erard, Bechstein, Chickering, Bösendorfer, Steinway all claimed that Liszt favoured them above the others. In fact the competition between these companies probably helped to improve the quality of them all, thus encouraging composers to push the boundaries even further. By the time Prokofiev was writing the mammoth cadenza in his Second Piano Concerto (1912) the total string tension on a concert grand piano would exceed 20 tonnes.

Liszt's abstract sonata

The restraint of the abstract did not come easily to Liszt. He was by nature a storyteller, a man of the stage, a theatrical prophet who burned to communicate a poetic-romantic vision. But in his case the stage was not set for an opera. Rather, it is Liszt himself who is the character, the subject.

The vast majority of his works bear descriptive titles. As Noah naming his animals, or as Santa Claus wrapping even the most modest gifts in shimmering paper, Liszt imposed the flourish of an appellation to most of his pieces. Études became a 'Wild Chase' or 'Evening Harmonies'; nocturnes became 'Dreams of Love'; waltzes were 'melancholy', 'Mephistophelian', or even 'forgotten'. But when it came to his sole work in sonata form ... nothing, merely *Grande Sonate pour le pianoforte par F. Liszt.*

Just over a hundred years earlier, and just under a hundred miles away from where Liszt was living in Weimar, a Mass was written in the same B minor key. It was Bach's only known complete work in that form. That the Lutheran from Leipzig would not write many Masses is understandable, but that Liszt, a man of such manifold talent, energy and years, would write only one sonata is puzzling. However, it is significant that the one he wrote is a masterpiece, and that he took great care in its construction (evident in the many pastings-over and corrections in the manuscript). It is the work that proves beyond all doubt that Liszt's compositional genius was not just that of the inventor, the innovator, the elaborator – but that of the supreme architect as well.

Both Liszt concertos in the same concert?

Although performing two concertos in one concert is a lot more playing (and rehearsing) than for a usual engagement, it was a common occurrence in earlier generations. Eileen Joyce was known to play up to four concertos in one concert, and Artur Rubinstein would play multiple Mozarts or Beethovens or both Brahms concertos in the same concerts. It's interesting, though, that he ruled out playing both Chopin concertos together: 'They are too similar.' But both Liszts?

Definitely! In fact they work beautifully and revealingly on the same programme because their differences (and similarities) show us much of what makes Liszt so innovative. They are the same length, around twenty minutes, but the First is four movements contracted into one unit, whereas the Second is one unit expanded into multiple sections. They both use the compositional technique (virtually invented by Liszt) of transformation of themes – a few small motivic cells become building blocks for the whole work, or, in Liszt's case, more like costumes for characters in a drama – but the 'plot' of each concerto is very different. Their beginnings could not be more contrasting in mood: the First assertive, confident, swaggering, the Second dreamy, exploratory, tentative. Yet their opening three bars use the same motive: two descending semitones.

Liszt was almost certainly at his most creative in the act of

improvising, and his two concertos are like spun-out cadenzas
that were later tightened into concert works of superb architectural proportion.

Why Chopin's B minor Sonata is harder
to play than Liszt's

We all like grading things – marks out of ten, five-star reviews,
best in show and so on. Even Liszt's own edition of the 32
Beethoven Sonatas lists them in ascending order of difficulty,
beginning with op. 49 no. 2 and ending (of course) with op. 106,
the *Hammerklavier*. Some of the choices in the middle seem
puzzling or random – I don't know, for example, why he would
rank op. 26 as harder than op. 10 no. 3 – but it's still a fascinating list, and topic.

Liszt has a reputation for writing music of the greatest difficulty, and some of his earlier études and transcriptions do
indeed reach to the edges of the possible; but the pieces that
we hear regularly (the mature works) are much less hard than
they sound. In fact, that is part of the genius of Liszt: to make
something sound more difficult than it is. He understood the
keyboard and explored its possibilities like no other composer
before him, and he laid the foundation on which everyone since
has built. His glittering effects, which rendered his audiences
open-mouthed with admiration, involve a principle of maximum effectiveness and minimal effort. Horowitz took this 'spec-
tacular simplification' a step further with his transcriptions.
Even in his straight performances of other people's pieces, he
often left out notes; lots of them sometimes. Has anyone – even
Arturo Toscanini who was conducting on the occasion – ever
noticed that in his 1940 recording of Tchaikovsky's First Piano
Concerto Horowitz misses out the final left-hand chord in every

bar of the last movement's main subject? Nevertheless, even if his war horse *is* missing this shoe, it still gallops along with matchless excitement.

Neither Chopin's nor Liszt's B minor Sonata has as a principal (or even secondary) aim mere virtuosity; they are both serious works, beautifully crafted, highly expressive, but in completely different ways. Here are a few points about some specific contrasts between the two pieces:

LISZT: Can sound good even on a bad piano.

CHOPIN: Needs a fine, refined instrument.

LISZT: Apart from the fugato section the piano writing is not contrapuntal.

CHOPIN: This piece, like many in Chopin's last years, is full of counterpoint.

LISZT: It is painted mainly in bold colours – emotionally and pianistically.

CHOPIN: Most of it is shades, hints, suggestions, half-lights.

LISZT: The mood is larger than life; it is onstage, in public.

CHOPIN: The mood is often restrained; behind the scenes, personal, private.

LISZT: Unashamedly romantic and 'Byronic'.

CHOPIN: Balances carefully Classicism and Romanticism.

To play either piece wonderfully is as difficult as it is to play *anything* wonderfully – but a bad performance of the Liszt can still convey something of the heart of that piece, whereas a bad performance of the Chopin will probably miss the target altogether.

Why Liszt's B minor Sonata is harder
to record than Chopin's

Studio recordings tend to favour works of intimacy, as long as you can get into the right frame of mind, and as long as the piano is responding properly. It has to do not just with the absence of an audience but with the kind of introspection involved in playing something over and over again, the self-examination, the aim to take one's inner vision about a piece and fix it forever. Out of over sixty CDs the one I found most enjoyable to record was of Mompou's piano music. These pieces are perfect to listen to alone, and they were perfect to record alone – with just a red light for company.

In a concert the Liszt Sonata can take wing, even to the point of carrying the player to unknown places. It's one of those works where you feel the power of the narrative from the first moment. Its sweep, its bold character, its magnificent gestures, inspire and are inspired by a 'live' audience. In a good performance the whole hall can be on fire from the struck match of the first staccato octave Gs in the bass, to the climactic flames, which will lick around even the last seats of the balcony. In the isolation of a recording studio on a Tuesday morning this kind of drama can be difficult to conjure up. By the time the pianist has played enough for the engineer to get the right sound, sometimes for up to an hour, not only has physical tiredness set in, but the emotional fuel has been used up a little too.

But the repetition of passages in search of tonal and textural perfection is part of living with the Chopin Sonata, and intimacy is part of its character. To find the perfect transparency and balance between melody and accompaniment in the first movement's second subject is a lifetime's project. To judge the pedalling so that a seamless robe is wrapped around the coloratura singer in that melody, as flexible as a fine fabric's response to every turn and twist, is one of the countless and never resolved challenges when playing the piece. Rarely in a concert does it work in every bar, and each wrinkle along the way can undermine confidence and courage. Alone with the red light there is time to explore, to examine, to experiment. Chopin's domestic drama, too subtle for many stages, can unfold unhindered in front of a microphone.

Chopin and the development of piano technique

Two names are pivotal in the history of piano technique: Chopin and Liszt. Both came from a similar pianistic background, the classical callisthenics of Czerny, Hummel and Co., the meat of scales and the potatoes of arpeggios, but where the young Liszt was dazzled by Paganini's acrobatics, Chopin was dazed by the sweet melancholy of Bellini's bel canto. If Liszt, in his early opera paraphrases and études, seems like Samson pushing down pillars, causing the whole temple of conventional pianism to tumble in cascades of figuration, Chopin is more like Solomon reaching out for one of the Queen of Sheba's more exotic perfumes.

This analogy of 'reaching out' is not idly chosen, for it is to this that the distinct contribution of Chopin can be traced. A much quoted and classic example of Chopin's new approach to the keyboard is the first étude from op. 10 (the set is dedicated to Liszt). Here the routine, arpeggiated figuration covering the span of an octave (and covering endless pages of piano music of the time), becomes extended by two notes to a tenth, requiring a new technique of rotation. One could say, literally, that it becomes 'more than a handful'. No longer are the fingers alone sufficient to execute this passage; the wrist and arm have to be used, and thus Chopin 'elbows' his way to a new panorama of pianism.

The examples in these études are as numerous as they are astoundingly innovative. Never is a pattern repeated, such is the fertility of his invention. The 'black-key' étude (no. 5) forces the player to adopt a new hand position on the keyboard. The cramped, curled finger shape favoured by an earlier generation of pianists is not possible for extended passages on the narrow black keys. One has to develop a more fluid, flatter finger position. It is interesting to note that Chopin liked to begin his students with the B major scale (containing the most black keys) rather than the usual C major scale to help develop this hand shape from the start. The second étude in A minor whispers its chromatic secrets between the three weak fingers, developing independence, strength and a limber legato. In the op. 25 set of études this overflowing inventiveness continues. The octave étude (no. 10) presents the idea of the legato octave, the cantabile octave; the 'double-thirds' étude (no. 6) features a new 'sliding' fingering supplied by the composer; and the 'Winter Wind' étude (no. 11) takes a further step in the technique of rotation, razor-sharp zigzags shredding the keyboard into chromatic ribbons.

Despite the influence of Hummel, especially in the concertos, Chopin's astonishing keyboard innovations are unthinkable without his harmonic development. He didn't just take Hummel's writing and stretch it into more elegant shapes. Where Hummel seems satisfied with a carbolic-soap virtuosity – clean, fresh, bubbling, with a fresh-faced exhilaration – Chopin tends to dab his passagework with rare oils and perfumes. A comparison of the development sections of the two composers' concertos is highly revealing. One's first reaction hearing them side by side is surprise at how indebted Chopin was to Hummel, but after closer examination Hummel seems merely to be the caterpillar to Chopin's butterfly.

Due to the early influence of Bellini, a 'singing' approach to the keyboard, both lyric and coloratura, is essential in all of Chopin's music. It is never enough to 'rattle out' the notes, even in the most obviously virtuosic of his works; every phrase must come from the throat and lungs as much as from fingers and arms. Pedalling, tone production, voicing – in all of these Chopin was the great innovator. These qualities had all been required in earlier piano compositions of course, but where before the pedals had had a mainly functional use – padding out textures and aiding legato – now they become tools of infinite nuance. Chopin's counterpoint too reveals itself in a more specifically pianistic way. Inner voices are highlighted, not, as in Bach or indeed Beethoven, for their melodic or motivic importance alone, but more tellingly because they supply a coloured filter to the harmonic lens.

Every one of Chopin's works includes a prominent piano part. For a composer who wrote for such limited forces, his genius is all the more remarkable. Without the benefit of Liszt's larger-than-life personality – the international performing career, long life, social connections, intellectual breadth, twinkling eye – Chopin was able, by the sheer quality and originality of his work, to be inseparably identified with his instrument.

Chopin, Rothko and the bowler hat

Chopin died in October 1849. Although he had struggled with ill-health for most of his adult life, his seven-month visit to the UK in 1848 could well have accelerated his decline as he shivered his way from London to Edinburgh and back, stopping in various draughty, damp places. His last London address was 4 St James Place. From his front door, he would have been able to walk in about three minutes (I timed it) to the front door of

James Lock & Co., the famous hat shop, at 6 St James Street – trading at the same address since 1676.

Only weeks following the death of Chopin, a certain William Coke II (who was later to become the Earl of Leicester) walked into Lock's to collect a newly commissioned hat. He had requested a design that would be extremely strong, and low enough in the crown, so that his gamekeepers would not have it knocked off by the branches of trees as they rode through his estate – Holkham, in Norfolk. He took the prototype hat outside and stamped vigorously on it with his full body-weight. When it remained intact he was satisfied. He paid the price of 12 shillings and returned home carrying what would become the most important hat in modern history: the bowler, named after Thomas and William Bowler who had actually manufactured the hat across the river in Southwark.

It was the first hat ever made that would bridge social gaps rather than delineate them, donned as it was by tramps and toffs – just as Chopin was perhaps the first low-born musician in history successfully to enter into the society of the aristocracy . . . on *his* terms. The bowler became a symbol of the middle class: those both upwardly and downwardly mobile could brush off its brittle dome, place it on their heads, and step into the street without remark or censure. It was also a hat much favoured by the Jewish communities of Europe, culminating in its immense popularity in the Weimar Republic. Significantly, there are few photographs of Nazis wearing bowlers.

Marcus Rothkowitz arrived in New York from Dvinsk in Russia (now Latvia) in 1913 at the age of ten, escaping with his family from the terror of the pogroms. Although they immediately moved out to Portland, Oregon, he returned to New York in the mid-1920s and began to study art. By the late 1940s he had moved towards complete abstraction and eventually became

part of the group of painters known as the Abstract Expression-
ists. But, despite this, his work is by far the most 'Romantic' of
those who were his contemporaries. The blur and burnish of
his mature, pulsating canvases seems to draw the viewer into
a hypnotic, mystical world; and if 'Romanticism' suggests the
subjective vision of the individual, I cannot think of any paintings less conducive to being shared than Rothko's. They have to
be experienced in deep silence and solitude. Although they were
created in an era of publicity and pop, their uncompromising
seriousness forces us to an inner desert to view them.

If Rothko was arguably the most Romantic of the modernists, Chopin was certainly the most Classical of the Romantics.
Not just because in their form Chopin's works are always polished and perfectly shaped, but also because he rejected titles
for his compositions – those nametags on the baggage of individualism that Schumann and Liszt culled from poets and from
their own inner thoughts, first-name secrets whispered into the
ears of the audience. Chopin's titles are mere husks – abstract
words revealing little except the length and outline of the work
to be played: pencil drawings that the melodies and harmonies
would colour in.

Two Slavs in the West, at two seminal artistic moments . . .
changing people's ideas, creating inimitable masterpieces.
Rothko had as deep a love for music as for art, and, according
to his son Christopher, Mozart was a particular favourite. Chopin
too loved Mozart above all others, and the first work to show his
prowess to the world was his op. 2 *Variations on 'Là ci darem la
mano'* from Mozart's *Don Giovanni*. After hearing it for the first
time, Schumann declared, '*Hut ab, ihr Herren, ein Genie!*' –
'Hats off, gentlemen; a genius.' I wonder if Mr Lock of St
James Street would have concurred.

The reflection above was written as a (tongue-in-cheek) experimental justification for using a photograph on a CD cover of myself wearing a bowler hat standing in front of a Mark Rothko painting.

Debussy: piano music without hammers

When I strike a note on the piano, more is heard than that note alone. The other strings vibrate with sympathetic overtones forming a halo over every tone – a veritable choir of angels. Claude Debussy is perhaps the first composer to write with those pianistic overtones specifically in mind, to harness them consciously as part of his creative process. Although it was the orchestral work *Prélude à l'après-midi d'un faune* that Pierre Boulez described as 'the beginning of modern music', it was at the piano where Debussy's revolutionary new approach to form and timbre was developed.

With *Pagodes*, the first piece of his triptych *Estampes* (1903), we hear something totally fresh. Debussy had heard Javanese gamelan music at the Exposition Universelle in Paris in the summer of 1889 and had written with great admiration about its complexity and sophistication, but his use of its tonal colour (loosely, the pentatonic scale – the five black notes of a piano) is not so much a translation of a foreign text as it is a poem written in a newly learned, fully absorbed language.

Composers, especially in France, had regularly utilised exoticism in their works (Saint-Saëns and Bizet spring to mind) but it remained a decorative detail, a picture postcard, a costume. With Debussy the absorption has gone to the marrow. It is a transfusion of blood, flowing in the very fingers that conjure up these new sounds at this old instrument.

Igor Stravinsky commented that he 'was struck by the way in

which the extraordinary qualities of this pianism had directed the thought of Debussy the composer'. Debussy's discovery of new sounds at the piano is directly related to the physiology of hands on keyboard. It is impossible to conceive of most of Debussy's piano music being written at a desk, or outdoors (despite his frequent use of *en plein air* titles). No, this is music made as moulded by playing, as dough is folded with yeast to create bread. As the fingers reach the keys, sound and touch seem to fuse into one. The keyboard has ceased to be a mere function for hammers to strike strings. It has become a precious horizontal artefact to caress. This is music *of* the piano as much as for the piano. The poet Léon-Paul Fargue wrote that Debussy 'would start by brushing the keys, prodding the odd one here and there, making a pass over them and then he would sink into velvet'. 'He gave the impression of delivering the piano of its song,' Fargue added, 'like a mother of her child.'

When he played in public, Debussy preferred to keep the lid of the instrument down, and, apparently, at home he would cover the top of his upright piano with cloths to muffle the sound. 'One must forget that the piano has hammers,' he said. Although it requires a superlative technique to play Debussy well, his widow, Emma Bardac, made an interesting observation: 'Many pianists should bear in mind that if they play Claude's music and someone tells them how wonderful their technique is, then they are not playing Debussy.'

The American pianist Jerome Lowenthal told me he was backstage in Paris in the 1950s when he overheard an old lady speaking to the pianist at the end of a concert.

'My father said that people always play *L'Île joyeuse* too quickly.'

'Oh,' replied the pianist, 'and who is your father?'

'Claude Debussy.'

Debussy's piano music is perfectly conceived for the instrument. But it isn't just that it fits beautifully under the hand or sounds wonderful as the vibrations leave the soundboard and enter the ear. To play the opening of *Reflets dans l'eau* (from *Images I*) feels as if the composer has transplanted his fingerprints onto the pads of your digits. The way the chords are placed on the keys (flat-fingered on the black notes) is not so much a vision of reflections – of trees, clouds or water lilies; it is as if each three-padded triad is an actual laying of a flower onto the water's surface. Later on in the piece, as the waters become more agitated, the cascading arpeggios are like liquid running through the fingers, all shimmer and sparkle.

In *Poissons d'or* (from *Images II*), the opening motive, a darting duplet of double thirds, is like trying to grasp a fish's flip as it slips out of the finger's grasp. In the central section, the slinky tune slithers with grace notes as the hand has literally to slide off the key as if off the scales of a freshly caught trout. In the first piece of this set, *Cloches à travers les feuilles*, the fingers are required to tap the keys (pedal held down, fingers pulled up) as if mallets against a bell.

No other composer feels to me more improvised, more free-flowing. But then the player is conscious of a contradiction as the score is studied more closely. Music that sounds created in the moment is loaded with instructions on how to achieve this effect. The first bar of *Cloches à travers les feuilles* is a case in point. It is marked pianissimo and contains just eight notes, each of which carries a staccato dot, but the first is also coupled with a strong-accented semibreve, the fifth has an additional dash, all the notes are covered with a slur and, as if that were not enough, Debussy instructs the pianist to play '*doucement sonore*'.

Children's Corner might be like so many toys in his daughter's nursery, but the workmanship behind every join and seam is of the highest fastidiousness. All of his pieces sound spontaneous, but every stitch (every dot, dash, hairpin or slur) is specific. This is not mood music, pretty sounds assembled at a dilettante's whim. Behind the bells and the water and all the poetic imagery is an abstract musical mind of the utmost intellectual rigour – an architect of genius, despite the small scale of the buildings.

If most of his piano music has a feel of improvisation about it, the two books of Préludes celebrate this in a special way. Until well into the twentieth century, a pianist would rarely begin in concert to play a piece cold. A few chords, an arpeggio or two, served as a warm-up as well as giving the audience a moment to settle down. This was known as 'preluding', and Liszt spoke of it as a technique to be learned by any aspiring pianist. Debussy's Préludes are perfectly crafted jewels, conveying more in their few minutes' duration than many an opera, yet they can also seem as intangible as mist – with titles, tacked on with ellipses at the end of each piece, like mere trails of perfume in the air. *Voiles*, the second from *Book I*, is 'sails' or 'veils', but somehow the confusion of term doesn't matter. We have been pushed away from the shore and the resulting imaginative journey is more important than any destination. Modernism indeed!

Debussy began piano lessons at the age of seven in Cannes as an evacuee from Paris at the start of the Franco-Prussian War, and he died during the final year of World War I, unable to have a public funeral because of the aerial bombing of Paris. The circumstances of his life, framed by his country's enmity with Germany, seem an apt symbol for his music's rejection of a kind of German aesthetic. His instinct to stay clear of classical structures, his elevation and celebration of small, ephemeral forms and his delight in the atmosphere of beautiful chords for their own sake, with no desire to find a specific function for them, was an audacious challenge to some more self-consciously serious German intellectual fashions of the time. Indeed, the *Golliwog's Cakewalk* (from *Children's Corner*) is a direct hit, with its cheerful celebration of popular culture and the cheeky quote from Wagner's *Tristan und Isolde* followed by the minstrel's scoffing sniggers.

When assessing a composer's place in history, there's always the question as to whether the tendency is backwards or forwards. Despite the opinion of Elliott Carter that Debussy 'settled the technical direction of contemporary music', and despite the impossibility of the existence of the piano music of modernists such as Olivier Messiaen or György Ligeti without him, I think the secret to playing Debussy's music lies in its Chopinist roots – he edited the Polish composer's works for Durand – and in his ties to his older, old-fashioned compatriots Massenet, Delibes and others.

Debussy might have stretched harmony and form into new shapes, but it seems to me that it is in a Parisian café, a Gauloise in hand and coffee at his side, that we glimpse something essential about his spirit. For all his sophistication, he could never resist the lilt and leer of a corny cabaret song, not just overtly, as in *La Plus que lente* (1910), but tucked away inside more experimental pieces such as *Les collines d'Anacapri* (*Préludes I*), *Reflets dans l'eau* (*Images I*) and *Poissons d'or* (*Images II*). He never left behind completely the romantic sentimentality of early piano pieces such as *Clair de lune* and the *Deux Arabesques*.

Although his taste for popular styles found expression in ragtime takeoffs such as *Minstrels* and the *Golliwog's Cakewalk*, it was his more serious music that was later to have an immense influence on jazz composers, from Gershwin to Bill Evans to Keith Jarrett to Fred Hersch. And not just because of a shared sense of improvisation. The repeated patterns, the piling up of sonorities, and the way Debussy would crack open a chord, finding creativity in the colour of its vibrations, found its way into their very DNA.

If the ghost of this Parisian ended up haunting every American jazz bar, it found its way east, too. Debussy might have discovered his own pianistic voice after hearing the gamelan, but by the end of the twentieth century the inspiration had reversed direction and his impact on Asian piano music is incalculable. From Toru Takemitsu to American minimalists to New Age Muzak . . . all owe Debussy virtual royalties.

Debussy and Ravel: chalk and cheese

It is sometimes said, 'Oh, that pianist is wonderful in Debussy and Ravel.' This is strange. Not that someone can't play both composers beautifully, but that it's presumed there's a necessary connection between the sensibility or skills required. Yes, they were both French, lived at the same time, shared the same publisher (Durand) and wrote music that could be termed 'impressionist'. (Monet's painting *Impression: soleil levant* has carried much diverse baggage on its shoulders.) But in soul, and thus in interpretation, the two composers are completely different animals.

Leaving aside detailed musical comparisons, let's just look through the keyhole into their bathrooms and bedrooms to glimpse some clues. Ravel's keen razor shaving clean the lines of his thin face; Debussy's wayward beard, carelessly trimmed, hiding loose folds of flesh underneath. The sharp parting of Ravel's hair versus Debussy's bush ruffled out of sleep. Ravel's tie selected then knotted with a keen eye versus Debussy's cravat twisted around a day-old shirt. Both men smoked cigarettes but whereas I can almost smell the nicotine fingers of Debussy in the photographs, I imagine Ravel's Gitanes to be masked by a rose-scented pomade, with not a speck of ash outside the ash-tray. And sex: Debussy's tumbling, voluptuous celebration of it; Ravel's repressed desire suffocating inside his immaculately tailored suits, his fastidiousness repelling intimacy – the love that dare not tweak his mane.

Ravel has been described as a Swiss watchmaker for his precision and the clear intent of every dot, every line, every slur; whereas Debussy could never be mistaken as a time-keeper. Many of his pieces could lose their bar lines or time signatures without losing their way. You always see the individual drops of rain in Ravel's mists, whereas Debussy invites us to look at the garden beyond, a blur through the moisture.

Pigeonholes are to be avoided in music, and to presume that a pianist will be equally at home in these two very different composers is dangerous. They are two French birds that simply do not sing on the same branch.

The three faces of Francis Poulenc

A reliable, reputable source told me once of an occasional routine of Poulenc when staying in Paris. In the late afternoon he would leave his apartment and go to the park where he would have a lustful tumble behind a bush with a willing soldier. He would then cross the park into the shadows of the Catholic church where he would slip into a dark confessional. After being absolved of his sins, and less than an hour after first leaving his home, he would return to a sumptuous supper, all ready to be served along with a decanted bottle of fine red Bordeaux.

Theology and morality aside, this circle from indulgence to 'Indulgence' to indulgence gives us an insight into the three different styles of Poulenc's music: the melancholy twists and turns of tunes sung wistfully over smoky, hazy harmonies (the sensual passion in the park); the pure and often strident Stravinskian tonality with its glinting major-seventh chords (the stained glass of the cloister); and the composer as *bon viveur*, the gleeful good humour of a naughty schoolboy stuffing himself with culinary delights (the feast of wine and rich food).

Poulenc's stock has risen solidly over the years. He was dismissed in the 1920s as a lightweight, a musical prankster from a privileged background, but his music developed in emotional power as his inner life became more complex. The shock of losing his dear friend Pierre-Octave Ferroud in a horrific car crash in 1936 propelled him back to the Catholicism of his childhood, and he remained a practising if struggling Catholic until his death. His letters to another friend, the baritone Pierre Bernac, reveal his torture of heart and his depression, but also his spiritual engagement and excitement as he was writing his operatic masterpiece *The Dialogues of the Carmelites*.

French spirituality has always been full of extremes, from the rigour of seventeenth-century Jansenism to the 'dangerous' laxity of the Carmelite nun St Thérèse of Lisieux, who died a mere two years before Poulenc was born. She saw her method of 'spiritual childhood' as if taking a lift to heaven rather than an arduous climb up a steep staircase. I'm sure that Thérèse would have been shocked by the sequence of Poulenc's nocturnal gratifications, but I think she might have been even more disturbed at any despair of forgiveness, or indeed at any inability to celebrate the blessing of good food and wine. True asceticism does not give up material goods because it despises them, but because 'goods' is precisely what they are.

My Mass and my tears of joy

My *Missa Mirabilis* and the M1 motorway will always have for me an unforgettable connection. In September 2006 I was staying at my mother's house in Cheshire during a week of concerts with the Hallé Orchestra and Sir Mark Elder. I took the opportunity of the free days before the evening concerts to gather together a year's worth of sketches I'd made for a Mass setting, commissioned by Martin Baker, Master of Music at Westminster Cathedral. It was an intense week of creation because I finished three of the movements in three of the days. They were stuffed into my briefcase, which sat on the floor next to me as I drove south after the final concert of the Manchester run.

When I reached Milton Keynes a lorry moved into the middle lane where I was cruising along at around 80 mph and I calmly moved over into the fast lane . . . at which point something terrifying happened. My car screeched out of control, swerving, spinning . . . then suddenly it was tumbling in somersaults across the three lanes. As it turned over four or five times many thoughts raced through my mind – one of which was that I would never get to hear the music I had written that week. Then, strangely, I realised that my car had stopped, on its side, with my door above me in the air, crumpled metal all around, and a strange smoky dust everywhere. I didn't feel any injury, and I knew I wasn't dead or unconscious . . . and then a ferocious survival instinct kicked in. I tried desperately to get out, but couldn't reach the door. Then it opened, and the arm of the lorry driver who had caused the crash was reaching inside to help my climb to freedom. I rescued my bags later, especially anxious to wrench open the mangled passenger door to retrieve my briefcase with the three completed Mass movements. I eventually made my way home in a taxi – glass and filth in my hair, a drying trickle of blood on my forehead, and tears of a strange joy wet on my cheeks.

The central idea of this Mass setting, and its central movement, is the *Credo* – in some ways the most problematic text to set because of its length and the non-poetic nature of the words. Instead of setting it simply in a descriptive way, I wanted to explore aspects of the psychology that underlies the whole nature of belief and doubt. The Creed contains line after line of densely packed, carefully articulated theology – as watertight and restrictive as Nicea could make it. I, like most Catholics, have said these words quickly, without thinking fully of the depth (or daring) of what is being expressed. What does 'believing' in these pregnant clauses actually mean? When I stand and affirm that the Holy Spirit 'proceeds from the Father and the Son', what am I saying? And what about those who have ceased to believe and yet still rattle off blithely the bold print in the Missal after the sermon and before the offertory?

In my setting of the *Credo* I divide the men from the upper voices as if innocence from experience. Only the treble/soprano and alto voices actually sing the word 'Credo', constantly interrupting the fast-paced mutterings of the tenors and basses. What at first is a youthful encouragement to believe becomes a despairing cry as the men's pattered rote appears to turn into defiant unbelief and the final clauses about resurrection and eternal life fizzle out. A last 'Credo' is sung an octave lower by the upper voices – quietly, as if tired and shattered from their earlier, futile exertion.

Before this drama unfolded, the *Kyrie* movement had introduced us to a gentler, less complex world of forgiveness, and the melodic and harmonic material is sweet and consoling. The *Gloria* is based on a rising scale and a falling zigzag, joyful and exuberant in its outer sections, more anxious in the central *Qui tollis* section where a few prophetic hints of the *Credo* appear, in the *Miserere nobis* for example.

The *Sanctus* and *Benedictus* seek to contrast the divine and the human. The angel's 'Holy, Holy, Holy' is something beyond the universe itself in grandeur and scope, and the music here is huge, broad, immense. In the *Benedictus* God has become man in the incarnation, and the music is deliberately and sentimentally intimate – as if two people are sharing a drink in a Parisian café, with a whiff of Poulenc perhaps in the harmonies, or maybe even the sound of a distant 1950s pop tune coming from a neighbouring café's jukebox.

The *Agnus Dei* takes the 'Credo' motive, sung by the upper voices, and develops it in a plaintive way, sung unaccompanied. All is restrained and quietly expressive until the third, louder statement of the text, where the response should be 'Grant us peace'. Instead of 'peace' the organ or orchestra plays a short interlude of mounting agitation and desperation based on chromatically altered fragments of the opening vocal chords. As this passage reaches its high point, with still no sign of *Dona nobis pacem*, the choir sings a full-throated *Agnus Dei* to the music that had accompanied the baptism clause in the *Credo*. Finally, as a climax to the whole work, the *Dona nobis pacem* is sung; it is a variation of the descending scale we first heard in the first movement's *Christe eleison*. The spell has been broken and all gradually becomes calm. The piece ends musically as it began, the *Dona nobis* sharing the same melody of consolation as the *Kyrie*. It is the Lamb of God who has brought the piece full circle, as well as bringing peace and healing to all of creation.

My First Piano Sonata: fragments of fragility

Sonata for Piano (broken branches)

Prelude (Autumn) – desolato – fragile – inquieto – piangendo – immenso – sentimento – malancolico – passionato – freddo – volando – ritmico – non credo – morendo – crux fidelis – Postlude (Spring)

Originally 'sonata' was a term used to denote a piece 'sounding' rather than 'singing' – for instruments rather than voices. It has had a rich history from the single-movement forms of Scarlatti through the Classical centre point of the Viennese classics to the outer boundaries of Boulez and Cage. For all its multiplicity, the term itself has kept meaning in its wordlessness and its seriousness: a sonata, regardless of form, is a statement – of unity, if not of uniformity.

My First Piano Sonata (broken branches) is constructed of sixteen small, inconclusive sections. The work is not a collection of album leaves though – of saplings existing comfortably in their own space – but rather branches from a single tree. And branches broken in three senses: fragments of fragility, related in theme but incomplete and damaged; an oblique tribute to Janáček's cycle *On an Overgrown Path*; and finally a spiritual dimension: 'I am the vine, you are the branches. Cut off from me you can do nothing,' said Christ to his disciples in St John's Gospel. The climax of this sonata is a section called *non credo*, based on material from the *Credo* of my *Missa Mirabilis*, which explores issues of doubt and despair in the context of the concrete affirmations of the Nicene Creed. The penultimate section, a wordless but metrically exact setting of the sixth-century text *Crux fidelis*, reveals another 'branch' – the wood of the Cross.

The sonata begins with a Prelude (Autumn) and ends with a Postlude (Spring). The music is identical in both except that the anguish of the former's G sharp minor is blanched into G major at the end of the piece. Branches begin their lives anew in the spring, and nothing is so broken that it cannot be healed.

My Second Piano Sonata: insomnia in a seedy bedsit

Piano Sonata no. 2 (Notturno luminoso)

The subtitle for my Second Piano Sonata suggests many images: the moon on a calm lake perhaps, or stars across a restful sky. But this piece is about a different kind of night and a different kind of light: the brightness of a brash city in the hours of darkness; the loneliness of pre-morning; sleeplessness and the dull glow of the alarm clock's unmoving hours; the irrational fears or the disturbing dreams that are only darkened by the harsh glare of a suspended, dusty light bulb. But also suggested are nighttime's heightened emotions: its mysticism, its magic, its imaginative possibilities.

The sonata's form is ABA and there are three musical ideas: one based on sharps (brightness), one based on flats (darkness), and one based on naturals (white notes) representing a kind of blank irrationality. The piece opens clangorously, its bold, assertive theme – sharps piled on sharps – separated by small cadenzas. Yearning and hesitating to reach a cadence, it finally stumbles into the B section where all accidentals are suddenly bleached away in a whiteout. Extremes of pitch and dynamics splatter sound across the keyboard until an arpeggio figure in the bass gathers rhythmic momentum and leads to the 'flat' musical idea, jarring in its romantic juxtaposition to what has gone before.

This whole B section is made up of a collision, a tossing and turning, between the two tonalities of flats and naturals, interrupting each other with impatience until the whiteout material spins up into the stratosphere, a whirlwind in the upper octaves of the piano. Under this blizzard we hear the theme from the beginning of the piece, firstly in purest, brilliant C major in the treble, then, after it subsides to pianissimo, in a snarl of dissonance in the extreme bass of the instrument. The music stops . . . and then, for the first time, we hear the full statement of the 'flat' material, Andante lamentoso. The music's sorrow increases with wave after wave of romantic ardour, deliberately risking overkill and discomfort.

At its climax the music halts twice at a precipice then tumbles into the recapitulation, the opening theme now in white-note tonality and unrecognisably spotted across the keyboard. As this peters out we hear the same theme but now with warm, gentle, romantic harmonies. A final build up to an exact repetition of the opening of the piece is blended with material from the B section and, in the last bar, in a final wild scream, we hear all three tonalities together for a blinding second-long flash, brighter than noon, before the final soft chord closes the curtain on these night visions.

My Third Piano Sonata:
tonality, dogma, modernism

Piano Sonata III (Trinitas)

Art, like life, moves ahead by reimagining and sometimes even destroying what went before. As new cells in the body form when old ones die and as it's natural for children to move away from parents (if only in tastes and ideas) so artists find energy both by building on the past at the same time as leaving it behind. This moving on can sometimes involve violent destruction as well as a more organic construction. But there has arisen a challenge for artists in every field over the past century: what if it's the destroyers whom we wish to destroy? What do we do when modernism is no longer modern? Where do we find ourselves when we are *après* the avant-garde?

It is a vast topic, and one that has significance in every corner of cultural life, but suffice it to say in the present context that around a hundred years ago atonality finally triumphed in Western classical music. The bending trunk that had supported dissonance's tonal tensions from before Bach to Wagner and beyond finally snapped. The resulting shattering of rules and the threat of anarchy's reign required a new system, a new framework. There was no going back to the old regime but new freedoms needed new structures. Arnold Schoenberg came up with a system of composition in the 1920s (twelve-note technique) where atonality (music separated from clear harmonic roots) would be guaranteed. In this construct each note of the Western chromatic scale appears just once in a sequence until all the notes are used up and the sequence begins again. The row can be inverted or reversed or transposed but, strictly speaking, it shouldn't be disordered.

Traditional tonality works by creating tensions that are resolved, by mixing familiarity and repetition as if signposts, markers along the way, paths to return home. Conversely the twelve-note system ensures that all roads are equal, that no note is more important than another, that all lanes lead only to each other – a nomadic, circular path where home is the journey itself. For many post-war years it was pretty much the only map in print for young composers who wanted to be performed, commissioned or broadcast.

I wanted to try an experiment with my Third Sonata: could I use twelve-note technique to undermine or at least to question the technique itself? Could I find a path outside the circle? Some tonal composers (Britten, Shostakovich and Barber spring to mind) had used note-rows in their works as symbols of modernity, as decorative or cynical nods to a musical establishment that had disowned them, but could a whole piece be constructed with this principle? Could a system designed to avoid tonality become one that unashamedly reclaimed it?

To begin with I used a note-row shot through with tonal implications. Not only does it begin in C major (notes 1 and 2) and end in its dominant G major (notes 10, 11 and 12) but thirds, both major and minor, are carved into the very contours of the sequence's twelve notes. The sonata is in three sections, with the first two using the note-row in a traditional manner. But at the centre point of the piece, the start of the third section, there is a scramble towards the top of the piano ending in a scream of a C major chord.

From here to the end of the piece the row is set free and commences a thoroughly eclectic journey. It begins as the harmonic foundation for a stately chaconne, then splinters into a minimalist motive of swirling, hammered loops. After a pause, we hear a super-soft descending scale of mini-clusters (as if played by an infant's chubby digits) as the accompaniment to a hymn tune under which the row appears as a sour shadow of dissonance. Then there is a passionate, pleading mantra using the row, then a radiant reappearance of the hymn tune now accompanied by crashing clusters played with a book or the flat of the hand – all these shuffled around seemingly at random until a long silence appears on the final page of the sonata. A sudden return to strict twelve-note technique occurs with twelve, short, soft, six-part chords made up of the original row and introducing a new row from the suspended notes held on top, as distant from tonality as I could make it. The sonata comes to a quiet close on the same notes with which it began – a C major chord.

Why *Trinitas*? Well, I like subtitles and as this piece was commissioned by the (Catholic) *Tablet* magazine I wanted to incorporate some spiritual or religious aspect in the creative process. When I realised that this piano sonata would be my third, that it was going to be in three sections, and that it would utilise major and minor thirds in its musical material, the Trinity seemed to be an appropriate tag. But then, as I continued to think of the dogmatic aspect of the twelve-note system, I could see a strange parallel with the Trinity – another dogma. Both are an ordering with numbers, man-made constructs, intellectual braces to aid recovery after a crisis, whether after the collapse of tonality or after the Christological confusion of the Arian controversy in the fourth century. Both dogmas have positive and negative elements . . . and consequences. The musical ones have already been discussed, but what about the Trinity?

At its best this non-biblical term, invented by theologians, was an attempt to convey the idea of the one God as 'relationship' within God's own inner life, with all the implications of wisdom (the Son) and love (the Spirit) which that implied. But it was also a doctrinal 'line in the sand' on an issue that is ultimately unknowable, and it proved to be the final straw in the embittered relationship that developed in the early centuries of the Common Era between Christians and Jews. It was, and was intended to be, the end of fudge. It also proved to be the end of the road. After the Trinity was defined, the two faith communities parted like a train divided and there began to develop, with increasing vigour, a tradition of anti-Jewish polemic in the post-Constantine Church's vigorous defence of orthodoxy. Perhaps it is not overly melodramatic to see a line stretching from Nicaea to Auschwitz.

I love living in the present eclectic age. I love the fact that the size of my collar or the width of my tie is not dictated by changing, authoritarian fashion. I love modernism now because, in the free-flowing twenty-first century, I'm able to choose it, and to play with it, and then leave it, and then take it up again. Its challenge to the status quo or to comfortable conservatism is ever relevant and refreshing – until it begins to enforce its own rigidity. Schoenberg did say (tongue in cheek perhaps, or maybe even with a dash of hope) that there were still pieces to be written in C major. Tonality in the end proved to be indestructible. Amid the debris of the post-war, post-Shoah years composers slowly began to discover it again as diamonds among the rubble. The snapped tree had begun to grow again.

Alfred Cortot: the poet speaks

There are only a few surviving films of my favourite pianist playing, but one extraordinary one is readily accessible on the internet: Alfred Cortot teaching the final piece of Schumann's *Kinderszenen*. He plays the short, one-page movement but also talks us through it – he is giving a lesson after all. But this is a transcendental clip in every way. First, phrases on the keyboard are caressed as if improvising, yet also as if those notes have lain under those ageing fingers for a lifetime. Then there are the words themselves – ideas of risky sentiment, but expressed with an innocence that charms us, even if they would be virtually impossible to utter today. Alain de Botton put it memorably once when he said, 'The great fear of us moderns: being naive.' Certain pure, powerful ideas can be expressed only when their author is open to vulnerability.

Beyond the tangibility of music and words is the sheer aura of the man towards the end of his life: the exquisite detachment and refinement of manners, the haunting vision in the piercing eyes. He is both unafraid to reveal his personal thoughts (almost with the intimacy of lovemaking) while at the same time keeping a profoundly respectful distance. It's just *impossible* to imagine him uttering a crude phrase or word, linguistically or morally. The clip also raises the issue of whether music can have a story or message behind it, in the light of Stravinsky's famous statement that 'music means nothing'. The title, *Der Dichter spricht*, is Schumann's own contradiction of this claim, allowing Cortot to take him at his word, and leaving us with a film-as-poem, a pianist-as-poet, and a peerless example of one of the great re-creative artists of the twentieth century.

Two formidable ladies

Most of us spend most of our moral lives in the middle – sitting on a fence much broader then the gardens on either side. Our days are filled with small acts of cowardice and laziness alternating randomly with small acts of generosity and kindness. The big gestures, whether courageous or cruel, usually pass us by – more often through circumstance than through choice. But, at certain times in history, circumstance demands of people difficult decisions, forcing them to confront virtue and vice in real situations, when such choices involve life and death . . . for themselves and for others. There were two female pianists in the last century, both Beethoven specialists and exact contemporaries, who did not sit on the broad fence like most of us, but who stood in the gardens on opposite sides with utter conviction and determination.

Elly Ney (1882–1968), it is said, was a 'fanatical supporter' of Hitler. She voluntarily joined the Nazi party in 1937, participated in 'cultural education camps', became an honorary member of the League of German Girls, and wrote adoring letters to 'mein Führer'. According to the pianist Edward Kilenyi, who was a captain in the US Army at the time, she would read extracts of Hitler's writings and soldiers' letters from the concert stage, and in Salzburg, where she taught during the war, she used to honour Beethoven's bust with a Nazi salute. After the war she was banned from performing in Bonn, and a request in 1952 for this ban to be lifted was refused. Her career, which had flourished in the earlier years of the century, never recovered, and just a few years ago the mayor of Tutzing, the small Bavarian town where she died, finally removed her portrait from the Town Hall.

Dame Myra Hess (1890–1965) could easily have escaped safely to America, where she had a huge following, at the outbreak of the Second World War, but she chose to abandon her international career and stay at home in central London during the worst of the bombing. After the outbreak of war all public places of entertainment were closed, but she convinced the government to allow her to start a daily series of concerts at the National Gallery, beginning on 10 October 1939 and continuing until 1946. Although all the paintings and sculptures had been removed for safe keeping, and occasional daytime air raids meant that the audience and musicians had to retreat to the basement, 824,000 people attended 1,698 concerts during London's darkest days. Dame Myra felt that music could give a genuine moral boost to people facing terror and hardship, and she was prepared to risk her life and livelihood for that cause.

Most of us fall between these two extremes, and our various shades of moral grey can fluctuate daily, depending on all kinds of varying circumstances. Some artists who left Nazi Germany were courageous, some selfish; some who stayed there were courageous, some selfish. Some began well but descended to evil and collaboration; others began badly but later discovered heroism and humanity. I mean to prove nothing by placing these two formidable ladies next to each other in this way, except, perhaps, to pose the uncomfortable question: is there a moral dimension to music? Can a person who does evil things be a great artist?

Josef Hofmann and Steinway:
two greats in an era of greats

It is often said that Josef Hofmann was the universally acclaimed 'greatest pianist' of his time. I knew about this reputation – Rachmaninov famously put aside performing Chopin's B minor Sonata after hearing Hofmann in the same piece; Horowitz, when visiting Steinway Hall in the 1920s and having Hofmann's piano pointed out to him, said, 'Please . . . may I just touch it?' But when we listen to the recordings of Hofmann today, can we see what these two pianists and just about all of their colleagues and contemporary critics were so enthusiastic about? Was he really the greatest during a golden period of so many greats?

He was born in 1876 in Podgórze, a district of Kraków, in the year the first modern Steinway piano was made. Although the Steinway factory opened in New York in 1853 and its first full concert grand (8 feet 5 inches) was produced three years later, it was only with the invention of the Capo d'Astro bar and the full cast-iron plate that a truly modern piano was created – just in time for the Centennial Exhibition in Philadelphia in 1876. (It's worth noting here, as an aside, that Hamburg began making its own home-grown Steinways only around 1910. Steinway was an exclusively American company for its first half century.) I think part of Hofmann's unique success and acclamation was that he was, by the time his career was in full flow, the first pianist to use the modern American piano properly, to learn how to play to and with its strengths.

Many European artists were uncomfortable with the Steinway. They found its action too heavy, its tone too brilliant, its bass too rich, its treble lacking the delicate silver strands of the Erard or the transparent, reedy baritone of the Bechstein. Moritz Rosenthal, during recording sessions in the early 1930s at Abbey

Road, complained to producer Fred Gaisburg that he could not get 'his effects' on Steinways, and asked for his favoured Bösendorfer instead. Gaisburg protested that the Steinway sounded cleaner, clearer on record and they ended up adjusting the action to suit the pianist's taste rather than changing the piano.

Chopin would probably not have been able to play more than a few bars on a modern Steinway. Liszt would have been restricted. Debussy and Ravel would have written very different music if they'd had modern Steinways in their studios. But Hofmann not only sat in front of it with the confidence and expertise of an experienced pilot in a cockpit, but he even invented one of its later features: the 'accelerated action', patented in 1940.

When Hofmann's bass chords crashed against the back wall of Carnegie Hall like huge waves, when he spat out repeated notes with the speed of steel pistons, when his melodies hung in the air like wheeling birds, he was directly influenced by the Steinway's improved dampers, hammers, iron frame, Duplex Scale system and the Capo d'Astro bar. Hofmann's assertive brilliance was breathtaking – and new. No one had ever played liked this before, and I think that is the main reason he was crowned king at a time of many princes.

Glenn Gould and modern recording

Some have claimed that Glenn Gould, with his notorious disdain for concerts and the public, would have felt vindicated by twenty-first-century attitudes towards electronic media. That someone can now record himself at home, editing the file to perfection and then uploading it to a potential audience of millions, would have been beyond his wildest dreams.

Let me begin by saying that I adore many of Glenn Gould's recordings, and I'm always happy to give him the benefit of the doubt, even in interpretations I don't like. To hear him play the *Lord of Salisbury Pavan* by (his favourite composer) Orlando Gibbons is a wonder, an example of his amazing and unique way of holding or lifting the slowest singing lines on endless horizons of poise. Not to mention his eccentricity, of course. I'm sure Gibbons would have dropped his cup of mead in astonishment at the slow, pecking ornaments in that performance – the original, decorative earrings recast into swinging chandeliers of attention-grabbing prominence. But nevertheless, he is unquestionably one of the greatest artists of the twentieth century, and his playing seems as fresh today as ever.

He was a man of many myths. The most telling for me is that he was an invisible recluse, making recordings as a purist musician's response to the emptiness and futility of modern concert life. In fact he relied on and was addicted to the most visible, publicity-conscious promotion of his times. He recorded with eyes fully open to his audience; it's just that he didn't want *them* to see *him*. He scrutinised them voraciously, but through the peephole of technology, safely at home north of the border, safely supplied with his pills and scrambled eggs, safely financed by the regular, large cheques arriving in the post from the offices of Columbia Records in New York City.

The days when an artist could record in a studio, under contract, for decades, for a major label, as Gould did, and make a lot of steady money for himself and his record company, are over. The most successful artists' recordings still sell a good number of copies, but only on the crest of the wave of their concert careers. CDs and downloads are spin-offs, not the central force of a professional musician's life. Indeed, some of these are taken from 'live' concerts. Many major orchestras now release only recordings of concert performances, either on their own labels or through internet-based downloads. Even pop artists

(Madonna, for instance) use recordings to sell concert tours, not, as in the 1980s, the other way round; and some artists are even giving away CDs or digital downloads for free – looking to box-office receipts rather than the cash registers of now-defunct record stores to make their fortunes.

Glenn Gould's prophecy that carefully controlled studio recordings would snuff out the public concert seems quaint and dated today, and many of our most recently built halls combine architectural splendour with meeting places for fine food and lively conversation. The concert is alive! Gould's idealism was ultimately all about control – of himself and the medium – and I think he would have been extremely uncomfortable in the modern pick'n'mix supermarket. It was fine for him to take an exposition from here and a coda from there and stitch them together with an expert and patient producer, but I can't imagine him welcoming ten thousand Joe Goldbergs doing the same on their bedroom computers – free, swapped, downloaded, or deleted as the fancy takes them.

I'm sure Gould would have loved the internet (I can imagine dozens of his alter egos in dozens of forums), and he would have written a fascinating blog, but if he had been starting his career now, rather than in the golden youth of the 1950s LP, it might have to have been on YouTube where he would make his mark – or miss his mark – in the cruel (and free) lottery of cyberspace's billion dancing bytes.

Happy (un)together

There cannot have been a more dangerous, free-spirited, unpredictable musician in front of the public than Ivry Gitlis. His career (strange word for something so kaleidoscopic), apart from concert-giving, found him studying with Enescu and Thibaud, jamming with John Lennon and Eric Clapton, acting under the direction of Truffaut and dipping his toes in (at the time) Palestine's Dead Sea with Bronislav Huberman – oh, and taking part in youthful spitting competitions with Josef Hassid.

I had met Ivry a couple of times but then a few years ago Steven Isserlis asked me if I would come along to Wigmore Hall where he would be interviewing the great violinist, and would I play something with him for this event. I was delighted to do this but we all agreed that there was no point in rehearsing. I knew that whatever Ivry did at 10 a.m. would be completely different by 12 noon when we were on stage, so we just decided to wing it. All I was prepared for was the unprepared creativity of his artistry.

We played the Paradis *Sicilienne* and Kreisler's *Liebesleid*. Having heard something about the life of this venerable legend in the interview for the previous hour, I sat at the piano already moved by the idea of playing with someone whose connections to the past were so rich. But then he began to play. The vibrating violin instantly became the passionate if slightly vulnerable voice of a lover, with words and songs and spit. And impossible to follow . . . if following means that every chord is together, every bar line reached at the same point. But it reminded me that strict ensemble was not so important to musicians of the past. Listen to chamber performances from the 1930s and everyone is following his or her own subtle path of rubato. Indeed, pianists from the same period are not even together with themselves. Their right-hand melodies rarely align exactly with the left-hand accompaniment, and both Mozart and Chopin spoke of this as an ideal to be sought. If rubato is too carefully planned beforehand it is like scripted lovemaking: false, hollow, stiff.

'Will you play at my funeral?' he asked me in the Green Room of Wigmore Hall afterwards.

'But Ivry, how can you be sure you won't outlive me?'

Die Meistersinger: Terfel is Sachs

Bryn Terfel is the Hans Sachs of his generation. When I heard him in the role for the first time in Cardiff it was stunning and overwhelming. As with his Wotan at the Royal Opera House a year earlier, he rode over the full orchestra with all the power in the world, yet constantly found lieder-like moments of intimacy and subtlety, drawing a character of multicoloured shades. He is one of the greatest actor-singers I've seen on stage, and when the Welsh chorus cried out, 'Hail! Sachs!', the poignancy was not unnoticed – a moment of national pride as character and (master)singer melded into one.

Although I'd never seen *Die Meistersinger* on stage, I'd known it since my enthusiastic teens. Wagner was my favourite composer for a while and neighbours at the time might remember it blaring out of open windows from our house on summer afternoons. I was reminded again on that occasion at the Millennium Centre how extraordinary is Wagner's genius. Through the sheer fecundity of his musical invention he is able to keep an audience riveted for close to six hours, despite an undramatic plot with awkward moments of comedy (some of the puns on birds and singing are claw-curling) and the final embarrassing paean of political hubris.

> Beware! Evil tricks threaten us: if the German people
> and kingdom should one day decay under a false, foreign
> rule soon no prince would understand his people; and
> foreign mists with foreign vanities they would plant in our
> German land; what is German and true none would know.

Some commentators have seen these foreigners planted in German soil as the Jews, and these lines have to be listened to with a pinch of salt worthy of Lot's wife. But in this production the director Richard Jones had up his sleeve a trump card that changed everything for me. The 'front drop' curtain was a collage of photographs of great artists from the Austro-Germanic tradition ranging from Bach to Goethe to Pina Bausch. As Terfel sang the words quoted above, individual photos from this collage were held up by members of the chorus. I think Haydn was the first one and I winced for a moment at the gesture . . . but only for a moment. Within seconds it all made sense. Wagner's political hawk was spreading its wings as a dove, and with the image of Simone Weil, the French-Jewish philosopher who died during the war in London on a starvation diet in solidarity with occupied France, my eyes filled with tears.

Wagner is a towering representative of a glorious cultural legacy, but we need not let him be a Beckmesser excluding those who don't keep his own rules of membership. German art has shaped us all and is greater than any one nation, having the potential (unlike that other Reich of recent, bitter memory) to last for a thousand or more peaceful years.

When Ernest twiddled the knobs

Ernest Fleischmann was not universally liked in the music business, but he was a good professional friend to me over the years. He was a man of strong opinions, of vision, of the sort of intense energy that swept all along with him or else pushed it aside. Despite disagreeing with him on a number of things (usually not voiced – he was not an easy man with whom to argue) it was always clear that he was passionate and deeply knowledgeable about music – the notes in the score and their vibrations in the air, not the vapid print or hot air that so often surrounds those notes today.

Ernest first invited me to play at the Hollywood Bowl with the Los Angeles Philharmonic in 1985. A pianist had cancelled and they needed a replacement. The conductor was Sir Charles Groves and the piece was Rachmaninov's *Paganini Rhapsody* which I had half learned a few years before and played once (badly) with a youth orchestra. I had a few days to get the piece back into my fingers and I remember flying out from Manchester to Los Angeles in a state of excitement and fear. I remember too the tremendous size of the Bowl auditorium as viewed from the stage. The heads of the audience in the back rows were as small as the notes on the page of my miniature score. I also remember being told that the old house Steinway I was playing on that occasion had probably been used by the composer of the work I was performing. A thrilling thought!

I returned to the Bowl many times over the years to play for Ernest, but on one occasion he joined in the performance. The amplified sound was fairly primitive before the shell underwent a highly sophisticated acoustic renovation in 2003–4. I was playing Brahms's First Concerto with Paavo Berglund conducting and at one point, early in the first movement, I struck one of the great, grand chords in the piece and heard something I've never heard before or since: the sound of the instrument *increasing* in volume with a great swell of sonority – impossible for a piano to do naturally, as its vibrations decay the instant they are created. It was a shock and I quickly recognised the hand of Ernest. His seat in the audience had direct control of the amplification system. He'd obviously decided that the balance was off (all the sound in the Bowl has some artificial enhancement) and he'd taken charge of the situation. I smile as I think of this example of the two sides of his personality: his concern for the music and his relish at being in control.

It is not altogether an admirable trait in human beings that they tend to like those who like them. If Ernest had not invited me back to play regularly over the years and spoken well of me to other managers I would probably not be writing these words. If he'd said of me what he apparently said of some others ('That man will never play again in this town'), my career in the early years might well have taken a different direction. But without him the Bowl itself would probably not have been renovated, Frank Gehry's Disney Hall might not have been built, the London Symphony would have had a dramatically different history . . . to name but three of the many pots that Ernest Fleischmann stirred and seasoned with his own unique blend of spices over a long career.

Douglas Steele's repetition

My first composition teacher, Douglas Steele, was more than a little absent-minded by the time I studied with him. He would sit at a rattly old upright Danemann in a teaching studio at Chetham's School in Manchester and play *Hommage à Rameau* from Debussy's *Images I* for me every week. About three lines down he would turn to me (every week) and say, 'Michelangeli holds down the pedal here.' Actually, as great as the venerable Italian pianist was, Douglas played this piece better. His sound, scooped out of the cantabile depths of the piano, was radiant, and his sense of rhythmic freedom was sublime, as if the bar lines were a row of trees swaying, breathing in the breeze.

It is said that there is a fine line between genius and madness, but as I sat next to Douglas week after week that line was blurred and irrelevant. The genius was in the sound he drew out of that battered old piano, and my lessons with him were a rare hour of sanity and joy in my otherwise stressful early teens.

RIP Joseph Villa

Joseph Villa, a great pianist and a dear friend, died on Thursday 13 April 1995, from complications resulting from AIDS. He was forty-six years old and at the height of his pianistic powers, although, through the puzzling lottery of musical careers, he never had the sort of success he deserved. Fortunately he made five commercial CDs (Liszt and Scriabin), and there are a number of live concerts floating about the internet, most remarkably two versions of the Second Sonata of Rachmaninov, which are possibly the greatest performances of this work to have been captured by a microphone.

It is in these that the clearest glimpse can be seen of the almost fearful energy and passion that could burst forth when Joseph played. A friend of his recalled to me an impromptu performance of Scriabin's Fifth Sonata at a party where the initial, distracted listening was suddenly transmuted into speechless fixation as Joseph conjured up the piece's wild frenzy. As the last, screaming arpeggios shredded up the keyboard, it was the audience's nerves that were in tatters.

Due to his almost empty concert schedule during the years we were friends, I was able to hear him live on only one occasion: when we read through the piano-duet version of Liszt's *Via Crucis* at his apartment. I remember his hands being incapable of just playing notes; every chord was coloured with the care and expertise of a great painter. He knew just how to handle the vast scope of Liszt's style – his epic gestures, his soaring vocal lines. What an irony this duet seemed when I visited him in the hospital a year or so later, his phenomenal powers smothered under the sterilised white sheets, and the burden of extreme physical weakness making his final months a personal 'Via Crucis'.

One particular interest we shared at the time was the traditional Latin Mass. In fact, we became close friends as we chatted over brunch after our weekly 'Tridentine treat' at St Agnes' Church in New York. I never saw him more passionate than when he was lambasting the modern liturgical abuses he witnessed. He would often make these views plainly known to cowering priests or trouser-suited nuns, and would sometimes even walk out in protest as guitars were 'untuned' before starting their strumming.

There is an inevitable sense of tragedy when such talent is unused or ignored or cut short, but some lines from the French philosopher Jacques Maritain seem to me to be an appropriate response:

> The philosopher is without consolation at the loss of the tiniest transient reality, a face, a gesture of the hand, an act of freedom or a musical harmony in which there radiates the faintest glimmer of love or beauty. He has his own solution, I must admit. He trusts that not one of these things will pass away because they are all kept safe in the memory of the angels . . . [who] will never cease speaking of them to one another and so will bring back to life, in a thousand different forms, the story of our poor world.

RIP Vlado Perlemuter

One of the highlights of my years studying at the Royal Northern College of Music in Manchester was the opportunity to play in masterclasses for the great French pianist Vlado Perlemuter. These classes were held in what was known as the 'organ room', and so it was appropriate perhaps that the first piece I played for him was the *Prélude, Choral et Fugue* by the great organist César Franck. It was inspiring to know that the small, quietly elegant man, seated on my left and wearing a woollen scarf, had studied the piece with Alfred Cortot, and had been at the centre of an incomparably rich time in Parisian pianistic life – either in direct contact or only a generation removed from all of the greatest figures in French music of the period. He seemed to like what I was doing with the piece, although he stressed the gravity of its mood, the seriousness at the heart of Franck's vision. 'Don't play this passage like Meyerbeer,' he commented as I turned the corner of a phrase with too sweet an inflection. 'Like a procession,' was his comment in the opening of the *Choral*, emphasising its liturgical spirit. He wrote some interesting fingerings in my score, including his suggestion to play the opening arpeggios with the right-hand thumb on the thematic first notes. I did this for a while afterwards but then I found that brilliant Steinway pianos were not really suited to it. It was too easy to find notes in the following arpeggios jumping out with a jangle, but I can see that on older, more mellow instruments if would have been an excellent way to shape that particular melody.

One of his passions was that one should never repeat a note with the same finger when it was part of a melodic line. This idea came into its own when I played the Fourth Ballade of Chopin for him with its tender repetitions in the main theme; this is an understanding of fingering and its role in shaping a phrase that comes to us from Chopin himself. What has to be calculated artificially with one finger becomes an organic phrase when the whole hand is employed, literally moulding the contours of the melody with elasticity and naturalness. The importance of the left hand was often mentioned too in the classes, not so much in the bringing out of voices, but in the shaping of the harmonic base under the melodic line. Thus Chopin études, where the difficulty appears to be in the fast-moving right-hand figuration, become virtuosic in the fullest sense when the left hand is played with total command and with a palette of subtle inflection.

For a man with such impressive musical connections it was refreshing to observe Perlemuter's modesty. Names that could have been dropped with regularity were quietly mentioned only to emphasise a point: 'Ravel told me to do this . . .'. Hard to argue with that! Indeed, so quiet were his comments at times that only those in the front seats were able to hear them. He was giving a lesson with people present, not entertaining an audience. He taught only repertoire with which he felt completely at home, and on the School of Keyboard Studies notice board was pinned a sheet with the works he was prepared to hear: all of Chopin, all of Ravel, but only specified, if fairly wide-ranging, selections of other composers. The omissions were interesting: no Russians, as I recall, which seems strange perhaps from someone with Polish-Jewish roots; and no contemporary works, less strange from one who had lived a long time and had seen many 'contemporary eras'. However, on one occasion, when we had some time left over, I did suggest playing Rachmaninov's Second Concerto for him. He laughed and said that it was not a piece he taught but he was happy to listen to it. He had nothing to say, not because it was particularly well played, but because it appeared to be outside his particular world of refinement and moderation and nonchalance. There was absolutely no sense of undermining the piece or of any condescension; it was simply in another language, which he found difficult or unnecessary to speak. For all of his Slavic and Semitic background, Perlemuter communicated musically with the purest of French accents. In repertoire where that was appropriate, it seemed at the time to be the only way it could be played.

RIP Shura Cherkassky

When most people die we feel as if the lights have been switched off. With Shura Cherkassky it's more like lights being turned on – for the concert is now over. The final encore has been played, the stage is bare, the flowers already withering, and the seats vacant under the harsh houselights.

Artur Schnabel once said, explaining why he would never play encores, that applause was a receipt not a bill. For Cherkassky it was more an invitation to open a bottle of champagne. Dinner might be over, but when an audience has changed in the course of an evening from customers to friends, who can be in a hurry to say goodbye? Sadly, that is what we have to do, although no one who heard Shura play or met him will ever forget his unique personality, both on and off the stage. His golden tone, like sunshine melting a bowl of the richest ice-cream (two of his 'favourite things'); his contrapuntal voicing, like a child wandering into all the rooms he's been banned from; or, for that matter, his walk to the piano – as if treading on crushed velvet. We shall try to keep our memories fresh with his recordings (particularly the 'live' ones), and will treasure among ourselves the many anecdotes that have now become part of musical folklore.

One such story comes to mind. I knew Shura a little and experienced, along with a number of extremely annoyed travellers one afternoon, a typical slice of Cherkasskiana when we happened to bump into each other at JFK Airport.

'Stephen, hello! How *are* you? Why don't we go and have a drink? Do you have time before your flight?'

I did and we took our places in the queue. I ordered a coffee and he asked for an orange juice. 'Is it freshly squeezed? Are you sure? Could you check that it's freshly squeezed?' The word 'squeezed' was almost onomatopoeic as his lips effortfully delayed each consonant. After much consultation, and a lengthening queue behind us, it was determined not to be freshly s.q.u.e.e.z.e.d but he decided to take the glass of Tropicana on offer anyway. Then the fun started. Out of his suit pocket, from under a monster fur coat, came a purse bulging to breaking point with coins. He spilled them all out in a jangle onto the counter – a vast pile from, it seemed, every country in the world. Then, as if practising scales at the slowest tempo, he counted each one out with a fat forefinger: 'Five cents . . . ten cents . . . thirty-five cents . . . oh no, that's a Canadian quarter.' That one was moved to one side. 'Fifteen cents . . .' and so on, to the mounting fury of the ever-lengthening line of people behind us and the girl at the cash register in front of us. To me he was a hero and a great artist, so I enjoyed this equivalent of an outrageous rubato, but I don't think the forty-eight people at risk of missing their flights were so enchanted.

Such oblivion to the world around is not something to be imitated, yet when transferred to the concert platform it can awaken in us a freedom from undue regard for what others think, unleashing the ability simply to do what we want to do. Constant self-questioning at home in the practice room, yes; but then complete self-confidence in the wings of the concert hall – if not at the cash register of a busy airport.

RIP Lou Reed

In my teenage bedroom – dark-purple ceiling, light-purple walls, joss sticks smouldering – I used to listen to Lou Reed. 'Take a walk on the wild side,' he suggested with that ironic, sing-song, cooler-than-cool voice. I didn't take his advice in the end and went back to Beethoven, despite years of neglecting the piano and neglecting to do my homework. But in those voice-breaking years as I lounged around in my flared jeans covering my (purple) platform shoes, and as the LP, scratched and coarse, spun lazy circles in the smoke, I did feel a certain coming of age. I felt maturity arriving as if a shoot in a plant pot pushing out of the brown soil (no, not that plant). I was wrong; I was still a kid; it was a false spring. But when I heard of his death and realised that such a force of nature as Lou Reed was now a dead leaf, beyond the autumn of life, I felt a strange and poignant sadness.

Rest in peace? Maybe chill is more like it.

Great Greens I: by way of an introduction

It struck me that of the few great people I've met over the years, three of them were called Green. By 'great' I don't mean famous, or witty, or talented. I'm thinking of something more powerful than those qualities – a sort of 'holiness', although not (necessarily) in a religious sense.

You sometimes meet people who have an aura, a presence that radiates something extraordinary. This quality can be something unpleasant: there are people who drain you of energy, who seem illuminated only by their own brilliance and plunge all others into darkness. But my Greens were men of quiet, inner strength who radiated a nurturing generosity to those who came in contact with them.

Gordon Green was my main piano teacher from when I was ten to when I was seventeen. He taught at the Royal Northern College of Music and the Royal Academy of Music.

Father Maurus Green was a Benedictine monk from Ampleforth Abbey. He received me into the Catholic Church in 1980 when I was eighteen, at St Mary's Church in Warrington.

Julien Green was the French novelist to whom I wrote

after reading his powerful novels and diaries and who invited me to lunch at his Paris apartment when I was playing there in 1996.

One thing that united them was a sense that they really *listened* to you in conversation. A kindly listening, a listening that encouraged confidence (in both senses of the word), a listening that was not a reluctant price paid for their next prepared monologue, a listening that was not poised with easy answers to the difficult questions, but was simply a pair of open ears connected to an open mind and an open heart. It's a rare quality . . . and they were rare men.

Great Greens II: Gordon and the smokescreen

We cannot choose our parents and, more often than not, we cannot choose our teachers either, at least in the early, formative years. However, if that choice had been available to me I could not have selected a more nurturing, stimulating or inspiring teacher than Gordon Green.

I rarely saw him clearly in the seven years I was his student as he was usually obscured by clouds of pipe smoke. Just as he was about to make a musical point he would reach for the matchbox, strike a match, then hold its flare against the charred pipe, tamping down the tobacco and drawing in deeply. Not since the Mount of Transfiguration were wisdom and clouds so perfectly united. As the smoke was billowing all around him his mind was weighing the issue at hand – how to pace, how to phrase, how to pedal. In my first six months of lessons (I was ten years old) I think we talked of pedalling more than anything else – feet as important to a serious pianist as fingers.

It has been said that in music silence is as important as sound, and this was true of Gordon's teaching too. Before he made any comments he would always think deeply. His suggestions were illuminating but tentative; he was anxious never to pontificate or to narrow horizons. A hand on the arm to guide, not a collar and leash around the neck. After he made a suggestion my hands would leap to the keyboard. 'Wait! Think what you want to do before playing.' Like a farmer, calm and heedless of the seemingly barren ground viewed out of season, he had a holistic approach to artistic development. He would never demonstrate because he didn't want the student to imitate him, but rather to think, to listen, to form a unique personality slowly and surely. Competitions would draw from him gentle contempt. Why face an evil, however necessary, before the appointed time? To jump into that circuit early merely meant that there was less time to develop musical maturity – and a *lifetime* is too short for that.

I had my lessons at his house in Hope Street, Liverpool, until he moved to London. I loved to look at his desk where letters of Proust lay alongside Liszt first editions – and tobacco tins. We would listen to some old recordings. 'Hear how marvellously Cortot shades the pedal at the end of the A flat Étude of Chopin.' The LP would turn round and round, and then, that moment of magic from fifty years earlier would shine through the speakers – a shimmer of sound that tickled the ear. I looked through the gossamer clouds at Gordon, his white goatee beard divided in two by a smile of total exhilaration, the pipe held in a cumulus cradle. Then his wife, Dorothy, would swing open the thick, heavy door and bring in a tray of coffee and biscuits. My father used to sit in on most of these lessons and I loved to hear them discuss pipes and politics. They both had rather radical, left-leaning views. Often in the afternoons of my morning lessons a guest would be expected: friends such as Sir Charles Groves, students such as John Ogdon or the young Scouser Simon Rattle, or some mysterious person needing a place to practise. On one occasion that person was Sviatoslav Richter, who was playing at the Philharmonic Hall further down the same street that same evening. I wish I'd hung around to bump into him.

Both Gordon and my father died when I was in my late teens – too early for me to appreciate fully their wisdom or to ask all the questions that have surfaced since. But, as well as being increasingly conscious of the sap of my father's artistic genes as the years pass, the roots of Gordon's early inspiration guide so many of my musical ideas to this day.

Great Greens III: Maurus and the smile

When I was in my late teens I decided to become a Catholic. Many friends and acquaintances since have found it puzzling why I would embrace something they have spent their lives trying to cast away. Suffice it to say that without Father Maurus Green O.S.B. (1919–2001) I'm not sure I would have taken the final plunge, however much I had dangled my legs in the water. I'm not talking about finding a latter-day Newman or Knox who could draw with brilliant clarity the clean, clear lines of Catholic doctrine; I already knew that I wanted to swim the Tiber, but I just didn't have the courage to face either the cold water or the possibility of drowning . . . and Father Maurus's warmth and gentleness made it possible.

I began attending St Mary's Church in Warrington, which had been staffed by Benedictine monks from Ampleforth Abbey since the late nineteenth century. It has always had a fine musical tradition. One of the early monks, the Reverend J. E. Turner, was a published composer whose fine, sturdy music was still being performed by the choir eight decades later. I ended up attending the 6.30 p.m. Mass to help out by playing the organ, and Father Maurus was nearly always the celebrant. St Mary's was cold and dark on those Sunday evenings, but when I arrived early to practise the organ I would see Maurus huddled in his habit, praying his breviary near the front. As I approached him he would look up from the book, his face lit up with a big smile, and suddenly there was no need for the electric heaters to be switched on.

I would also go along to the presbytery on a weekday evening for instruction. I was a fierce traditionalist in those days and was slightly frustrated by Maurus's unwillingness to snap closed the doctrinal pigeonholes. I wanted ultramontane assurances but he, reaching for another cigarette (he must have smoked hundreds during these sessions), wanted rather to talk about virtue, and the practical application of charity, and the Gospels, and Christ. He was no liberal (he would have taken issue with many of the things I've written about in this book) but I think he saw that I had already read enough Tanquerey or Frank Sheed and that I needed to learn something about why theology was written in the first place.

He was an excellent preacher, although not a brilliant one. I think a witty turn of phrase would have been seen as either immodest or unkind and so was left unuttered. In fact what I remember most about his sermons were their silent beginnings. He would simply stand in the pulpit and look around the congregation with a gentle smile. It might seem calculated or precious when described in words, but at the time it appeared as if he were praying for all of us, enveloping every one of us in a kind embrace. He was no plaster saint and was not without his faults (although I see him liking this part of his story much more than my earlier words of praise). He could be annoyingly vague at times, and his idealism and support for various causes could seem almost more a provocation than a conviction . . . and *very* occasionally I saw a priggishness surface. But it would have been unthinkable for him to be unavailable to anyone who needed to talk, or to cling petulantly to a fault after it was pointed out to him. (Someone should have stopped him driving though. He had a green Citroën 2CV which was held together with only rust and a prayer and he drove it, foot to the floor, with great lurches of the steering wheel.)

If much of his spiritual character could be traced to its Benedictine roots the rest can be traced to his involvement in the Focolare movement, one of several post-war organisations that arose in the Catholic Church as an expression of a new lay spirituality. This is not the place to discuss its history or teachings; these can easily be found on the internet, including accounts of those who have left the movement with negative experiences. I just know that it had a pivotal place in Maurus's life. He was the first priest member in the UK in the early 1960s. Its spirit can be clearly seen in the two books he wrote, *She Died, She Lives* and *The Vanishing Root*, both biographies of young members of the Focolare. I have to confess (sorry, Maurus!) that I don't like either of these books very much. Certain movements develop their own 'members-only' terminology, which can be perplexing or annoying to outsiders, and although the Focolare's spirituality of the unity of all people (Catholics, Orthodox, Protestants, other faiths or no faith) means that such particularity is not intended to exclude, it does make it seem like a closed door to some. Nevertheless, in the former book there is a prayer quoted by Maurus which I think sums up all that he stood and struggled for in his life:

Lord, make me a friend.
Grant that I may inspire confidence
in the person who suffers in anguish,

in the one who is searching for light a long way from you,

in the one who would like to begin again but doesn't know how,

in the one who would like to open his heart but doesn't feel able.

Lord, help me not to pass by anyone with indifferent face,

with closed heart, or hastened step.

Help me to attend at once to those who are near me.

Make me see those who are worried and bewildered,

those who suffer and don't show it,

those who feel isolated and long for friendship,

and give me the sensitivity which makes me meet their hearts.

Lord, free me from myself

to be able to serve you,

to be able to love you,

to succeed in listening to you

in every brother or sister you make me meet.

G. Volpi

Great Greens IV: Julien in the kitchen

I knew I was gay from the age of about five, indeed before I knew what it was. It was certainly unchosen. But when I chose to become a Catholic in 1980 I set in place a conflict that would occupy me for years to come (and is likely to continue to do so from the writing of these words until the last words I write). Then a friend told me of the French novelist Julien Green (1900–1997), considered one of the greatest men of letters of the twentieth century, and someone who had lived with and written about issues of homosexuality and faith throughout his life. Green has not been served well by his English translators on the whole, but I bought a number of his books and became fascinated with the voice behind them.

Of the three Greens he is by far the one I knew least. Indeed, apart from his books, my only contact with him was one phone call and one lunch at his Paris apartment in 1996. Our meeting made a huge impression on me though and I wrote a lengthy diary entry about it at the time, which follows.

I was in Paris to play a recital and I had invited Julien Green and his adopted son (long story) Jean-Eric Jourdan to attend. They weren't free that evening but invited me instead to their home for lunch the following day. My taxi arrived at rue Vaneau intentionally early by 15 minutes and so I was able to walk about the quiet, elegant streets in the 7th arrondissement gathering my thoughts and courage. I arrived at the building, punched in the security code Jean-Eric had faxed to me, then pushed open the thick black doors into a subdued courtyard with a vibrantly green garden at the end. There was another set of doors at the bottom on the right with another code. These opened to the scent of a thousand flowers and a stunning, museum-quality elevator, which I decided not to use. I bounded up the stone stairs and arrived at the first floor. Jean-Eric had said they were on the second floor but I wasn't sure whether France uses the British or American system of numbering so I rang the bell. Eventually a woman's voice called out. I knew instantly that it was the wrong flat but I replied, 'Monsieur Green?' Some mumbled words were spoken within, which I knew meant one floor higher. Up the second flight of stairs, a second bell and a warm welcome from Jean-Eric Green.

I entered the opulent, book-crowded hallway and immediately to the right was a study/sitting room. Eric called into it for Julien and an old man with a black cane walked very slowly out to meet me. He wore a dark brown, three-piece suit with a blue shirt and tie. The shirt had a white collar and the tie was broad, in silk, with polka dots in the same blue but a different weave. This legendary figure seemed so vulnerable that my nervousness instantly disappeared – as if I were meeting a child. Once he spoke, though, I could tell he was perfectly clear of mind. He had a kind, rather shy manner and was exactly as I imagined him from the book of correspondence I'd read between him and the philosopher Jacques Maritain. Eric was extremely talkative throughout my visit, which at first made it easier – there were no awkward gaps – but eventually rather spoiled things because Julien was slow and thoughtful and Eric would jump in and answer a question or change the subject or recall an anecdote.

We went immediately to the kitchen for lunch, a lovely old space with *vert anglais* tiles and paint. Eric was full of ideas and opinions: 'Chopin – all right hand. I think Field was greater.' 'We don't like Mozart very much.' Any topic provoked an instant judgement. Much slightly camp amusement, but from the few things Julien said in his serious, gentle way, I wished I'd had more time to talk to him. We ate cantaloupe melon, smoked salmon, cassoulet with no meat, the best brie I've ever had, and mixed strawberries and raspberries, finishing with (astonishingly, in Paris) Nescafé instant coffee.

I asked Julien if he read his own books. 'Only *Moira*. I think it's good, *non?*' he said doubtfully to Eric. He said he felt he could write no more novels, only his diary. He mentioned at least four times how much he loved my Schumann CD, especially the pieces from *Album for the Young* which he wanted to hear when he was dying. He was extremely effusive, making a special emphasis that I should understand his enthusiasm. He told me he had listened a number of evenings earlier and was profoundly moved, waking up during the night with the music in his thoughts. He commented on his love for Schumann and the music's extreme simplicity.

When I mentioned Jacques Maritain it provoked an affectionate memory. 'I saw him every day . . . he was my best friend really.' He was happy to praise Eric's novels. 'As good as mine . . . at *least*!' Then the telephone rang and Eric left us alone. I could hear his voice rising and falling with gossip and intrigue and the room seemed calmer without him. I asked Julien how he had returned to the Church. He seemed puzzled and began to describe how he found a Catholic book among his father's shirts just after the death of his mother. And then he told me how a priest, a Jesuit, had steered him towards becoming a monk. When I asked again what brought him back to the faith, he said he didn't understand my question, but then, understanding something, he told me that he had received a particular grace in the early 1950s. God had spoken to him: 'That's enough, Julien. No more, no more.' Or words to that effect. At that point his sexual desires left him for good. He then said to me, 'I wasn't expecting to say this to you.'

He spoke too about the differences between hetero- and homosexuality, and asked if I'd read about recent studies suggesting that these preferences were already fixed in the womb. 'So where's the sin? Oh, I don't know . . .' He suddenly seemed distressed. I wanted to bring him some comfort so I said something about there being little difference if these preferences happened before birth or in early infancy. At neither stage were they chosen. I then suggested that this particular cross might be a special vocation and that God was especially close to those who suffer in this way. [My own views on this matter were in a state of flux at this time.] Then Eric returned and the conversation became light again. Visits to England, the decision (reversed) to move to Italy, problems with publishers and translators, etc., etc. We went briefly after lunch into the drawing room – dark maroon-red walls with golden moulding along the ceiling. Heavy Victorian furniture from the family's American home sat along each wall and huge velvet curtains covered most of the windows. In fact the room was very dark, but rich and relaxing. A modern hi-fi system jarred alongside the bookshelf of first editions. On the way to the drawing room we passed many interesting things on the walls, including a Confederate flag and a signed photo of André Gide: 'He wasn't as bad as they say now. He was a good man, a good friend.' After a few more anecdotes by Eric about their rainforest experience with alligators and other things, it was time to leave. It was now 3.30 p.m. and I had arrived at one. I suggested calling a cab but Julien touchingly protested that the cab would take only five minutes as if he wanted me to stay. But I needed to catch my train to Rouen and didn't want to outstay my welcome. We took our leave warmly and I left. Ah, I forgot. I asked him about the changes in the liturgy. No hesitation: 'I want to hear Mass in Latin. I don't want to hear Mass in French.' It seemed so obvious to him. He spoke with love of God, his closeness and how he had always answered his prayers. 'I want now to die well . . . I have no fear of death at all.'

I cannot convey here the warmth and serenity of the man, his face always smiling and encouraging with anything I said to him, his gentle voice introverted but confident, and with that purity, that truth which Maritain mentions in his letters to Green. I told him of my love for the first volume of his autobiography, *The Green Paradise*. 'I don't know what I wrote really. It was a confession. I can say that it is *totally* honest.'

After his death two years later there was the publication of the final volume of his diaries (*En avant par-dessus les tombes*). I looked curiously, anxiously for the date of our lunch:

3 May. Yesterday Stephen Hough came to lunch. The previous evening we'd been listening to him on a record playing a Schumann sonata,* which had made an unforgettable impression on me. I'm sure I had never heard this sonata played like that before, that's to say with the combination of the composer's twofold genius: his passion, his frightening unleashing of strength, then the Schumannesque gentleness and charm. I realised yet again that there is a power in music that puts the spoken word in the shade. It is universal and irreplaceable. The pianist himself is charming, open, a convert from Protestantism; he talked to me about his faith and I told him about the way in which I had been converted. Immediately this strong bond brought us closer. I observed in Stephen's speaking voice a very slight singing quality; the voice of a musician.

* He must have meant the *Fantasie* op. 17, which was on that recording.

. . . AND MORE

What is your motto?

I don't have a motto as such, some phrase I carry around in my mental pocket like a talisman, but if there is a precept shadowing my life it would probably be this: *Everything matters; nothing matters*.

Strictly speaking, it is a contradictory statement: if one half is correct then the other half is false, and even more strictly speaking neither phrase is true in an absolute sense. But I think it holds a strange, creative tension in its paradox. Its juxtaposition of extremes is a springboard both to calm contemplation and to intense action.

Everything matters

What we do has implications – whether we consciously act with this knowledge, realise it later, or merely let actions wash into and over our lives with an absent mind. There is a potential for good or harm in almost every word we speak to another person, indeed in every facial gesture. A smile rightly timed can turn a person's life around.

The great spiritual writers categorise such mindful living as seeing God in everything. Or as turning everything into prayer. From the austere St Alphonsus de Ligouri (*Preparation for Death*) to cuddly, groovy Matthew Fox (*Whee! We, Wee*) the idea that we can relish the smallest acts of our lives and make them sacred is a rich mine of spiritual treasure. Everything matters. Everything is gold . . . if we want it to be.

This has many implications in the world of a musician – studying the score, perfecting one's craft at the instrument, cherishing every note, being attentive, daring to experiment, restless in pursuing ideals and goals.

Nothing matters

But there's a danger with the 'everything matters' attitude. We can become fixated, neurotic, obsessive about things. We can see only trees, whereas 'nothing matters' is the wood. Realising that our lives last but a micro-second in the universe's timeline can release tension, allowing us to relish better, to attend and to reverence more fully.

But 'nothing matters' by itself can leave us in the soapy suds of an endless rose-perfumed bathtub. We need 'everything matters' to see our ablutions in the context of a day to be lived. On a plane with a failing engine everything matters in the cockpit but nothing matters in the cabin.

From a musical perspective we can fuss so much with details that the architecture holding everything together can be lost. I remember coming across a teacher when I was a student who had brilliant insights into many things but whose students ended up paralysed. They needed to be reminded as they walked into that exam that 'nothing matters'. Not only can such an insight enable us, ironically, to do our best but it's related to the bigger question of success or failure as both being ultimately meaningless.

'Everything matters' is our telescope on the stars; 'nothing matters' is the night sky in which we see them.

Rilke, and poetry as the root of everything

Ich möchte aus meinem Herzen hinaus unter den großen
Himmel treten. Ich möchte beten

Rainer Maria Rilke

Sometimes I'm asked how the different arts I'm involved with interact with each other – music, words, painting. I think it all comes from a poetic impulse.

Poetry is a furnace. It's the fire that drives all art. 'I want to go out from my heart' – or, in one word: *ecstasy*. To leave behind the mundane, the routine, the predictable. The prosaic. Every work of art seeks such an evacuation. Such longing is at the heart of every heart; it drives every (good) religious impulse; it drives every (good) sexual impulse. To shed the skin-deep, to cast away the superficial; or, as Rilke puts it, 'to step out under the vast Heavens'.

Ich möchte . . . Ich möchte. Rilke's initial desire to get outside himself leads to his second desire: to pray. To ask, to demand, to long for . . . something. 'For I wish it so! What I wish I still don't know' was Marc Blitzstein's take on that same inner hunger.

Those who writhe and thrust on dance floors, who inhale and inject, who gag on flesh in strange bedrooms . . . we can only say it's fake, not that it's evil. When we are able to leave ourselves (*aus meinem Herzen hinaus*) then we can we pray, then we are fully human.

A poem is polished prose, cut like a jewel. The words mean everything and then they mean more. Every poem, every note of music is a prayer. *Ich möchte beten.*

Beauty, beauty, beauty

Towards the end of Alain de Botton's thought-provoking book *The Art of Travel*, he writes about 'possessing beauty' – how we hold on to things that have attracted us in our travels, and he refers to the writings of John Ruskin for some illuminating, provocative ideas.

'The art of drawing . . . is of more real importance to the human race than that of writing,' writes the great Victorian gentleman. Not because he wants everyone to become an artist, which he admits would be impossible, but because drawing teaches us to *notice* rather than merely to look. De Botton makes the observation that when we want to draw something we have to look at it for ten minutes at least. Point made: when did we last stand in front of something beautiful for that long and really examine it? I was sitting with a magnificent view of Prague's old city when I read this book and I tried looking intensely at the elegant buildings outside the window. I just couldn't manage it for more than about thirty seconds without my mind beginning to wander or lose focus. If I'd been sketching it with pencil and pad it would have been a different story.

I then went on to think about a musical equivalent of this, because music exists only in a passing of time, racing past us like the mid-nineteenth-century trains Ruskin so hated. It is utterly non-fixed, and to focus on one moment is to destroy the whole. It is a forest that we have to pass through, not a single tree that we can contemplate or capture. But if hearing and seeing beauty have different timetables they both require a sort of repetition in order to be fully appreciated: music needs to be heard many times, and the visual world needs multiple, if consecutive, seconds of looking. Only in such repetition perhaps can we grasp or hold on to beauty.

> How to kéep—is there ány any, is there none such, nowhere
>   known some, bow or
> brooch or braid or brace, láce, latch or catch or key to keep
> Back beauty, keep it, beauty, beauty, beauty, . . . from
>   vanishing away?

Gerard Manley Hopkins hints at this repetition literally in the lines above from his ecstatic poem, 'The Leaden Echo and the Golden Echo', but by the end he (the Jesuit priest) suggests a further step:

Give beauty back, beauty, beauty, beauty, back to God,
    beauty's self and beauty's giver.
[. . .]
Oh then weary then why
When the thing we freely fórfeit is kept with fonder a care,
Fonder a care kept than we could have kept it, kept
Far with fonder a care (and we, we should have lost it) finer,
    fonder
A care kept.—Where kept? Do but tell us where kept,
    where.—
Yonder.—What high as that! We follow, now we follow.—
    Yonder, yes yonder, yonder,
Yonder.

The 'art of travel' looks as if it requires a lifelong journey.

No poetry after Auschwitz . . . but music

'It is barbaric to write poetry after Auschwitz,' wrote Theodor Adorno, and George Steiner went further when he spoke of the death of the German language after Nazism. Sadly there are few, if any, languages in human history that can express themselves with a truly innocent tongue.

Replying to these two intellectual giants or entering the gates of Auschwitz . . . well, angels fear to tread. And silence is the only (beginning of an) adequate response. Except that true silence exists only in an artificial chamber, a radio booth, a scientist's laboratory. The quietest field is ever scurrying and spitting with nature's blood and sap.

For one person the vacuum of appropriate words was filled by music. The pianist, teacher and Terezín concentration camp survivor Alice Herz-Sommer, who died in 2014 at the age of a hundred and ten, claimed that, despite her being Jewish, Beethoven was her religion – a sort of appendix to Adorno, music appearing out of the charred ground when words have been burnt to ash.

Shortly before her death, Alice made the following comment: 'I think I am in my last days but it doesn't really matter because I have had such a beautiful life. And life is beautiful, love is beautiful, nature and music are beautiful. Everything we experience is a gift, a present we should cherish and pass on to those we love.'

Her lack of bitterness after losing her husband and many friends and family members in the camps, and the optimism and joy that seemed to fill her every day are immensely uplifting to read about. Indeed, the word 'miracle' came so frequently to her own lips: 'The world is wonderful, it's full of beauty and full of miracles. Our brain, the memory, how does it work? Not to speak of art and music . . . It is a miracle.'

I could never have said all of this to her, growing up as I have in circumstances of peace and prosperity; it is an obscenity to cast easy words of comfort into the cauldron of someone else's suffering, a form of Adorno's 'barbarism'. But she can say those words to us. She has the right to tell us that 'everything we experience is a gift' when there was a time in her life when everything was being taken away from her. The beast for her has, inexplicably, miraculously, been tamed – through music.

Beethoven is my religion

Alice Herz-Sommer's striking statement that 'I am Jewish, but Beethoven is my religion' raises a number of interesting questions: Beethoven the man or Beethoven the musician? Is a composer a creator or a conduit for something greater than him- or herself? If so, a conduit for what? From where? Does great music have a moral influence . . . or not?

One of the things that kept Alice alive, physically and psychologically, during her terrible war-time suffering, were the concerts she gave with other inmates in Terezín. But the chilling fact is that the men operating the ovens and the evil political system fuelling them also loved and celebrated fine music. Those men would return home from a day of killing and weep over Schubert songs. It's a moral conundrum that challenges any easy assessment of the mystery of human behaviour and its capacity for evil.

Of course, Alice's comment about Beethoven was not meant to be read theologically, and for someone who lived through such toxic times a suspicion of religion is understandable. But maybe there is a path shared between great art and great living, which is what religion is ultimately about. To lift us out of ourselves, to point beyond, to awaken a sense of the 'other' . . . all of this can flow from music. As nuclear power can keep a life-support machine working as well as destroy a city, so music can inspire us to great things as well as anaesthetise us when we have become monsters.

'I have had such a beautiful life,' said Alice not long before she died. If Beethoven can be the source of such serenity then who am I to argue? He is certainly a composer who takes us to the rarest spiritual peaks, whose striving and struggling, whose ecstatic highs and lows are some of the greatest musical expressions of the human spirit in history. But then I can't help wonder: who does Beethoven worship? I imagine that Alice by now has discovered the answer to that intriguing question.

The expectation of change: dis-ease in twentieth-century art

L. P. Hartley wrote in the introduction to his novel *The Go-Between* (1953), both as an explanation to critics why he depicted a Golden Era over fifty years earlier and as a defence against being accused of decadence and outmodishness:

> There is [an] element today with which novelists of the past did not have to contend. There is not only change but the *expectation* of change [italics mine]. Sixty years ago changes were neither apparent nor thought to be pending, and in writing of the present the novelist believed he was also writing of the future. He had the benefit of that illusion – the illusion of stability so helpful to fiction.

The 'expectation of change', whether vast social change or merely the imminent need to move apartments, makes a certain kind of root-forming impossible. Few people take the trouble to renovate a bathroom in which they will shower for only a few weeks; few people invest energy in a relationship that will last only a few hours. The 'exile' is not so much someone living far from home or someone with no home, but someone with no *fixed* abode: the sadness of a short lease; the restlessness in possession of an expiring passport.

The 'requirement of originality' is another of the twentieth century's curses, closely related to Hartley's 'expectation of change'. No creative artist wants to duplicate (or at least to be seen to be duplicating) another artist in the same field, but it was never an obsession until after the First World War. Originality originally came as if by surprise, when one was not looking for it. The integrity of creation resulting from the struggle with material was the fruit of a clear focus on the material itself, not on those who might later view it or hear it. We have now lived through generations of artists in all disciplines where a concern for originality is often the only concern, the overriding arbiter of importance or quality. It's a view blind to the distinction drawn by George Steiner between a word derived from 'origin', suggesting roots, a source, the past – and 'novelty', a jingle of superficiality, an unformed idea's already jaded smirk, one mid-afternoon's warmed-over trend.

I think Rachmaninov would have been struck by the L. P. Hartley quote and I think the idea of unease with change and the compulsion to be original was a central backdrop of anxiety to the least known of his piano concertos – the Fourth op. 40, discussed earlier in this book. In this work's wild seesaw between romantic gesture and twisted harmony, between melodies breaking down and rhythms snapping to attention, Rachmaninov unwittingly ended up writing one of the most original works of the twentieth century.

Teju Cole and neutering poets

'Spring is coming. Please remember to spay or neuter your poets' – a plea from the brilliant writer and photographer Teju Cole that appeared on Twitter a number of years ago. I, and a few hundred others, retweeted it instantly and savoured its piquancy. But then a dissenting voice arose within me . . .

One thing that has infected the arts since the World Wars (initially after the First and then even more fiercely after the Second) has been a fear of sentimentality. Twentieth-century artists came to regard Victorian culture and Victorian expansionism as the same lumpy cornice to be removed from a decaying edifice. With this new aesthetic came the demolishing of much beauty, inside and outside buildings, inside and outside human lives.

I understand Teju's desire to muzzle mawkishness but might not such an attitude risk stifling the courage that anyone needs to create anything at all? I often see the results of this in the timidity of musical emotion heard in many masterclasses. I will sometimes ask students to exaggerate a rubato to the absolute limits in an aim to loosen them up. They smile, take a little more time than usual and then stop with embarrassment.

'No, *wildly* more than that! How far can you go? Go to the edge!'

Boys don't cry, thus the eyes in our audiences remain dry too. Composers too have been infected. Cynicism (parody, iconoclasm) has no limits in the composition departments of our universities or music colleges, but if you stray too close to sentimentality there is an instant, mocking derision.

Of course, in all of this I'm being an advocate for the Devil. I can't bear the soggy pap of bad poetry or bland, banal, beige music. I love the sharp knives of much cutting-edge culture. I, too, wince at the kissing kittens on the chocolate box. But for those who wish to perform music from a less emotionally bashful era (Elgar and Rachmaninov, for starters), it is essential to overcome cynicism and emotional fear. That *portamento* slide, that exquisitely turned phrase, that seductive inner voice, that ripe modulation . . . all of these have to be believed in. No spaying, no neutering.

So the next time spring appears, please give everyone a pen and notebook. Celebrate those trees. Exult in those daffodils. Take joy in those birds in the park, those lighter evenings, those warmer mornings. Risk the kitsch. Place a heavy bet on the meretricious. 'April is the *coolest* month' – well, not necessarily.

Architecture as eureka in Sydney

Because we listen to music in time I think any eureka moment with sound will always be a work in progress – a *series* of moments strung together like an animated film. There might be one chord (or frame) that punches us in the stomach or runs a feather down our backs but the real impact of the experience is culminative. Elgar tried in *The Dream of Gerontius* to convey the electric shock when the soul of his character is given a flash sight of God and then responds with an agonised, 'Take me away.' But even here the build-up in the orchestra, the moment of silence before the chord and the exquisite subsidence of sound after it, before the tenor's blazing entry . . . it's the sequence that creates the effect. It's all of a piece.

For me only the visual and in particular buildings really have the power to take away my breath in one explosive instant. The impact of a great edifice is immediate, but then we can stand there holding it in our gaze, embracing its outline with awe. For this to happen with music we need to play the piece again, either in sound or in memory, but a great building seems to freeze time itself. We look at its stillness and become still ourselves.

Cathedrals often do this but so do many secular spaces as well. The Sydney Opera House, when I first saw its white mosaic flesh, was a flash moment. I had travelled the seemingly endless distance to get to Australia for my first tour in 1991 and in those days artists were put up at a hotel at the Optimo end of George Street where the Sydney Symphony and the Australian Broadcasting Corporation had their studios. After a large breakfast, and already in love with Sydney's white-gold morning light, I walked for thirty minutes towards the harbour. Eureka! There was the monument we've all seen in postcards – a familiar face, but now seen breathing for the first time. Perched on its haunches by the ocean with sufficient energy for a whole continent, yet also at rest in the harbour with ease, with confidence.

I've walked past it countless times since and never without feeling I was altered – if only my passing mood. I've gazed at it from every possible angle; I've watched its tiles change hue with the changing sun and clouds; I've run my hand along its cool, chaste contours; I've looked out from its dressing rooms or its Green Room cafeteria across the harbour on dozens of occasions over the years. It's an example of how great buildings, almost uniquely, can produce eureka moments repeatedly. They expand time into the space of their presence. They push aside the air that surrounds them in a way a painting cannot do. Even a sculpture, the closest relation, is somehow movable, however heavy and monumental. We place it somewhere, whereas a building *is* a 'where'.

Mastromatteo's obsession

One of the nicer things about growing older is that some people you knew years ago and who showed promise are now at the stage of fulfilment. I first met Anthony Mastromatteo in New York in the early 1990s, before he had squeezed his first glob of oil paint from his first plump tube. One day he showed me a poem he had written – on a large piece of exquisite paper, unfolded within a larger hardboard folder. I don't remember the poem now except that it was about ten words long, but I do remember how it was intensely etched in razor-to-the-wrist precision of penmanship. In fact it was almost impossible to read the words because the eye was so captivated by the shapes of the letters. Some years later he told me that he was taking art classes, and his rise from first breath to breathtaking brilliance was alarmingly swift. In a matter of months, exquisite pieces in pencil and oils had been produced. I proudly own the very first oil painting he did in class – a small portrait of an old woman in gently fading colours, an image of cataract-unclarity and blurring memory.

Tony now has a successful and flourishing career – indeed, one of international stature and acclaim. Using the style and technique of *trompe l'œil* hyperrealism he has explored for a number of years the subject of the comic strip. It is as if Vermeer had decided to send away the woman (and her pearl earring) and stick an old *Superman* magazine cover on his Delft wall instead. Of course the subject matter calls instantly to mind Roy Lichtenstein, but where he was painting contemporary culture and questioning the value of 'art on a wall' itself (and I do love his iconic pieces whenever they shout at me from the walls of a museum), Mastromatteo, fifty years later, with a technique from five hundred years earlier, is exploring a much wider range of issues . . . memory, beauty, nostalgia, reality. The comics depicted are no longer contemporary 'pop' images; they are faded . . . torn . . . dated. There is nothing light-hearted about these paintings, nor are they cynical or whimsical: they are heart-rending. And the grubby, torn tape that usually affixes the image to the imaginary wall is often the most beautifully painted object in the whole composition. They are images from a lost adolescence discovered in a dusty attic; memories cutting into the present, their fiction suggesting terrifying facts: the sadness of the lonely collector shuffling in the back of a junk shop; the disposability of pulp magazines . . . now lining forgotten drawers, now stained at the bottom of a birdcage, now wrinkled and blotched like the contemporary faces of those who first bought them.

After decades of 'high art', and particularly Abstract Expressionism's frequent conceptual contortions in post-war New

York, the Pop artists wanted to return to the people with a splash – to celebrate ordinary tastes, lives and images with innocence and simplicity. Indeed, the word 'vulgar' derives from the Latin *vulgaris*, meaning 'the general public'. The splash now has dried, whether of Andy Warhol's silkscreens or the garish, measled images on Lichtenstein's canvases. They were limited in conception and are now imprisoned by their epoch. What allows Mastromatteo to step into their aesthetic shoes is that, unlike their rubber sneakers, his 'footwear' is hand-made of the finest materials . . . threaded with gold, studded with jewels. Before we start (or need) to think about what the images actually mean, we are immediately intoxicated with the technique and precision. In fact, as utterly, mind-blowingly 'realistic' as his paintings are, our mind truly begins to bend before the unreality our eyes insist on. The dance of discernment between the three visual negatives (a cartoon that is not a cartoon, stuck on with tape that is not tape, casting shadows that are not shadows) makes us dizzy.

In his 2009 painting *Obsession*, he takes a small, perfectly painted cartoon image of Wonder Woman, already a miracle making us gasp with its technical audacity, then he reproduces it nine times – a throbbing, flesh-and-blood Xerox machine. This is virtuosity spinning dangerously into space. We squint with the artist; we feel the pain of his narrowing eyes in the detail, which then broadens out to a stare approaching insanity. We don't know where to look on the canvas, but we can't take our eyes away from it. If we look at one torn square, the others draw our eyes with a maddening siren call. And yet, in an email to me, the artist spoke of this act of image repetition as an act of worship: 'For me the brutally faithful representation of the object becomes the generation of a sign or icon.' At the end of the day (or the end of our tether) there is a strange, deep, restful joy at beholding something so completely, gorgeously perfect . . . and ordered. It becomes a liturgy, an endlessly repeated act, which is not without concept but beyond it.

The ring of silence: the pots of Anna Paik

I've known Anna Paik for years as the spouse of my friend and colleague Leon McCawley. I've always liked her paintings and admired their technical virtuosity, their contemplative strength, their Asian undertones – as if a subtle spice were flavouring the Western subject matter. But over the past few years she has begun painting Korean pots and these pieces are absolutely astounding. They ring with silence. There is a timeless quality to them that forces the viewer to leave behind the reference points of daily life and enter another world, another zone.

It's partly because the gentle colours and shapes are simply pleasing and soothing to the eyes; it's partly because the aura of mystery behind the objects depicted is by definition unresolved: a pot is made to contain something, we think, and these paintings (unlike Vermeer's milk jug or Cézanne's tumbling fruit bowl) celebrate the self-sufficiency of an empty vessel. Neither a stag's head nor the needling embroidery of a tablecloth distracts us from the sacred spheres.

Beyond these thoughts, I realised, as I looked at one and then another and then another, that earthenware can remain when human bodies are dust. A pot, even when broken or cracked, measures its life in centuries not decades. And their emptiness is not a void but a symbol: if we approach any work of art with that emptiness that suggests receptivity and space we are more likely to be filled and fulfilled.

Paul Klee at Tate Modern

There was a wonderful show at Tate Modern in 2013 called *Making Visible* – a survey of the quiet, small, gently lyrical paintings of Paul Klee. The exhibition was cleverly arranged in chronological order, showing the amazing variety of his work. There are no clear 'Blue' or 'Rose' or Cubist periods as in Picasso, and there is no progression to abstraction down an ever-tightening grid as in Mondrian. Rather, Klee's style remains constant and distinctive from beginning to end but with an array of recurring characters along the way.

I left the museum charmed, refreshed and fascinated . . . but unmoved, as in feeling I was standing in the same place emotionally and spiritually as when I entered. Despite pieces with pleasing shapes and radiant colours there seemed little *depth*. The pigment was always playing on the surface. Fish might have been swimming underneath but we were shown only the sparkle of the sun on the rippling water.

After the final room of paintings I arrived at the shop and realised, looking at the shelves of merchandise, that Klee's doodling calligraphy seems almost designed for reproduction. There are works of art that can never be adequately photographed (from Rubens to Rothko). It often has to do with size, but also with texture, with scope, with inner intensity. But Klee's pieces seem as if they were made to be borrowed for postcards or posters – indeed I had a few Blu-tacked on my bedroom wall as a teenager. Part of this has to do with the medium of Klee's pieces (so many of them are both small and on paper) but it goes deeper than that.

To me they are underwhelming . . . but I think that's the point. Klee was a fragile bird's claw in an angry twentieth-century world of fists, a tweet in an epoch of screams. In fact the greatest shock of the show for me was noticing the dates and country of creation. Many of these pieces came to life in Germany amid the deadly devastation of the First World War, and later works date from the beginning of the curdling of culture in the Nazi era. But nothing seems to have affected his work. The shapes, the colours, the subject matter all remain restful or quirky: no *Guernica* here.

To borrow Harry Eyres's teasing inversion of James Bond, 'stirred, not shaken', I was certainly not shaken by this show. And stirred? Well, only if that means the gentle turn of a spoon in an afternoon's cup of tea. But later, rethinking my visit, I realised that there's a quiet soulfulness in Klee, which avoids the self-consciousness of 'spirituality' and which I missed on this occasion. I was expecting the paintings to be powerfully communicative whereas instead they are the hushed source of their own contemplation. I'm ready to see them again.

Almost the same: van Doesburg and Mondrian

Theo van Doesburg is the painter whose work you see in a museum from a distance and think it's by Mondrian and then see the card underneath and realise it's not. But actually there are significant differences between the two. Van Doesburg's colours are more romantic, his shapes softer, the temperature slightly warmer than in Mondrian's refrigerated, disinfected world. There is more butter in van Doesburg's sauce. Even with the limited palette of a piece such as *Composition XIII*, note the gentle lines and soft greys, like a cottage with sloping walls rather than an apartment with razor-bladed angles. Where later Mondrian takes us to an abstract world of chilly perfection, and Josef Albers repeats his schoolroom geometry lessons with polished confidence, van Doesburg's shapes seem to dream and dance.

Nevertheless, in the end, Mondrian does seem to have the 'edge'. His pieces bear repeated and lingering viewing in a way narrowly missed by his contemporaries. Perhaps it's the Webernesque brevity and transparency of his work, the utter discipline of utter simplicity, and his absolute trust in line over pigment, in counterpoint over the harmony it produces.

Gerhard Richter not naked

I own a Gerhard Richter . . . well, it's an autographed postcard bought from an auction house in Germany for around 40 Euros. The curious thing about his signature on my card is that it's upside-down – or the printing of the image on the postcard is. My initial thought was a disappointed, disillusioned consideration of the tailor where the emperor goes for his suits: 'If the artist himself doesn't know when his painting is upside-down then what chance do the rest of us have?'

But this is missing the point of abstract art. It is of value because it pleases or disturbs our vision as a celebration of colour and shape. It doesn't have to *mean* anything or *represent* anything because it relies on the viewer (or rather directly on the viewer's eye) to find its purpose. In some ways it asks more of the spectator than a country scene or a portrait of a princess. With these we can stand back and simply admire the control of the artist; with an abstract piece we need to lean forward, not to interpret or 'recognise' but to absorb, to be engulfed by something that plays directly on the pupil of our eye.

The great abstract canvases of Richter (or Rothko or Pollock) bypass the mind, with its calculations and associations, and force us to stop thinking, to stop imagining – to enter another dimension. Because the imagery is somehow naked, we come to realise that the emperor doesn't always need to be dressed.

Old Masters: either we kill them or
let them die naturally

I visit quite a lot of art galleries on my travels. It's one of the joys of being in major cities with an hour or two to spare on the day of a concert.

One thing that brings a rush of anxiety to me though is being informed that such and such a famous piece has been 'restored'. Not that I think there's any automatic merit in preserving a dirty, muddy canvas blotched with soot or candle wax for nostalgia's sake when it would have begun its life sparkling and dazzling with bright colours. But there is a real dilemma to face: how much can we clean grime before we begin removing paint? If a finger on a hand is missing should we replace it? If colours are faded can we simply touch them up? What is the point at which precious pigment becomes disagreeable grunge?

Every painting (and every restorer) will provide a different answer to these questions, but whatever the decision made the person restoring must approach the throne with fear and trembling. A painter told me once that apparently Ingres was reluctant even to touch up his own earlier work. I fear some restorers have no such scruples. I've visited galleries where an old triptych has been restored and I've been convinced that two or more different people (with four or more different eyes) have been at work, so different were the choices made of pigment on the three panels. Granted, the colours would not have been wan and pale or a soup of brown mud when they were originally created but were *those* the colours on the artist's brush? Who can tell? And that's the problem. We know the flaking surface of the untouched picture is genuine – art with centuries of wrinkles – but to my eyes many restored pieces look as if a plastic surgeon has stretched flesh across an ageing cheek. Aunt Mildred might look sprightly these days, but she never actually looked like *that*, even as a frolicking maiden. Often the choice ends up being: do we kill a piece by restoring it, or do we let it die by doing nothing?

When staying a few years ago on the Tuscan–Umbrian border I visited many places to see the frescos. Because of the technique of painting a fresco, as a wall crumbles so do these images. In the Basilica of St Francis in Assisi restorers were faced with a task on a totally different scale after the devastating earthquake in 1997. When a vast panoramic image lies on the floor in dust there's little choice but to start afresh. What has been achieved there is extraordinary, even heroic, although it did seem strange to me to see tourists gazing up at a modern artist's medieval pastiche with the same awe as they would at the surviving masterpieces from the original walls and ceiling. But, unlike a painting hanging on the walls of an air-conditioned museum, here to restore was to rebuild.

I left the crowds and walked across town to one of the oldest churches in Assisi, Santa Maria Maggiore, which had been the city's cathedral until around 1035. There were no visitors or souvenirs in sight and there was an uncanny, electrifying silence inside the stone space. I then glimpsed a priest and deacon saying Mass in front of a fresco reredos, hidden at first on a side altar – imperfect, crumbling and frail. It was utterly exquisite. The irony is that this fresco in its ancient fragility was revealed to modern eyes only in 1997 after that same earthquake. Apparently some meddling restorer in 1640 had covered up the older image from around 1560 with an 'improved' version. It's somewhat reassuring that even in ancient times taste can be questionable.

And in modern times . . . I've noticed that some of Mondrian's iconic white boxes are beginning to crack, barely a hundred years after they were painted. Should we fill in the monochrome fissures or just let nature take its course?

Maths and music: joined at the hip or walking down different paths?

A number of years ago I took part in a brief but interesting discussion on BBC Radio 4's *Today* programme with Marcus du Sautoy, Simonyi Professor for the Public Understanding of Science and Fellow of New College, Oxford, and John Humphrys, one of the programme's presenters. It followed on from a debate at Oxford University with the motion 'Is music the act of sounding mathematics?' Marcus was in favour of the motion and I was asked to join the discussion on the radio as a voice against it.

Is there some special affinity between maths and music? People always say there is, as if it's a perfectly obvious equation. But I think the ultimate issue in this debate is a subjective one: even if music is underpinned with mathematical principles, does the musician have to be aware of them in the act of creating or re-creating the notes on the page or the sounds in the air? I hope not, as my own abilities in maths at school were . . . well, let's not go there. But there are more objective issues involved in this debate.

Mathematics is a lean subject. It aims to prune away the superfluous, the redundant. It has an eagle eye for clarity and it delights in rules that can be proved or definitions that can be demonstrated. Ambiguity is anathema to the mathematician. Going off at tangents, fanciful decorations, illogical diversions . . . all of these would put me at the bottom of Marcus's class. As he put it in an article for *Science Spectra*, 'Music of the Primes': 'Mathematicians like to look for patterns.' But the elements that would cloud the mathematician's mind (tangents, decorations, diversions) are at the very heart of most great music, especially from Romanticism onwards. It is so often at the moments when logic is put aside that magic is conjured to life – and it is the bending and blurring of patterns (noticing them but then deliberately confusing them) that rescues music from mediocrity and is the trademark of the greatest composers. Until the early nineteenth century the link between maths and music was perhaps clearer. There is often a sense that composers from the pre-Romantic era were working with similar tools to mathematicians – a search for clarity and order. But so were theologians. Science and religion were seen as allies in the same intellectual debates, and the theologian and the mathematician were often the same man. Then, by around the 1820s, there was a breakdown, a parting of the ways.

Deliberate ambiguity

Schubert's greatest work happened when he gave up the need to 'make sense'. Take the strange, wandering harmonic progression in the middle of the second movement of his Sonata in D major D. 850. This irrational ramble has no structural purpose at all except to induce a kind of haze of uncertainty before returning to the main subject. It is mind-wandering ('sleepwalking' in Alfred Brendel's apt phrase). It doesn't return, it isn't developed, yet it's a moment of supreme genius. It is absolutely the opposite of a mathematical way of thinking. Schubert is not looking for 'solutions' but delighting in vagueness, allowing the chaos to remain unresolved with no attempt to offer an answer. Further examples of this in nineteenth- and twentieth-century music are literally countless.

Non-structural elaboration

If a mathematical formula could be stated in, say, 30 words, why would someone want to use 230 words? But music is constantly adding superfluous decoration, limitless ornamentation, carefree embellishment. The very form of variation is one example of this. A more telling instance is Schumann. How frequently when the singer has finished the song does the composer give to the piano a brief, wordless commentary as a coda? These extra bars add nothing to the strict logic of the song, but they are ruminations of exquisite beauty. Strictly speaking, they are an indulgence tagged on. After all has been said or sung, there's something more.

Time-keeping and rhythm

It has been said that rhythm and arithmetic are 'playing to the same beat'. I don't agree with this. It's not 'beat' but 'pulse' that is of central importance in music. The analogous relation of pulse to the human heartbeat is not without significance. Great music (and music making) involves the irregular, the unpredictable. In fact, a metronomic beat often kills a performance because its mechanical predictability is ultimately slack and dull, lacking the tension that comes from the push and pull of rubato. One of the reasons folk music's vibrancy is so hard to notate is because of its irregularity. It keeps time and takes breath with heart and lung, not as a machine. It is never exactly the same twice. Mathematical equations are by definition repeatable. They aim to capture, to hold, to prove something in as final and immovable a form as possible. But the 'final' cannot exist in music because it lives only as a sequence of sounds passing in time. The score might be frozen on the page but the reality flows past/into our ears. We don't, we can't, 'capture' it. I'm aware that many composers from the mid-twentieth century onwards have specifically used mathematical principles to create their works, but this is both a departure from tradition and an exception that proves the point. These works use numbers as a sort of extra-musical theme or inspiration, not as the defining feature of the sounds we actually hear. They are like the wire mesh under the sculpture's torso, providing structure and support – a point of creative departure. Maths in this music is the Diabelli waltz, not the thirty-three variations spiralling upwards in ecstasy from it.

I don't believe composers think numbers when they think notes. Maths is an immortal diamond; music is a human heart.

Sport and music: on the same team?

I confess that, with the exception of Wimbledon or an exception-ally flashy snooker match, I have a bit of a blind spot with specta-tor sports. But there are some interesting and perhaps surprising connections linking the performance worlds of sport and music.

First, being a musician is a much more physical activity than is often presumed. Muscles, tendons, joints and their related reflexes need to be trained to the highest level of flexibility and skill. On the other hand, the athlete or sportsperson requires a deep inner strength in addition to any obvious, external phys-ical prowess. The training of mind and concentration is at least as important for a prizewinning weightlifter as the bulging biceps bending the sleeve of the polo shirt.

Then there's the issue of consistency in sport, so often the key to success. It isn't so much about superhuman skill but about sustaining quality in an almost dogged way, never losing focus round after round. We see this clearly in an extended tennis match: a first set of the greatest brilliance is worthless if the next two sets are filled with mistakes. Plodding accuracy can triumph – no contest – over maverick genius.

To sustain a musical career over many decades requires a certain consistency too. Many young players have a first 'set' of pieces polished all ready to go as they collect their gold medal at the competition gala, but not a third, let alone a sixth . . . and at best a handful of concertos. That's one issue, and it is about numbers. Beyond that it's the consistency of energy and creativity that matters and that is the requirement for a lifelong career. The ability to draw something fresh out of familiar repertoire year after year.

So far sport and music are on the same team. But they part company at a deeper human level because the fallibility of the greatest musicians is their special treasure. I would argue that it is only when an artist reveals a certain vulnerability that genius ignites. When it seems inconceivable for an instrumentalist to fall off the 'bar' (technically or musically), there is no tension, attention is lost, fizz has fizzled out. A perfect human face (if it exists) is empty of eroticism; a performance that comes to a close without a bruise or a cut is bloodless, lifeless.

The main reason for taking part in competitive sports is to try to win, but in music there are no real goalposts. Any trophies are phantoms, shadows in the footlights. It's the main reason why music competitions do not exist. Oh, wait a minute . . .

The curse of the perfect number

I met a woman once who told me that the thermostat in her apartment was set to an unchanging 24 degrees Celsius, from January to December.

We can't (yet) control the sun and clouds but we can create a home bubble of thermal perfection. But rather than a fixed temperature, maybe we could have a slight drop in the temperature during sleep, and then a gentle increase when our waking bodies pad down for porridge on a dark morning? A lowering during that workout on the exercise bike, a raising for that curl-up on a sofa with a book?

Actually we miss out on some of life's greatest moments of pleasure when we assume such control over our hots and colds – the steps towards a blazing fire after a long, frosty Christmas walk, or the modern delight of entering a cool, air-conditioned building after the external heat and humidity of, say, Singapore. It's not without reason that that country's first leader, Lee Kuan Yew, cited air-conditioning as the greatest invention of the twentieth century.

I suppose I'm old enough to have been influenced by some of my grandparents' 'make do' mentality. Living through rationing and the deprivation of two world wars made it impossible for that generation to demand the luxury of the perfect environment. 'Is the temperature all right for you, sir?' asks the limo driver. The cars of my childhood had two options: heating off or on; windows open or closed. I get hot and bothered with anxiety when offered the chance to lower the heat from 22 to 21.4 degrees. Is this really why my heart is unfulfilled? Happiness as a matter of six degrees of deprivation?

As I'm reaching the final stages of writing a piece of music I like to add metronome markings because, although a performer's tempo choice can change from hour to hour, these numbers still give some broad indication of shape and character and, more importantly, of relationships between different sections. When I first started to write my Third Piano Sonata, the stark, cold opening was conceived at a crotchet = 60, the pulse of a heartbeat. But after the piece was finished and as I was checking through proofs for publication, this just seemed too slow – a heart beating comfortably at home rather than with excitement and energy on a stage. A red line scratched through and changed it, warmed it up to 72. Exact numbers in music can be deceptive too.

The idea that anything in life can be perfect or fixed is a dangerous one. Imperfection is perhaps one of the definitions of being human, and patience with other people's imperfections is an essential part of being humane. Mind you, sitting nervously backstage before a concert, with the audience gathering, hands getting colder and clammier by the minute, it's always good to spot a thermostat on the wall and then to hear it hiss into action as the dial is turned to the perfect number.

The essence of underpants and the lap of luxury

I am aware that I appear to spend most of my life in the lap of luxury. I don't see myself as recklessly decadent (who does?) but compared to those for whom a slice of day-old bread is a feast, or clean, running water a miracle, I am guilty of culpable indulgence.

It is safe to say that at no time in history have humans been more aware of and also, to be fair, more concerned about such global inequality. This knowledge should spur us on to ever-greater generosity but our wheels of altruism constantly risk getting stuck. A terrible crisis hits the news and suddenly donations rise, but then time passes and the crisis disappears from the news and we carry on as before. I honestly don't know the solution to this except to keep the issue always in sight and keep helping out as we can, even in the smallest ways.

But that's not what I want to write about here. I want to *defend* luxury, to unpick the preconceptions of cheap or expensive. I want to make the point that although a bag of the best Darjeeling Second Flush is much more expensive than a box of PG Tips teabags, it's a lot *less* expensive than a daily cup of coffee at McDonald's. A bottle of Andy Tauer's delightful, smoky Lonestar Memories perfume might well be more expensive than a week's wages for some, but one squirt (it's all you need) is a lot cheaper and healthier than a Mars bar – and a bottle could well last you for years. It has often been said that a hand-crafted pair of shoes is better value in the long run than a pair bought in a high-street sale. The former, if looked after, will outlive you, whereas the latter can be cracked and useless after one rainy season. If we decide to continue drinking tea and buying clothes, it might well be that the luxury brands are not quite as extravagant as they seem.

There's another side to this issue: those expensive designer clothes that are not any better than their generic twins. I remember being appalled, seeing the price tag on a simple white T-shirt (made in a developing country) listed at over $100 and distinguished from others, it seemed, only by a label; not to mention hearing once in Singapore about a T-shirt (this time with a design mass-printed on its white torso) that cost over $400. Why do people buy such things? I don't think it's just to show that they can afford it and therefore they must be rich, powerful and worth something.

Paul Bloom, in his fascinating book *How Pleasure Works*, talks about the 'essentialism' in how humans look at objects. We know a cake shaped exactly like a tiger is not a tiger, not only because we bite it rather than it bites us. We know that there is an inner essence to things. There is a 'tigery' something and there is a 'cakey' something and we know this goes beyond (inside) the furry stripes or the chocolate chips. St Thomas Aquinas, via Aristotle, talked about substance and accidents to try to make clear the distinction. Bloom points out that when we put on designer clothes we are subconsciously wearing and responding to the *essence* of the product. The logo or colour is only the accident; it's the hidden (unspeakable?) connotations that are the substance. Even if unseen, designer underpants cling to those who buy them with a comforting hug that is due not merely to their properly fitting waistband or padded pouch.

So much for some of the subconscious reasons we shop like

this – blindly, blithely; but there is an urgent ethical need for these hidden connotations to be unveiled and then changed. We need to be constantly reminded of the injustice involved in producing and purchasing this flimsy underwear. We need to 'taste' the sweat in the sweatshops, to look into the eyes of the oppressed faces of those slaving in the factories. And we need to keep doing this with the monotony of the machines themselves until the unseen pleasure such garments might give us unravels . . . until it trickles away, leaving solidarity with those who make our clothes the most sought-after logo of all.

Do musicians tend to be socialists?

When Margaret Thatcher died in 2013 some voices were raised on social media asking why there was so little respect for her or regret about her passing from musicians. I have no way of measuring this but it reminded me of two points about musicians: we tend to be fairly apolitical (or at least politically naive), and we're only a few generations away from being the equivalent of servants, thus naturally left-leaning.

I was out of the UK as a fun-loving student during much of Mrs Thatcher's time in Downing Street and, as I didn't own a television in New York or read the newspapers, she was a shadowy figure in my memory. Indeed, I recall one morning in 1982 walking along a practice corridor at the Juilliard School and meeting my friend Ezequiel Viñao.

'Did you know we're now officially at war?' asked the Argentinian composer with a grin.

'Oh, are we? Gosh. Anyway, let's go and have a coffee. What are you working on at the moment?'

Many musicians in the darker years of the twentieth century took a heroic stance against dictators and their atrocities, but some who continued to live in totalitarian countries during these times seemed unwilling to engage in politics. Perhaps we can criticise what we perceive to be their collaboration or pusillanimity but we must remember that musicians do not usually work with (their own) words; their intellectual inspiration tends to have a different focus. Where prominent writers are expected to have a socially, politically responsible voice, musicians sometimes find meaning only in the voice that produces melodies with vocal cords.

I think it is safe to say that most musicians have predominantly liberal, left-wing views, and it's worth remembering that the superstar, highly paid musician is a recent phenomenon. Before the twentieth century, to be a successful musician was to be one who was employed. A few, such as Liszt, Paderewski and some singers, had phenomenally lucrative careers, but they were rare – and Liszt gave all of his money away, travelling by choice in a third-class railway carriage.

In most situations a musician was like a cook, someone brought in to provide a specialised service. Even when the more celebrated ones *were* offered a place at an aristocratic dining table, they were often seen as something of a performing monkey. Fast forward to the twenty-first century. Someone was telling me only the other day that when playing a concert in an English country house a few years ago, he had had to arrive via the servants' entrance. I rest my case, 'but not on the Queen Anne desk, please'.

Robert Mann, a founding member of the Juilliard String Quartet and its first violinist for fifty years, told me that he never passed a busker or street musician without stopping and contributing some small change. He saw them as colleagues – less successful ones perhaps, but still 'comrades'. And Gordon Green believed that musicians should be paid less than refuse collectors because they were doing something they enjoyed and which carried its own reward.

Whether such socialism is foolish naivety or heroic idealism is a matter of opinion, but what is certain is that, however many recordings are sold or tours sold out, the sound waves themselves are free. Musicians, at their best, have kept this insight alive, reluctant to grasp or exploit something so fragile, so universal – like the natural beauty of lilies in a field. 'Even Solomon in all his glory was not arrayed like one of these,' as someone often accused of socialist leanings put it.

The Final Retreat: my novel of desire and despair

When I was a teenager, in Warrington, a local Anglican priest committed suicide. As someone who was about to convert to Roman Catholicism, and was even considering a priestly vocation, this shocked and moved me deeply. How could someone whose life was meant to bring comfort to others be so desperate as to be unable to find comfort himself? But it was not just the issue of ending a suffering life (or the question of sin and salvation involved) but the disgrace. Shame was in the air and as little as possible was said about the affair in the community – although there were whispers that he might have been 'one of those . . . queer'.

Many years later, I came across James Alison's brilliant book *Faith Beyond Resentment*. In a moving introduction James writes about his friend, Father Benjamin O'Sullivan, a monk of Ampleforth Abbey (a musician too), who had killed himself the evening before a story was to run in a Sunday tabloid exposing his sexual relationship with a man. A tape recorder had been hidden in the bedroom of the London flat where they were to have an intimate encounter. My parish in Warrington,

St Mary's, was staffed by priests from this monastery and I found the whole story heartbreaking. What internal turmoil was involved in these two cases, what desperation in their tragic final moments. 'My God, my God, why have you abandoned me?' Could these words have had a more apt, a more poignant voice than from the mouths of these two lonely priests?

My novel *The Final Retreat* came out of subconscious reflections over the years on such issues and also on how far the idea of a 'wounded healer' can be stretched. Having not become a priest myself (and, thank God, not being subject to such desolate thoughts as these two men) I still wanted to write something about it. This novel is not autobiographical in any way – not just because I'm blessed with an optimistic nature but because the background and circumstances of Father Joseph's life are totally different from mine – but it does explore some issues, both sexual and theological, that have been on my mind since childhood.

My fictional character, Father Joseph Flynn, is a middle-aged priest whose faith and life are in tatters. He goes to see his bishop in a last-ditch attempt to find a solution to his hopeless situation and the bishop, a kindly, sympathetic man, suggests he go on an eight-day, silent retreat for prayer and reflection before any decisions are made about the future. Apart from short, daily meetings with a sanctimonious spiritual director, Father Joseph speaks to no one. But he writes. Page after page of a diary-cum-memoir in which he explores his state of soul, the loss of his vocation, his sexual addiction, and the blackmail that is destroying his life. The novel's form as a set of notebooks discovered after the priest's death attempts to convey the restrictions of time and space on a retreat – eight days in a cramped, ugly bedroom – but also for this priest the very act of writing becomes a form of artistic release as he allows memories to unfold while enjoying the process of finding words to express them.

The book works on three levels: musings on faith and religion; Father Joseph's life and family background; and the untold story of the bishop and the Nigerian priest. The interest and significance of these levels is in reverse proportion to their coverage in the book – we watch the story unfold through the wrong end of a telescope. Only glimpsed at is the 'untold story' of Father Chiwetel and Bishop Bernard who each make just three brief appearances in the novel. It's a big, bold tale but it's deliberately kept hidden, merely hinted at, a melody unsung. It is the 'twitch of the curtains' at the beginning and end of the book.

Father Joseph's life is told as flashbacks: memories of his childhood with a religiously obsessed mother, and also of his sexual encounters, deliberately non-erotic in description but explicit, aiming to shock with stabs of four-letter words as if he is lashing out in frustration and bitterness. Then finally there are spiritual reflections, both meditations on the Scriptures (the Nativity, the woman caught in adultery, the woman with the alabaster jar, Judas) and on theological issues (the Mass, Confession, Hell, Salvation, the Jews, homosexuality, etc.).

The atmosphere of claustrophobia is important: the narrowness of the retreat and its mindset contrasted with a more colourful world outside, the intimate world of the flesh. I want the reader to experience the utter weariness of Father Joseph, someone too tired to consider changing course, his life wasted, on the (last lap of the) wrong track. Religion represents all that is dull for him: the boredom of a dreary parish's daily grind and the winding down of late middle age. Sex makes him feel alive; it is exciting, symbolic of freedom and ecstasy and a lost youth.

The feast days on which the action of the book takes place are all relevant. It opens on the feast of St Jude, the traditional Patron of lost causes, and closes on the feast of Charles de Foucauld, who died at the hands of violent men – a hint perhaps that Father Joseph's own death might not have been suicide. But if a killing, by whom?

Although there are only a few passing references to music in the novel, its construction was influenced by musical composition, not just in the poetic use of words that form rhythmic patterns or that sing in and out of tune, but in the structure too as themes and motives return and form counterpoint with each other. The opening scene was conceived as a theme that, after its initial statement, disappears until the end, its return creating an arch. Indeed this circular form is related to my first three piano sonatas, each of which begin and end with the same material. Then there's the altered chord: at the beginning of the book the bishop signs his name † Bernard and at the end Bernard x – the cross of episcopal authority becoming a kiss and recalling Father Joseph's musing in short-story form about the death of Judas Iscariot where the traitor ends up being the one truly faithful disciple. Is Bishop Bernard a traitor to the Church, or is his weakness and vulnerability its ultimate hope?

But if there is a musical dialect as such it is more Sibelius than Tchaikovsky. Melodies are hinted at rather than fully sung. Ideas are deliberately left incomplete, left to be finished by the reader/listener. Another analogy might be seen in the world of painting – Howard Hodgkin, whose brushstrokes spill outside the frame, or some of the pieces of Clyfford Still, where the body of the painting remains calm but on the outer edge something seemingly unrelated is pulsating with turbulent life.

This book is infused with memories of priests I've met and known over the years; many were heroic souls serving joyfully and selflessly, but there were others whose eyes brimmed over with distress and suffering. Some stayed in the priesthood, some left, still others never took the plunge, hovering on the outside. One New York priest in particular comes to mind, someone I saw regularly celebrating Mass in the 1990s. Externally cheerful (too cheerful, perhaps) but, if he was caught off guard, I sensed tears in his smiles. He died young. Father Neville, Father Joseph's spiritual director for my fictional retreat, is based on some priests I've come across – over-confident, cold, prudish, bullying, never seeming to have any doubts or problems.

Why has the Catholic priesthood wanted to present itself over the centuries as perfect, as impregnable? Well, since the child-abuse scandals of the past two decades this facade has crumbled and our priests are now humbler as a result . . . and fewer in number. Nevertheless this novel doesn't touch on the paedophilia issue at all (all of the sex in it is legal, even if not loving) but in the demise of Father Joseph and of Judas we can see perhaps a glimmer of hope in the most anguished situations: if there is anything 'good' about the Good News it's that no one and nothing is irredeemable. As Father Joseph writes in one of his notebooks as he meditates about the separation of sheep and goats at the Last Judgement: 'Goats are extinct.' Somehow I trust that the final embrace of the Good Shepherd who risks losing ninety-nine sheep to save just one would have been joyfully experienced by Father Benjamin, by the Anglican priest from Warrington, and by my fictional priest, Father Joseph Flynn.

If I ruled the world

A musician ruling the world? Well, first there would be a lot less music, and the music that remained would be lower in volume. Banished would be music as wallpaper, music to block silence, music to fill empty space – enough! Jingles in lifts, jingles on airplanes, jingles on the phone as you wait to speak to the bank – enough!

Speaking of phones, I would ban marketing calls from loan

and credit-card companies and I would make illegal their slick, Brilliantined envelopes, which thicken our doormats. Waste of paper, waste of mental energy, and lethal for a pianist whose finger can suffer a paper cut ripping open their often disguised contents.

On a more serious note, I would launch some green offensives: solar power in every building and lights off in all public buildings at night. The daily glitter of city skyscrapers competing with the stars is an unnecessary, unforgivable decadence. Food waste is another atrocity that is reducible if not completely avoidable. Every restaurant should be forced to recycle its leftovers for animal consumption – and they should create fewer leftovers in the first place. Drastic reduction in plastic and a total ban on straws. And, please, liquid soap in hotel rooms, not those fat tablets, which end up squished into rubbish bins, imprinted with one stray hair from one stray night.

Aside from bigger issues of worldwide hunger, disease, conflict and equality (I'd need to consult my team of experts on those), I would address some aspects of domestic education. I would make sure that every school day began with fifteen minutes' communal silence, meditation, deep breathing, prayer, what you will . . . but please, no music. Out of silence is born concentration and from that comes learning. I would extend this to universities and to workplaces: bosses, secretaries, janitors breathing the same air of tranquillity in a fifteen-minute truce.

And, back to school: languages. I remember begging one of my primary school teachers to let us learn French instead of wasting time digging around in the classroom sandpit. Fifty years later, I'm left neither able to garden nor to speak French. Two equally fluent languages should be the norm for any child entering secondary education. This is the case in many countries, except the English-speaking ones.

Still at school, I would require an hour once a fortnight of music (classical, I'm afraid) appreciation. A gentle but systematic journey through music history, unlocking the treasures of the greatest composers and their masterpieces. And every child would have to learn a musical instrument. Why would this be a priority, other than for this world ruler's self-interested prejudices? Well, in the West one of the greatest curses in a mostly blessed age is distraction and boredom amid plenty. Learning a musical instrument is one of the best ways to discipline the mind to do *something* for more than a minute's duration, a plunging rather than a surfing into an activity requiring skill and involving purpose. It engages the whole person in something physical, mental and (at its best) spiritual. Concentration, or 'attention' as Simone Weil put it, is part of living a civilised life, with happiness derived from well-being rather than mere well-feeling. Paying attention, to people or to ideas or to ourselves, is oxygen for the soul. A constant flitting from gimmick to fad to video clip is to attempt to grow the tree of life in an inch of soil. Learning a musical instrument is not the only solution to the problem but it's one good one – and an easy one to implement.

As I jot down these thoughts I'm reminded how frightening this business of power is, how easily ruling the world morphs into re-creating the world in our own image. What courage it takes to leave things undone; what wisdom is involved in refusing to meddle in other people's private lives. If youth is wasted on the young, how much more dangerously is power entrusted to the powerful. Few people hunger for power who hunger for the good things it can achieve. Power should always be handled as if on short-term loan, or as if it could explode in our faces at any moment.

So I'm not really enjoying this hypothetical 'being the boss' business. I know that every day I ruled the world I would be looking keenly to find someone to take over from me as soon as possible. But before they did, I'd make sure I had secured a nice flat overlooking the water somewhere warm, Sydney perhaps, from where I could relax, read, sip leisurely on a glass of wine and think about what I would do if I ruled the world.

Pleasure

Pleasure is like a magnet guiding our every move in life. It was the evolutionary path that led all of us to the place where today we live and move and have our being. It's the carrot guiding us to do what's good for us and avoid what's bad for us. Food and sex, to take two obvious examples, are pleasurable because they ensure our existence. Pleasure is simply the way our bodies are designed to function, whether that pleases us or not.

And yet, if someone said to us, 'All I live for is pleasure', I think we'd find it rather strange, even a little disturbing. I don't think we'd entirely trust that person, or take him or her seriously. We'd have the sense that anything or anyone that got in the way of their pursuit of pleasure would quickly become dispensable. 'All I live for is . . . music or money or justice or my family'; these might seem limited by themselves and we might have different reactions to a life built on any of these categories alone, but at least they somehow make *sense*. We might be hardwired to live guided by principles of pleasure, but it has to be as the fruit of something else. If we pursue it as an abstract ideal, outside the tangible *goods* (important word) that bring it to us, it will most likely turn bad. To reach out and grasp the bubble of pleasure is to pop it. To enjoy those bubbles requires us to let them float past. To shape our lives by pleasure alone would be like forming the rooms of our house with sheets of wallpaper but no walls on which to hang them.

Pleasure is an essential part of being human and, therefore, has within it a spark of the divine. Even though as a Catholic I believe that all things created are essentially *good*, I'm only too aware that religion has probably been the main force trying to root out pleasure across our planet, across the centuries. Let's not even talk about sex, which has been fenced around and poisoned within an inch of its life . . . despite the fact that we sort of need it to keep this show on the road. Music has been banned in some Islamic cultures, and dancing has been banned in some Christian cultures – so many things that flavour our lives with joy and ecstasy have been the subjects of suspicion and repression.

And yet, understood correctly, fasting or celibacy are not about despising pleasure, but rather acknowledging its importance, its value . . . and its potential corruption. When a monk gives up food he is voluntarily giving up something *good*, something to be treasured, something to be grateful for. When a nun gives up family life it's similar, or should be; she wants to offer God the most precious gift possible. And beyond this life, it is only by some analogy with pleasure that the promise of life after death (heaven) has made any sense – *eternal* pleasure: if we deny ourselves pleasure now we can have it later for ever and ever, another kind of carrot. Of course we need a taste of it now to tempt us to its permanence later – but this is not the time or place to explore such a conundrum.

I think the important issue is the *pursuit* of pleasure rather than the pursuit of the good things that carry pleasure in their trail. The roots of pleasure are the acts of a good life – well-being rather than well-feeling. Avoiding pain at all costs will not give us pleasure, but conquering our fear of pain might well help us along the way. And sharing pleasure (or making others happy) is one of the surest ways of experiencing pleasure or happiness ourselves. All this leads us to consider one of the main paradoxes of pleasure: we grasp it either as an anticipation of the future or as a reflection of the past, but it *grasps us* (usually without our control) in the present. We often look forward to a holiday or look back on a birthday party with greater pleasure than in the moment of experiencing it. We savour pleasure in the past or in the future; the present moment of its visitation flies past too fast.

And so to music. It is the perfect example of this pleasure principle in the arts. Whereas with a book or a painting we control the time in which we experience the beauty, with a piece of music the beauty is carried along in the passage of time itself, a 'passing' (a journey and a decay) which *is* the pleasure. The notes vibrate past our ears, *into* our ears, in a sequence of sounds. Music does not have a 'moment' like the first bite of a rhubarb crumble, or the climax point of lovemaking, or the very last day at work before the holidays; music's magic evaporates in front of our ears, leaving only an echo, a memory behind. Yet the very handicap of its transience is its greatest asset because it enables us to enjoy it over and over again. It creates its own time-frame of relish, unlike books or paintings . . . or buildings, as I discussed in an earlier reflection. And even though the sounds disappear, in classical music the score remains, the formula that can be mixed into potency once more – musicians as the witch doctors of these 'controlled frequencies'.

Related to this is one of the reasons I believe music needs tonality. It is part of the internal swing of pleasure and pain mirroring that of our lives. We desire, we crave the pleasure of concord after the pain of discord. And to refuse to resolve is to prevent the future repetition of the very pain that in turn allows the resolution. It is to freeze-frame something that has meaning only in ebb and flow. It is to halt the intangible 'procession', the journey that *is* music. For me (although I readily admit that others have an opposite and perfectly valid viewpoint), music that is irresolvably atonal has nowhere to go. It is a hamster on a wheel instead of a horse galloping freely in the fields. I love a lot of atonal music but it no longer excites me when it is no longer creating tension against its opposite. Take away tonality from atonality and you are left with . . . A.

Music is intangible. The existence of the vibrations is *real* of course – measurable as sound waves and controllable as such; but these waves are beyond touch in the way the music they create touches us. And here music is related to perfume, another art form existing for the purpose of pleasure. Perfume requires a chemist's expertise and it isn't literally intangible, of course – from bottle to spray we see and feel the liquid – but its effect on us is indeed unseen and mysterious. It awakens memories and it alters moods in a very similar way to music. It is also a 'time traveller' – passing, evaporating and changing with us, as it blooms and then dies on our skin. Perfume is as 'useless' as music, but it has been said that great art, by definition, has to be useless. The minute we harness it, try to use it for a purpose other than to appreciate its intrinsic value, we de-struct the magic . . . and undermine the pleasure.

Holy smoke

I always wanted to be a tobacconist. From my childhood I liked to collect cigarette boxes, and my favourite game was to prop them up and pretend to sell them. 'Twenty Capstan Full Strength? Certainly, sir!' Of course, I would have been unemployed by now. In my youth many more people smoked, and there were many specialist shops. Apart from glamorous cigar stores such as Davidoff, do any outlets thrive or even survive today by selling only tobacco-related products?

I'd messed around with smoking quite early in my teens, puffing at some of my father's Burma cheroots, sneaking one or two of my mother's Benson & Hedges Gold. I even bought some ghastly herbal cigarettes, which, when lit, smelt as if the wastepaper basket had caught fire. But my real joy was to go into those old tobacconist shops with their brass scales and burnished-oak counter-tops and look up at the shelves stacked with different cigarette packets: Senior Service, Sobranie, Black Russian, Woodbine, St Moritz. I would ask people about the old brands – Passing Clouds was my favourite, in its pink packet. I loved the smell of the silver foil-covered paper that lined the cardboard boxes with light-brown dust caught in the folds. And then to open up the wooden tobacco jars filled with virtual hair-clippings of aromatic delight: the bitter Latakias, the fruity blends, the vanillas, the spices.

Then my coming of age. On my seventeenth birthday my father took me to a tobacconist near Albert Square in Manchester to buy my first pipe and my first ounce of tobacco. I chose a rough-finished black briar with a flat bottom and some rather sweet-smelling tobacco, the sort that makes people say, 'Oh, I like the smell of pipe smoke.' I also needed a pouch, of course – soft leather on the outside and rubber inside, which would keep the tobacco moist and fresh. Then there were pipe cleaners and a reamer, which would scratch off the burnt charcoal from inside the bowl. I had one with a tamper on the end, which saved using my forefinger to press down firmly but not too deeply on the smouldering nest. I remember my teacher, Gordon Green, having a yellow pad on his right forefinger from tamping down endless bowls of Gold Block.

One pipe is not enough for even the occasional smoker. The wood needs to rest and breathe between smokes. By the time I stopped smoking I had between thirty and forty pipes. People forget that the pleasure of pipe-smoking is not just in the taste or the narcotic fix of tobacco. A beautifully polished bowl with a straight grain that balances perfectly in the palm is a work of art and something to caress with pleasure. Much wood is discarded in the factory before the best pipes are finished. Mouthpieces too are important. Plastic is totally out; it had to be vulcanised rubber. And then there are the racks on which to keep them, and the travel packs. Because I was smoking when touring in the earlier part of my career I had quite a few leather zip-up bags, which would store four to six pipes and all the kit. I used to smoke constantly while practising and I learned a lot of my concerto repertoire while clenching a pipe between my teeth. Rachmaninov Third's racier passages would shower hot ash onto my trousers if not carefully judged. No wonder I've never liked wearing shorts at the piano.

And then I stopped. I don't really know why. I never had an addiction to tobacco and could go for days without thinking about it, even though it was always pleasurable when I relit my pipe. Occasionally my tongue would burn after my third bowl of the day, and I did think that my teeth and breath would not improve over the years if I continued smoking. Today buildings all over the world are completely smoke-free and the sight of smokers huddled outside doorways is common in most cities. I get an occasional twinge of regret when I think of the old days. There is no easier way to relax than to sit down in a comfortable chair with a book and a pipe. And my pipes sit there still, filled with dust now rather than ash. My silver Dunhill lighter is in a drawer somewhere too, black with tarnish.

I hope smoking never completely disappears, even though I now hate the waft of cigarette smoke in those restaurants that still allow it. But for me the passing clouds have passed for good.

Beef Stroganoff and a bag of bones

New York is more than a second home to me. I've lived in Manhattan longer than anywhere else, although not always in the same apartment. I began at the YMCA on West 64th for about a week, then moved to West 79th to the (at the time) dingy Imperial Court Hotel for about a month; then, as I settled into my studies at the Juilliard School (1981–3), I found a sublet at 235 West 71st Street, a room with bathroom in the formidable Anna Borsuk's spacious apartment.

Madame (as I had to call her) Borsuk was a relic of another age, in her case pre-Revolutionary Russia. When she arrived in the United States she had a brief career as a silent film actress, but then married, left Hollywood behind, and entered into the samovaric world of pre-war New York. 'Rachmaninov signed my piano . . . Chaliapin used to come to visit and would always sing for us,' she told me, her arms gesturing, her painted eyebrows arching as if the rattle of a cinema piano were accompanying her exaggerated movements. By the time I knew her she was truly a bag of bones, held together with sinews of memory, make-up, henna and the hauteur of an older world – but a great lady nevertheless.

One evening she decided to cook for me: Beef Stroganoff. It was absolutely delicious.

'Madame, this is wonderful,' I exclaimed. 'Could I possibly have the recipe? I'd love to try to make it some time.'

'Well, dear,' she replied. 'I don't like to give it to people. You see, it all goes back to when I was in Paris. General Stroganoff wrote it out for me himself.'

I can't verify the facts of this (I never saw the handwritten recipe), but it's one of the best name-dropping stories I know from a distant world where so many things seem like one more, perfectly enchanting fairy-tale.

Electronic books: the end of one kind of intellectual snobbery

We might not judge a book by its cover but we do often judge people by the books they read. I have to confess I usually try to see what my neighbours on a flight or train are reading, and I will sometimes categorise them by the titles in their laps. Like most people I have a history of intellectual snobbery. My (hardly read but much handled) copy of *Finnegans Wake* found a resting place in my school satchel for many months alongside my sandwich box. I even started setting it to music – although its 'riverrun' dried up abruptly after a dozen or two uncomprehended words. But with ebooks all of this changed. No one can know whether we are reading Homer or Harold Robbins as we swipe the screen to change pages. In fact, one of the drawbacks to these electronic devices is that we can actually forget the exact title of the book we are reading because it no longer passes before our eyes each time we pick it up.

Throughout my youth I remember seeing paperback copies of *A Town Like Alice* by Nevil Shute. It was omnipresent on bookshelves in bed-and-breakfasts, in dentists' waiting rooms, on dusty tables in junk shops next to the faded figurines and cloudy salt cellars. Library copies of it were well borrowed and smeared with many dated stamps. It was there on shelves waiting to be checked out, and it was there on trolleys wanting to be reshelved. I would never have read it myself then. My reading was the books kept in Warrington Library's back room, marked with an 'A' in the card catalogue – meaning 'adult': *Tropic of Cancer*, *Last Exit to Brooklyn*, *The Naked Lunch*, *Lady Chatterley's Lover*. They were not on the open shelves but had to be requested and Constance Trimble (Miss) with her grey tweed skirt, tight bun and half-moon glasses would bring them back to the counter with a highly disapproving look. 'You do know what sort of books your son is reading, don't you, sir?' she said cuttingly to my father on one occasion. I think he felt that this fourteen-year-old was better left to roam free than to be subject to censorship.

Then I came across *A Town Like Alice* in an online advertisement just a few years ago. I was instantly taken back to my childhood, to this book I had avoided, and I couldn't resist clicking on the link to read the synopsis. I bought it instantly and started reading it (hidden behind the Kindle screen) with great pleasure. Apart from the exotic interest of war-time Malaya and the post-war Australian outback, its domestic scenes seemed to me more fascinatingly old-fashioned than Dickens. Pre-1960s Britain: rationing, gentleman's clubs, homburg hats, offices with leather-top desks, telegrams, fountain pens, the colonies, smoking, always smoking. I think Miss Trimble would have been surprised at my choice, but approving.

Good Americans

I was leaving Nashville Airport one September afternoon in the lashing rain. We drove up to the airport's exit barrier and there was one of those wonderful, strong, glamorous old ladies you meet in America, seated calmly in the booth, waiting to take the toll money. It's a fairly mundane job at best, but she managed to make it something dignified and memorable with her feisty charm. In fact she was really as much onstage as I would be later that week in my concerts with the orchestra – and she knew it. In fifteen-second slots during her shift she has the undivided attention of maybe thousands of drivers a day. She was unhurried but efficient, hair perfectly styled, face carefully but subtly made up, clothes understated but well chosen, movements graceful. She assured us that the rain would continue. I believed her.

And she was right. The next morning the rain was still pouring down and, as I reached the concierge at my hotel, I asked him if he had a hotel umbrella I could borrow. 'We have none left here, sir, but I could get mine for you from my car in the garage. It'll just take a few minutes.' I was amazed at his generosity and was not quite sure what to say. Then immediately an elderly lady, standing with her husband to the left of us, said, 'I'll just run up to our room. I have a spare umbrella up there which you can borrow. We don't need it today.' In the end I just decided to take a run for it, splashing my way across the road to the hall, but I thought about this later in the day. Such totally open-hearted warmth and magnanimity seemed to me uniquely American. A hotel employee in London might help you out, but it would be done (or most likely not) as a servant obeying a master – with impeccable grace, but full of non-spoken baggage about who was in a superior position of power or duty. That morning I just experienced spontaneous acts of kindness, from two people, in the space of fifteen seconds.

Then there was an occasion at Kennedy Airport. I got onto the plane for the long flight to Seattle and, planning to spend the journey working, I reached into my briefcase to retrieve my computer. An empty space. I'd left it at the security point. The last few passengers were getting on the plane. What was I to do? I explained the situation to the flight attendant and she let me leave the aircraft to go to the boarding gate.

'Be quick, though. We're closing the doors in ten minutes.'

I raced up the ramp and approached the man who was tapping my flight's final details into the computer at his desk.

'I've left my laptop at security. Could you possibly phone there to find out if they've found it?'

'I'm sorry, sir. I have no way of doing that now.'

'But what am I to do?'

'You can go online and file an enquiry there. It's nothing to do with us. Different department.' He said all of this without looking at me, engrossed in his task of closing the flight. No empathy, no attempt to help.

A woman was standing by and overheard this exchange. 'I'm on the next flight to Seattle. I could go and retrieve your laptop and bring it with me.'

I was dumbfounded. 'Are you sure? That would be amazing!'

'Of course. It's no trouble at all. I have a few hours before my flight. Describe it to me and tell me where you're staying in Seattle.'

'Oh goodness, no! I can arrange for it to be collected from you.'

We exchanged email addresses and I gave her my hotel details. The following morning my laptop was at the front desk. It had been hand-delivered by this stranger after midnight on her way (out of her way) home.

I might be wrong (I hope I'm wrong), but I can't imagine such natural, unforced, spontaneous acts of sheer generosity happening in Europe.

Thanksgiving for Thanksgiving

Once a year, at the dark end of November, Thanksgiving Day arrives in the United States. It's one of those marvellous reminders of the good sort of innocence and naivety you can find in that country – like the unembarrassed willingness of audiences to cry at beautiful music, or to stand up and cheer after a performance. People think of America as the ultimate place of modernity, but there is much there that clings on to older fashions and customs – like journalists who write for the *New York Times* being required to refer to *Mr* Hough. And you're more likely to see shirts and ties and polished wing tips on a special occasion at an American university than at a British one.

Thanksgiving is one of those traditions that it is impossible to conceive of being invented today – it would be considered sentimental, meretricious, priggish, phony. But it remains as fervently observed as ever, a day in the year for a total shutdown of work and a putting aside of cynicism, if only in name. Yes, it's an occasion to stuff ourselves like turkeys, to loll around in a drunken stupor, to gorge on pumpkin and pecan pie, but the word is so direct – *Thanksgiving* – that it's almost impossible not to be directed to its original intentions in some small way.

As adults we often long to recover the delights of childhood but find that part of our weary maturity has remained adolescent as we grow up, with all the lanky arrogance of the teenager who has just read his first chapter of philosophy and feels ready to give a lecture on it. The immaturity of those pre-college years can stick with us and risk our being ingrained for life with habits of scoffing and scepticism. Actually I think it has affected the whole of society in some way, with a *Monty Python*-like response ready for every innocent or tender situation.

Dag Hammarskjöld, the Secretary General of the United Nations from 1953 to 1961, whom President John F. Kennedy called 'the greatest statesman of our century', gave us one of the pithiest quotes of wisdom I've come across: 'For all that has been – Thanks. For all that shall be – Yes.'

Willa Cather, Thanksgiving, and the soul of America

I recently re-read Willa Cather's *My Ántonia*. She is one of my favourite authors and one of the few who can bring tears to my eyes. I think that we can understand America much better after reading her, not just because she writes about pioneers and the rich land for which they felt the compulsion to be 'thankful', but because she highlights important aspects of the American experience. One of the common themes she returns to is the poignancy of leaving a small community (village, town, city) and moving to a bigger one . . . and then going back to the old one again as a changed person.

Lucy Gayheart is a late novel dealing specifically with this topic, intriguingly combined with a musical theme. Simplicity or sophistication; the world of soil and sweat or the subtlety of intellectual and artistic pursuits; salt of the earth or spice in the sauce. It ends up being an analogy of the universal experience of leaving the parental home, finding our own more 'sophisticated' way of doing things, and then (sometimes too late) realising that there was wisdom at the old hearth after all.

It is common to hear disparaging remarks about the boring Midwest, even (especially) by Americans. The two coasts are glamorous, their history stretching back in the West to the Spanish missions and in the East to the pre-Revolutionary settlers. Movies, finance, intellectual pursuits, tourism, museums, government, beaches. The middle seems dull, conventional and provincial in comparison. In reality there is something of a foundational significance about the Midwest. It is the bread basket, the reservoir, feeding not only stomachs but somehow the soul of the country. Its determined, heroic spirit is filled with a goodness that is at the roots of America itself. Cather understood this profoundly and although she lived most of her life in the very centre of New York's intellectual hotspot, Greenwich Village, she wrote with passion about the heroism of ordinary folk and about Nebraska where she had spent her formative years.

Parents teach us to say 'thank you' from an early age and it often becomes a habit, a turn of phrase with little meaning, but Thanksgiving is an annual opportunity to discover once more that gratitude is not only a matter of justice (everything we have in life is a gift) but of joy. *Dignum et justum est* – it is right and just to give thanks, and doing so makes the gift itself more precious.

Working hard by letting go

Monks in the Middle Ages spoke of work as prayer. Farming, studying or building, the rhythm of the toil was meant to lead to contemplation – not as a distraction from the task at hand but a heightened form of concentration and reverence.

To work hard is not to wrinkle our brows, tense our muscles, and lose sleep; it is rather to relax into full attention and focus – whether that work is washing dishes or operating on someone's brain. In the same way as the body's muscles gain power and endurance when they are loose, so our minds expand and our memories increase in capacity when we approach our tasks with gently confident absorption.

To aim at perfection in our tasks is fine as long as it does not require or envy the perfection of others; we should seek to find fulfilment in the very act of doing something with no other purpose than the good of what is at hand. This can truly become something exciting. That homework waiting to be done (and it has to be done anyway) can be a path to joy. Try it out first of all with something simple: go to the sink in your kitchen and wash something with care, love, complete attention, and to perfection. Not only do you now have a clean cup, but wasn't it fun too! Now take something you like to eat – a chocolate bar, for instance. Eat it with complete focus on what you're doing; chew slowly and enjoy the sensation in every part of your mouth. Take a full minute doing it and feel your body tingle with delight. Our bodies, paths to our souls, are crying out to be touched. They are like neglected old people who are never visited in their homes and long for company and stimulation.

It brings us back to that wise, old, hackneyed chestnut: to live in the present moment. A whole philosophy has been created out of the observation that the past and the future are phantoms; they don't exist. Only the now exists. Yet how often do we sit having a meal looking forward to the next meal and not enjoying the present one properly? Or we walk through a museum and never really look at anything in detail. We stand before one painting and have our eye on the next, or on the guide book, or on the gift shop, or on the attractive person who has just entered the room . . . and we miss out on them all. Or we read something on the internet or in a book like this and take nothing in, but are just aware of a sort of daze of distraction and dissipation, flipping aimlessly from one thought to another.

We should eat and read and, indeed, do everything with meditation and love, our senses as windows on our souls. Not because we ought to (Father Gerard Hughes SJ spoke in his writings about a 'hardening of the *oughteries*'). No, a bush in full bloom demands our full attention, in the present moment, because it is a wildly erotic, stimulating sight of cataclysmic power.

So to music. Just as we draw sound out of our instruments rather than pushing it in, so when we begin to study a piece of music we should stand before it, empty but attentive, waiting for its inner life to be revealed to us. One of the dangers in listening to too many recordings of a work we are learning is that we can be prevented from a personal exchange with the composer. We have already arrived at the house with second-hand baggage rather than being free to accept the unique hospitality that every piece will offer to us.

Unless we play an electric instrument, our pianos or violas or oboes will be slightly different every day, the wood slightly older, the humidity or temperature marginally changed. They exist in the present moment too. And the musician playing will be different too: you are a few seconds older now than you were when you began reading this paragraph.

The final irony is that we 'play' our instruments (what a marvellous verb that is in this context), but we have to work very hard in order to acquire the skill to master them. Yet if we can play and work (and taste and see) with full attention, we might be closer to the sort of contemplation that those monks were aiming for when Gregorian chant was contemporary music.

Pascal: the brilliant sun or a warm fire?

> Curiosity is only vanity. Most frequently we want to know only to talk. Otherwise we should not take a sea voyage in order never to talk of it.
>
> Blaise Pascal, *Pensées* no. 152

Although this aphorism is meant to guide us on an ascetic path to humility – to avoid boasting and tittle-tattle – there's more there than meets the eye. Firstly I think it can be turned upside down and used as a path to sensual delight in the material world, probably to the horror of its author. Indeed, if we cannot take delight in a 'sea voyage' without feeling the need to speak about it, the problem is not so much with the 'talking after' as with the 'taking of'. We should be able to do many pleasurable things and take joy in them for what they are . . . in that very moment. The danger outlined by Pascal is not so much one of pride or vanity, but of lack of gratefulness and 'presence'.

Second, never mind our talking about them. To listen patiently and kindly to someone else's enthusiasm for something that delighted them is one of the chief ways to build friendship and trust. But I get the feeling Pascal is interested only in his own holiness, his own avoidance of sin, his own relationship with God. Why do I fear that in keeping his own counsel – in his own room, mortified and pure – he might well have missed that encounter with the living God after all? His intellectual brilliance was like the sun, but sometimes we just want to sit by a warm fire.

Monks do it best

And I don't mean religion.

I don't drink liqueurs often, but when I do I like Chartreuse the best – the strong, green one, of course, made to a secret recipe by French monks for over four hundred years. And when the great gurus of scent, Luca Turin and Tania Sanchez, published their *Perfumes: The A–Z Guide*, their top choice for a lavender cologne (it happened to be among the cheapest too) was one made by the monks of Caldey Island, off the coast of Wales. Painter Fra Angelico and composer Tomás Luis de Victoria, clerics both, were arguably the greatest artists in their fields in their era, and let's not forget that hospitals, schools, universities and hotels all began, in idea and realisation, with those cloistered men and women.

I've stayed at quite a few monasteries in my time and they are full of surprises. The first being how hard these men work – in the field, around the property, in the school. Then the surprise of how 'normal' most monks are. There is usually a 'no nonsense' quality to their kindness – an infinite willingness to listen, if combined with a sometimes brusque unwillingness to indulge. There are exceptions, but there's usually a lot of joy bouncing off the stone walls, despite the general rule of silence: humour and words need not necessarily be inseparable companions. And, as monks will offer hospitality to anyone of any faith or none for only a voluntary donation (however small, if you can't afford more), monasteries are still the best bargain around for a weekend away from it all.

The traditional rule for monks had them rise in the middle of the night for an hour of prayer known as Vigils – sleep broken because the world and humanity is (still) broken. I was heartened recently to read that at Caldey (the place with the best lavender perfume) it was the favourite hour of the abbot. He wanted the community to hold up in prayer all those who were restless, lonely, in desperate situations, in hospitals, in prisons . . . in their darkest hour in that darkest hour. This is a custom hard to imagine in the secular world: a group of sleepy men or women getting out of warm beds every night of the week to trek down to a frostbitten chapel to spend an hour in distant solidarity with those in pain of various sorts. It's easy to see this as a waste of time, but so many things of value in our brief lives could be viewed that way. Music merely evaporates into thin air but what riches it leaves behind.

So perhaps it's comforting to know, when next we lie awake with insurmountable worries at three o'clock in the morning GMT, that a few craggy old men on a craggy island off the ancient coast of an ancient land are wishing us well, and they're making quite an effort to do so. And perhaps in our own sleepless moments, if we join in solidarity (it need only be a few seconds) with all the millions around the world who suffer, we become monks ourselves, alight in our bedrooms across the darkened wastes. Just don't try to make your own Chartreuse!

Myself or my brain

It's axiomatic to think of the human body as flesh and blood, but what about its status as dust as its atoms disappear in the renewal of themselves, apparently every seven years or so. Not one flake of the flesh that today is me, Stephen Hough, writing these words, will exist in another decade. All body cells will have been replaced and thus I'll be completely different . . . but really the same, if a little 'older'. I knew about this but I hadn't quite understood the idea that it happens to our internal organs too – even our brains. And if we have had, say, a kidney transplant twenty years ago and that organ has replaced itself around three times since the operation, it is still not 'me' but the donor; even if the donor is now dead, his or her DNA is living on in, and giving life to, another body. Mine.

Thinking of brain transplants takes us to the world of science fiction, but with our own renewable brains is it really plausible to accept blithely that our consciousness (our 'us-ness') resides there in some simple, materially quantifiable measurement? As we ponder this, plunging with our brains ever deeper into those same brains' transience, can we not see a glimpse of the *possibility* of immortality? A 'me' somehow alive, conscious, clinging on to identity outside (inside) the flying, dying atoms?

Daring to hope in Alzheimer's despairing inner world

I read an article once by Father Daniel O'Leary in the *Tablet* magazine – a beautiful, provocative, moving meditation on Alzheimer's disease called 'Silent Grace of Forgetting'. All of us face the possibility of dementia in varying degrees, either in our own future lives or in the lives of those we love. Its threat is to suck out the personality of the person, leaving behind an empty husk or, worse, a familiar body filled with unfamiliar malevolence – a strange enemy impersonating a dear friend. It's disturbing when it's not damned terrifying.

In his article Father O'Leary dared to explore a possible spirituality behind this dreadful disease, the need for our care-filled reverence, for us to *be* the memory for the person, 'to hold the fragments of a life together'. He points out that 'it is not our minds alone which make us human', and makes the further incarnational point that it is 'through the senses that the inner shrine is reached . . . The graciousness of the carer's eyes . . . the touch of the friend's hands . . . the dignity of the helper's composure [and] of the carer's voice, the radiance from his or her physical presence.'

He continues: 'Embodied love is the sacrament of invisible grace that somehow touches the fretful, demented mind and soul, and, beyond all our explanations, works silent wonders.' Then, quoting Rosalie Hudson's chapter in the book *Ageing, Disability and Spirituality*, 'Perhaps the person with dementia – freed from all pretension, totally incapable of spiritual self-examination – might be an icon of God's grace in us.'

Wishful thinking, rubbish, pie in the sky . . . I hear the reactions. But as we face such a dark place, is not the attempt to go there accompanied with such thoughts of compassionate care worth trying? To let go of our own fleeting, fragile cleverness, our propped-up cardboard images, even as they are forcibly prised out of our feeble hands? Yes, of course, we must be tireless in looking for a cure for Alzheimer's and for every possible means of prevention but, when the passage is inevitable, dare we go 'gentle into that good night'?

Going gentle into that good night:
the blessing of hospices

I was asked a few years ago to become a Patron of St Rocco's Hospice in Warrington, something especially delightful to me as it is a return to my roots. I lived my young, healthy years (from five to thirty) close by in Thelwall and Grappenhall.

The importance of hospices in our communities hinges on a number of related issues:

Care

Most obviously hospices are places of physical and spiritual relief for the terminally ill and for those who love them. Hospices aim to alleviate pain, fear and despair. To achieve care not cure is already to fulfil their purpose, and their service to the families of the sick is as important as to those who are actually being treated.

Honesty

Leading on from this is a burst of bracing honesty: despite the fact that some people do recover and return home, the principal function of a hospice is to be the last stop on life's journey and not to flinch from admitting it. To stare death in the face like that requires great courage from all involved.

Value

Hospices are like beacons in a community, unspoken declarations that human life is important in every moment of its living. They are a challenge to the prosaic, the utilitarian, even to the 'logical' in our moral lives. Human life is beyond measure, beyond price, and the healthy person's life, bursting with vim and vigour, becomes more valuable when he or she cherishes the one who is fading away on the last lap with the last breath. Both are equally precious.

Perspective

Hospices alert to us a true perspective on living: life as fragile; success and beauty as a mirage; time, in every one of its luminous moments, as finite. There's nothing good in suffering as such, but if unavoidable and freed from isolation and shame it can be seen through, seen beyond, in the kind company of others.

Hospices alert us to the fact that life means more than life. Being born is a terminal illness, to breathe is to face death, we cannot alter that; but we have totally within our power to care daily for those next to whom we find ourselves standing, sitting or lying.

Suicide? Let me assist you

I'm deeply aware that thorny moral questions such as assisted suicide involve stepping across minefields – and ones that risk exploding in the face of others rather than ourselves. This particular issue is not an abstract argument that can be teased into unanimity by typing some self-assured thoughts on a laptop. It involves the day-to-day lives (and deaths) of people who are usually in the most desperate situations – by definition beyond hope in their own eyes. So I tap the keyboard gently, cautiously – with the delete and question keys ever in sight.

I think there are three, delicately balanced and complexly interacting issues involved in this discussion:

1. The morality of the act itself: is it intrinsically wrong to take one's own life?
2. The state of mind of those assisting the suicide: is their

aid truly disinterested, and what does it mean to have compassion?

3. The state of mind of the person ending his or her life: can such a person make a rational, responsible decision if they are depressed or in pain?

The first point is probably the clearest. Few people think suicide is anything but a tragedy, but there *is* a logic behind the position: 'My life belongs to me and I have every right to choose how I live it and how I end it.' Furthermore, people throughout history have killed themselves, and if the determination is strong there is very little we can do to prevent it. But we risk basing our laws on passing moods as fickle as clouds in the sky unless we can face this question squarely. If suicide is *not* intrinsically wrong, then say so and have it available for anyone who requests it at any doctor's surgery. If it *is* intrinsically wrong, then the law should not facilitate or encourage its occurrence.

The second point is not so clear and has been much discussed. The two crudest scenarios are the busy, successful son or daughter for whom the parent's illness is an inconvenience; or the brother, say, who stands to gain financially from the death of the terminally ill sister. These situations exist, if sometimes in an almost subconscious form, and we can easily recognise the wrong involved. But outside these clear cases, what about the thousand permutations of love, responsibility, obligation, guilt and even hatred, that course through every family's history? Are our relationships with our relatives so pure and fundamentally benevolent that under that stone of compassion there could never lurk a worm of resentment? How do we measure our compassion? Where do we draw the line between alleviating the suffering of a loved one and encouraging them to end it all?

The third point is, in some ways, the most crucial and least discussed. Never mind the motives of those assisting the suicide, what about the mindset of the person wanting to end their lives? If a young person, in perfect health, were to go to her doctor and ask for the means to kill herself, would we find this acceptable? Why is it that we find such a request made by someone who is old, or in pain, or depressed, more tolerable? What is the moral logic of denying suicide for the well and facilitating it for the ill? Is someone better able to make a rational decision when sick and in pain than when twenty-four years old and healthy? Depression is in some ways the state of someone not 'in their right mind', and yet it seems to be a central requirement for permitting assisted suicide. I believe we are close to social hell when an old woman in a nursing home who is worried that she is a burden on her family is encouraged in that anxiety with smiling, sanitised legality. Coercion or browbeating can be effectively employed with the lightest touch when we are dealing with those who are weak and vulnerable, and the idea that it is selfish for the terminally ill to want to continue living is diabolical – a horrific turning of the moral tables with frightening implications for every lonely bag of bones sitting in a hospital bed needing only an affectionate touch to light up her eyes. We may want to appear compassionate and morally responsible but we are really making subjective decisions about worth and value. Why not come clean and say what we are thinking . . . that the old and sick have less reason to live than the young and beautiful?

It's not that I'm particularly anxious for spouses and relatives to be placed behind bars, but if we develop a mindset and a legal framework that encourages the idea that, as we get old and ill, the sensible, selfless, courageous thing to do is to end our lives, I think we will have regressed as human beings.

Dignity?

Dignitas – the name of the clinic in Switzerland where people can go to end their lives. One of the problems with talking about assisted suicide is precisely this word and the sense that it is axiomatic that someone old and incapacitated lacks dignity.

I had an experience with my dear old composition teacher, Douglas Steele. He ended up in a nursing home and was pretty mad, but still an absolute delight to be with. The last time I went to see him I opened his door and he was sitting on a commode with his trousers around his ankles. 'Come in, dear boy,' he shouted with a laugh. 'I shan't be long.' I was a little shocked at this ultimate example of indignity, but then I saw past the physical aspect of it as I looked up at the impervious, smiling face of my old friend, his extraordinary greatness of spirit unaltered. He dressed himself and, after telling me some confused stories I'd heard hundreds of times, he sat down at the piano and played a piece he said he'd written but was really by William Baines. It was all quite crazy but I left feeling great joy.

I had also seen him during moods of terrible darkness with an incapacitating depression he'd had sporadically since the Second World War. I can't help but think that on a bad day, with 'compassionate' relatives offering advice and blinded by his own dark mood, he might have been forced to agree that life is worth living only when it is dignified, and thus encouraged to end that life. On the day we met, in the nursing home, on the commode, William Baines resonating from the small upright piano, he flung dignity to one side and we both revelled in the childlike glee that resulted from it.

But on the other hand . . . some different thoughts on end-of-life issues

I'm sometimes suspicious of those who say that they believe in eternal life, Christians who claim that when we die we don't die – 'life is changed not ended', as the liturgy puts it. If they really believed this, would it not make end-of-life issues less anxiety-inducing? If that child with the incurable illness – pain medicated just short of the wire of the unendurable, tubes writhing out of bloody, raw crevices – were a mere hour away from an eternal embrace by the eternal Lover why the panicked insistence on prolonging the last hopeless moments on earth, at whatever cost? Is demanding a sufferer's month of utter pain (motor neurons' conscious but immobile torture) really to be pro-life? And (this is dangerous, I know) is a mistake, or even a medical misjudgement, *such* a disaster if that person immediately enters everlasting bliss? When Christians march and chant and hold placards and accuse and threaten, are they not often indulging in the worst kind of political point-making, promoting an 'us v. them' superiority, which is fundamentally, and ironically, contradicting the heart of the message of Jesus?

God allows death. He could stop it yet, as every second strikes, lungs cease to breathe, hearts cease to beat, vital organs atrophy and rot. We go to the ends of the earth to prolong life; God points down from heaven in destruction. This can seem completely arbitrary and random at times: a universe of cruel chance. But if we buy into a life-giving God, we have to accept the death-dealing Deity too, on a scale more massive than we can imagine. A black hole of slaughter at the heart of the Divine.

Maybe our clinging on to blood and bone should not be the issue after all. To 'let go and let God' is to welcome death and embrace it – Sister Death, as St Francis of Assisi described it, tellingly feminine. Tomb as womb. If the Gospel (Good News) means the destruction of death's dread, maybe we should stop trying to block something that has ceased to matter. Perhaps the terminally ill are being given a ticket to ride, so who are we to delay their journey?

Encouragement, falsehood, and Auschwitz

'Encourage' is a beautiful word, and to give encouragement is certainly one of the most attractive human virtues. Courage is something else. Although we understand that it is not about lacking fear but about doing the right thing in spite of fear, it can still seem intimidating. Its assertive strut of strength, action and risk can appear terrifying for all but the most self-confident among us. But encouragement is gentle, non-threatening. It looks outside itself; it raises another's hopes without raising its own profile. Good parents, good teachers (good confessors) know all about this. I've had all three.

Is it acceptable to lie in order to encourage? In the striking and moving novel *The Last of the Just* by André Schwartz-Bart, we hear of the Jewish tradition that in every generation thirty-six just men are born, the *Lamed-waf*, to take the burden of the world's suffering on themselves. The novel begins in York in 1185 when Rabbi Yom Tov Levey's martyrdom so moved God that he promised the rabbi's descendants a just man in each generation. After a few chapters, hurtling through history, we reach the extended story of Ernie Levey, who was killed at Auschwitz in 1943. During his final harrowing train journey, packed tight into a sickening, excrement-thick carriage of death and despair, he tries to comfort the terrified children who are still alive about their dead companion, assuring them that he is only asleep and repeating to them in rhythms matching the train's forward movement that in the Kingdom of Israel everyone will be happy and parents will be reunited with their children. A woman in the carriage confronts him in anger, digging her nails into his shoulder, asking him how he can tell them that it's only a dream. He replies, through tears: 'Madame, there is no room for truth here.'

Of course the theological question arises as to whether he was in fact, if unknowingly, speaking the truth, but beyond that perhaps there is a 'truth' in human compassion that is greater than 'facts'. The invisible bonds that join us together in society can be, should be, stronger than the material world we can grasp and measure and destroy. To bring healing to a soul, especially a child's, is to conjure up the fire of creation itself. 'Let there be light!' The Big Bang, the first First, might well have been, above all, an explosion of love: the universe's orgasm.

. . . AND RELIGION

Rock or tree?

People think of faith as something solid, a rock against which a tempest can rage, a fixture of stability when all around is in turmoil. 'You are Rock and upon this Rock I will build my Church' (Matthew 16:18) was Christ's response to Peter's confident affirmation of belief. But to me faith is more like a tree. It is mostly stable and supporting but it is alive and changeable and unpredictable too. And it gets damaged in the storm sometimes. And it can lose its leaves. Mine has undergone many autumns over the years.

I have gathered in the following section some spiritual reflections, written across different periods of my life, sometimes buoyed up with confidence, sometimes shaken up with questioning.

Empty hands

How wonderful that we can give others that peace which we do not possess. Oh, miracle of our empty hands.

This quotation from the novel *Diary of a Country Priest* by Georges Bernanos goes to the heart of the matter for me in matters religious. Any spirituality begins (continues and ends) with an overriding sense of our permanently empty hands. It has been said that the most important condition for being able to pray is a profound awareness of our inability to pray. In some ways any peace I myself might have (my neat solutions confidently arranged and ready for quick dispensing) is the worst thing to offer someone whose heart is riven with suffering. It is too often cheap, ready-made wisdom. It's not that if I'm sad

I need someone equally sad to sympathise; I just don't want a smug, smiling face beaming at me, trying to cheer me up.

I've been to Confession countless hundreds of times all over the world. If nothing else, I have probably saved thousands of pounds in psychiatrists' bills! The overwhelming majority of these priestly encounters have been positive – brief, sensible, understanding and genuinely encouraging. One memorable occasion was in New York when I popped into the Franciscan Church on West 31st Street. 'I'm an alcoholic,' said the priest in the midst of one of the most humane, gentle and uplifting five minutes I have ever spent. A few years later this particular wounded healer, Father Mychal Judge, would become world famous as the first certified fatality on the morning of 9/11, killed in the midst of service as chaplain to the firefighters.

Sometimes having nothing to say enables us to be living sacraments, outward shells containing (who knows how?) inward grace, conduits for blessings we do not possess ourselves. It's not dissimilar to playing a concert, perhaps: re-creating sounds I didn't write; moving an audience when I'm not in the mood; heart speaking to heart without the need for words.

I am not a Catholic pianist

Julien Green once wrote that he was a Catholic and a novelist, but not a Catholic novelist. I think the distinction is more than merely a way to prevent limitations of subject matter and moral judgement; it has to do with the difference between God's responsibility and ours in the creative process.

Music's abstraction removes that specific dilemma facing the believing writer, but when asked about the relationship between my musical and spiritual life my initial reaction is that there is none. My faith shapes *me* (although not as much as it might), and then that 'me' plays the piano or composes. Faith does not work directly on the materials at hand. Whether I play a good concert tomorrow night, or whether settings of religious texts I've written are inspired, has nothing to do with whether I prayed before or during the process. This relates to an important insight of Catholic spirituality: the entire material world, after the Incarnation, is now forever infused, perfumed with God. This is a step beyond seeing the goodness of Creation: yes, everything is *made* by God, but, after Christ, all that 'good matter' has had Hands of benediction extended over it in a new way. After Emmaus, every crust of bread is sacred; after Cana, all water can become wine.

Caravaggio's religious works are greater than Holman Hunt's not because he was a firmer believer than the good Englishman but because he was a better painter – and his notorious case is, delightfully, the exception that proves the exception: 'God makes his sun rise on the evil and on the good, and sends his rain on the just and on the unjust' (Matthew 5:45). Artistic genius and our delight in what it produces is an example of the profligate overflow of God's grace and goodness, given without limit or condition. In fact, an artist's complacent confidence that his faith and good behaviour will lend him God's help in a special way is likely to find *that* the very obstacle that gets in the way of greatness – a log in the artistic eye preventing him from seeing the 'world in a grain of sand'.

Where faith does have an impact for me is in the mental health that results from its vision of ultimate reality – the broad-shouldered realisation that becoming like children, as Christ commanded, is not to make us immature, but to encourage us to see life as a playground with so many swings and roundabouts, and buttered scones at home at the end of the day. If I walk onto the stage with concerns about wrong notes, critics, applause, fame . . . I will not play as well as I can. Of course I could always believe that I myself am God, but I fear that deity would be *far* too exacting and narrow! People regularly report an increase in physical and mental energy when they start to pray or meditate, forming in us an inner silence that is an essential part of concentration. To be able to hear each note, each bar, each phrase, both individually and as a related whole, requires an ability to see and to hold many parts in unity – a key to any life of contemplation. Avoiding distractions, creating new and better material out of mistakes, balancing self-demand and self-esteem, are all qualities that unite a musical and spiritual life. The hidden, daily annoyances of cancelled flights, noisy hotels, bad food and inferior pianos are a constant ascetical challenge. The patience required in the course of a tour to meet, with kindness and attention, hundreds of new people backstage or at receptions is a real call to holiness – much like a priest at the door of his church who tries to greet each person as if they were the most important in the world . . . at least for those few seconds.

It was nice, when I was setting the words 'dona nobis pacem', to know that they were a prayer, and that the 'nobis' included my friends and those thousands of people in the course of a year for whom I play. But don't blame God if the music I wrote for those words does not sound inspired.

Could God exist?

Some Christians kind of wish God didn't exist, or at least the kind of God who prohibits doing those things we most want to do. And some non-believers might wish that they could believe in *something*, that there was some benevolent purpose behind the seeming absurdity of it all.

I don't have any reasons that could actually convince anyone (even myself) of the existence of God. If faith is not the opposite of doubt but of certainty, then reasons for that faith might be called 'reasons not to be sure'. A few pointers help me to think about the issue, starting with not asking, 'Does God exist?', but whether there is a possibility of that existence.

One of the reasons atheism falls short for me is in its lack of someone/something to thank for those moments of ecstasy we experience in life, those gifts that have no human source. I wrote earlier in this book about applause and how it was more a necessary release for those in the audience than an appreciative token for those onstage. Gratefulness is like a silent, interior ovation, an overflow in the presence of unspeakable blessings; and, for me, that release is more natural, more cathartic, when there's Someone to thank.

Everything in life is a gift. And, beyond that, all things *receive* existence, in an unbroken chain back to grand zero. Nothing (no thing) just appears out of the blue. I therefore find it a small step from that axiom to the likelihood that some Power had to strike the first match at some beginning of the beginning; and not just a Big Bang of random energy producing random results, but something focused and ultimately 'sense-able'. We *can* know things . . . and in a universe without design we couldn't. You know that the book or screen you hold in your hand right now will not turn into a dodo because you know dodos are extinct . . . oh, and 'things' don't behave like that anyway. We call it science (*scientia* means 'knowledge' in Latin) because its constant search for new knowledge is based on the foundational fact that there *is* such a thing as 'knowledge' in the first place.

The priest and broadcaster Father Cormac Rigby's suggested definition of faith was 'being open to the possibility that God might exist', an open door for an open mind. It's a neat way of admitting that there's no way of forcing belief on someone, as well as gently reminding God that the gift of faith is promised freely to all.

'Could God exist?' A hymn from the ninth century puts it well: *Ubi caritas et amor, Deus ibi est* ('Where there is charity and love, there is God').

I think that's an existence (of God, and for me) that's worth living.

What if God doesn't exist?

I was on my way to try out pianos for a Royal Festival Hall recital a few years ago when I saw a poster on the side of a bus: 'There's probably no God. Now stop worrying and get on with your life.' Then, two minutes later, I saw another one. I felt exhilarated. My mind had been preoccupied precisely with *my life*, how to 'get on with it', how to play my recital the following afternoon without worrying about nerves, the voicing of the piano, whether my suit was pressed – all the material things that swim around us and in which we swim. And then, on the side of a bus, I was reminded of God. I stopped worrying and enjoyed . . . well, at least the rest of that afternoon.

Much was written at the time about this poster campaign, but I liked it because it was so absolutely British – an inverted and eccentric version of the 'Prepare to meet thy God' sandwich boards held up by the bewhiskered Victorian gentlemen of the Temperance Society. Its real aim was surely to annoy rather than to convert, but that's true of much Christian preaching too. At least it's a blast of fresh air in a stale debate, even if I know very few 'moderns' who actually do allow God to interfere with their enjoyment of life.

I'm not sure I would like a world without atheists – and I don't mean that ironically. There are too many moments in history when freethinkers and 'heretics' were ahead of the game in their understanding of, and heroic championing of, human rights. This is still true today, and a world peopled by only 'Christians' would probably force me to become the first atheist. But I do have two problems. First, the concept of negativity in the word 'atheism'. You can't call a negative a thing, because it's a 'no-thing'; and 'humanism', which is the best attempt to label it some-thing, seems small to me: a pinprick of a species on a pinprick of a planet in a pinprick of a galaxy. Alone again, naturally. We are left with, well . . . me. Or, even worse, with the faceless inhumanity of matter – so big it doesn't really matter. So nothing matters. I'm in my little shell with my semiquavers (shaken not slurred). I can try to 'stop worrying and enjoy my life', while it lasts, but haven't we all found that it's when we try to make *other* people's lives more enjoyable that their happiness splashes back onto us? Unplanned. Unexpected. It's a lesson I first learned from religion.

My second problem is that attacks on belief are usually reduced to pointing out the perceived stupidity of the believer. My maths results at school were so poor that I am reconciled for ever to a low assessment of my intelligence, but I have met too many people (and read, and played the music of, and looked at the art of too many people) who had religious faith and were simply not unintelligent. I might disagree with their views, but a scattergun aim at their IQ is a waste of bullets. Religion has caused more violence and suffering in the history of the world than anything else . . . except love and human relationships. There has been more bigotry and intolerance in religious societies than anywhere else . . . except in those societies where the experiment to outlaw religion has been applied.

Karl Marx famously opined that 'religion is the opium of the people'. Such a quality is not a good thing – although sometimes it might not be such a bad thing either. If an elderly woman is lying in hospital, incurably ill, with no visitors, wouldn't it be crass and heartless to wrench the rosary or Bible out of her hands? In the final reflection of the previous section I discussed something similar in the example of Ernie Levey. We give anti-depressants to people – why not give God, if it works? Studies do seem to suggest that people with religious beliefs live longer, healthier lives, and what do we have, in certain desperate situations, to take God's place?

Some atheists found the word 'probably' in the poster to be a cop-out, but in fact it's a wager – like Pascal's infamous one. It says, 'If you put a bet on God not existing you'll probably walk away a winner.' Pascal had the reverse point: 'If there's a chance God exists, you have everything to gain by believing in Him and everything to lose by not.' Both are games, of course, and Pascal's veiled threat seems rather narrow and petty to me. But what if the thought of God's existence or God's presence actually *helps* us stop worrying, lightens our heart, makes getting on with our lives that bit more joyful, more fulfilling – both for us, and for our neighbours?

Religion's moth-eaten tapestry

So 'religion is the opium of the people'. Alain de Botton, instead of using this idea as a stick to beat believers, requests instead that the smouldering pipe be passed along to him for a puff.

His much discussed book *Religion for Atheists* has been credited for initiating a new era of 'soft atheism' – or humanism with a human face. One critic suggested it was more like pastoral care for the unbeliever than aggressive evangelism from a secular viewpoint. Ironically I think that the book might end up being more of an encouragement to believers to value their heritage than it will convince non-believers to change their attitudes.

Here are words from de Botton's website describing the book:

Religion for Atheists suggests that rather than mocking religions, agnostics and atheists should instead steal from them – because they're packed with good ideas on how we might live and arrange our societies.

Among the ideas for which he wants to be a magpie are how to:

build a sense of community
make our relationships last
overcome feelings of envy and inadequacy
escape the twenty-four-hour media
go travelling
get more out of art, architecture and music
create new businesses designed to address our emotional
    needs

Christian critics raised the importance of the centrality of truth in any assessment of the value of religion, but there are some other aspects to this issue that have not, as far as I know, been fully explored in the context of de Botton's book and its ideas.

Although some Christians might be reluctant to admit it, 'faith' in God is not the only fuel propelling the religious experience. Guilt and fear have also been powerful incentives to those energetic believers who built schools and hospitals, went on missionary journeys, who attend weekly church services or provide heroic charitable support. One of the anxieties expressed in Counter-Reformation theology was that if 'faith alone' is all we need, then how can we make people behave well? 'Faith without works is dead,' said the Apostle James in the New Testament (James 2:26) . . . but not just works. Obligation under pain of sin has been an incentive ensuring strong attendance numbers at Catholic Masses through the centuries, and many a priestly or religious vocation has been kept in the air on wings of guilt as well as love – not to mention fidelity in matrimony.

I'm not sure that truth alone is enough to keep believers believing and dealing well with these issues (community, relationships, feelings, etc.); perhaps there needs to be the counter-melody of guilt and fear too. The tapestry of religious belief and practice is often knotted, tangled and moth-eaten, and nothing is so suspicious in religion as neatness and order. One of Catholicism's strengths (shared with Judaism) has been its awareness and acceptance of this and its admission that mixed motives are an unavoidable and natural part of being authentically human. The Church is not a perfect community of saints but rather a dragnet with good and bad fish all mixed up together (Matthew 13:47) – a different kind of 'truth', difficult sometimes to welcome, but ultimately humbling in the best, most healthy way.

To return to opium, if atheism's claim that nothing to nothing is the universe's non-plan, then nothing really matters that much in the end – including my smoking of the pipe of delusion and escapism. If I were languishing in solitary confinement until death in a prison cell (whether falsely or justly convicted), atheism would provide me with no reason to live, whereas faith and contemplation could actually bring me unspeakable joy, even in those most desperate circumstances.

Summarising his thoughts, de Botton asks, 'Even if religion isn't true, can't we enjoy the best bits?' What I've discovered over the years is that the very best bit of all is the possibility that it might actually be true – or at least the One whom 'religion' so awkwardly, inadequately tries to represent.

Do not touch me: the wisdom of
Anglican thresholds

Occasionally I like to attend Choral Evensong, the Church of England's evening service, adapted after the Reformation from the monastic hour of Vespers. It is a wondrous phenomenon. Even the word 'Evensong' is poetic, and it seems to chime in perfect harmony with England's seasons: autumn's melancholy, early-evening light; the merry crackle of winter frost; spring's awakening, or the lazy, protracted sun strained through the warmed windows of a summer afternoon.

Evensong hangs on the wall of English life like an old, familiar cloak passed through the generations. Rich with prayer and Scripture, it is nevertheless totally non-threatening. It is a service into which all can stumble without censure – a rambling old house where everyone can find some corner to sit and think, to listen with half-attention, trailing a few absent-minded fingers of faith or doubt in its passing stream.

Most religious celebrations gather us around a table of some sort. They hand us a book, or a piece of bread, or speak a word demanding a response. They want to 'touch' us. Choral Evensong is a liturgical expression of Christ's *Noli me tangere* – 'Do not touch me. I have not yet ascended to my Father' (John 20:17). It reminds us that thresholds can be powerful places of contemplation, and that leaving someone alone with their thoughts is not always denying them hospitality or welcome. Furthermore, the singing from the choir involves us yet leaves us free; we don't have to enter into it if the music has entered into us. The connection is made. It needs no name. We are known. We are accepted.

Heaven's above

I spend a lot of time on planes. I dislike almost everything about the experience – the enclosed space inside, the vast space outside, the stale air, the inhuman velocity – but I often pray best when hurtling along at 500 miles an hour. With the annoyances of security queues, late departures, lost luggage, rude flight attendants, cramped seats, the inability to sleep, and warm, plastic food, who needs a hairshirt or an all-night vigil?

Once a plane has taken off into the skies we are utterly helpless. It is one of the rare occasions in life (unless we are incarcerated or incapacitated) when we have no control over our physical circumstances. It is a material acting out of the spiritual state of abandonment – putting everything into the hands of God. We can press the button to summon an attendant, but to reach God we do not even need that. An interior glance and we are in touch with the Pilot who is steering everything in calmest skies. When the journey is smooth, and clouds below look like so many playgrounds of fluff, I can feel a childlike gratitude for the simple gift of being alive. In turbulent weather I recall the Gospel passage of Christ in the boat on the Sea of Galilee, asleep on a cushion in the midst of a storm of such severity that all were in danger of sinking (Matthew 8:24).

I often find myself thinking more acutely of the bigger issues in seat 13C. From Mars, Bach would probably still seem of interest, but outside of the Milky Way even he would be an insignificant speck, his sounds over in under a second, his complete works less than one dot of dust. This is good to contemplate, because *all* life is either worthless or of infinite value. To think that this particular person's life is not worth living is to fail to see the ultimate insignificance of all existence. Unless we are clinically depressed or natural nihilists, such thoughts should make us value every minute we have. Things *do* matter – and none more than human life itself, from cradle to grave. The tenderness and vulnerability there in all the greatest art is from the same root as the fragility of one who cannot lift an arm, or a heart.

G. K. Chesterton discovered that thinking of the smallness of humanity, paradoxically, made him feel more at home in the world. We didn't choose to be here and then find that our choice was well or ill advised; we found ourselves here, not *against* our will, but *beyond* our will. By our own fireplaces we become larger than life. It *is* wonderful to smell toast or chestnuts on the edge of burning; it *is* wonderful to see and hear logs splitting into glowing, red shards. I know that the smallest nut or bolt in the plane on which I'm flying tomorrow has its place of importance in whether we stay up in the air or not. And the smallest nuance or rhythmic adjustment in the piece I'm playing tomorrow (micro-seconds, micro-decibels) can turn a good performance into a great one.

But I'm sometimes still fearful and doubting as the plane's wheels leave the ground. Like the disciples in that Gospel story I rush to wake up the slumbering Christ and, again, hear the gentle rebuke: 'Why are you afraid?' Yet it is this very sense of our weakness that enables us to begin our spiritual journey. And we are beginners every day of our lives. To be 'born again' is the rising from sleep at the start of each day, and the constant awakening from every stolen nap along the way: prayer, the cup of tea we share with God as we recover the energy to take off again.

Becoming Jewish and staying Catholic

One day, with time to kill, I was browsing in a bookshop and came across *Becoming Jewish*, a guide for those who want to convert to Judaism, by Steven Carr Reuben and Jennifer S. Hanin. I found it fascinating, partly for the subject matter (how do you become a Jew?) and partly for the open-mindedness on the part of the authors about which strand of Judaism might appeal to the curious reader. Four separate paths or traditions were described with equal clarity and respect. Becoming Jewish is not just a question about what you have to *believe* but what you have to *do* – learning Hebrew, undergoing circumcision, or various other lifestyle changes. Obviously the more Orthodox the more there is to do and the harder and longer the process.

Those born Jewish do not really have to do anything to remain Jewish, but those choosing to become Jewish have to embrace the new path completely – at least at first. Similarly with Catholicism. The convert is required to affirm all Church teaching; there can be no pages missing from their Catechism. As Father Richard Rohr said, 'You have to start conservative.'

Leafing through that book made me realise again that every Christian has to start (and remain) Jewish; Christianity's foundations are (and remain) the God of Abraham, Isaac and Jacob. While it is perfectly understandable that Jews should consider Christians to be in error it is wholly unacceptable for Christians to see themselves as separate from their Abrahamic roots. This theological truth is something that has begun to be rediscovered only in the past fifty years or so, in the aftermath of the Holocaust and the Second Vatican Council. The role that Christian theology played over the centuries in the creation of anti-Semitism is as indisputable as it is shameful.

A great mistake was made when early followers of Christ saw themselves replacing Judaism with a new chosen people based on ticking the right confessional boxes. The Jewish people's precious insight, and a much misunderstood one, was that God chose them unreservedly: not, in the final analysis, because by doing so He rejected others (and the Jewish Scriptures are full of reasons why that choice was not made based on good behaviour), but that God's connection with humanity was a personal embrace, and that the Chosen People, as a beautiful flower, were meant eventually to fill a vast garden – Abraham's descendants 'as numerous as the stars in the sky and as the sand on the seashore' (Genesis 22:17). Christ's development of this idea, as an observant Jew, was that this choice of God was both personal *and* universal.

The dominance of Roman law and Greek philosophy throughout earlier Christian history now seems a stumbling block not just to interfaith relations but to an understanding of our own faith. Might we find a safer way to preserve the integrity and relevance of Christianity in our present century and beyond at the synagogue as much as at the church?

Is it Christian to single out the Christians?

In the twenty-first century Christians are statistically one of the most persecuted groups in the world. It is often claimed that not enough is said by Western political leaders about the atrocious terrorist killings that take place from time to time, particularly in Pakistan and the Middle East. A gunning down of worshippers during a church service is Terror with a capital T because its aim is intimidation through fear. I'm a weekly churchgoer; it could be me.

Has the response by the West been an example of cowardice as some claim, a politically correct reluctance to support Christians as one of the religious groups most under threat? I am conscious thinking about this that I would be as horrified by an attack on Hindus in their temple, on Tories at their conference, or on students at a rowdy nightclub as I am by violence against Christians – my own group.

If one had to make a list of Christ's most powerful, revolutionary insights one of the most important would be the undoing of that human 'reflex' to want to be part of a special, privileged group or clique. To see Christianity as a club or a cultural identity is to negate its very soul – not to mention the madness of cliques within the cliques when denominations fight and fume. The God Christ preached and lived was one who is Father to all and who views everyone as beloved because everyone was created and is upheld in love. That inclusive insight is Christianity's front-page headline.

We might not like it, but Christians are not God's 'favourites'. We might like even less the fact that God loves terrorists as much as he loves well-behaved little me. This is not to suggest turning a glib, blind eye to evil or injustice, far from it, but it is to suggest that any Christianity worth preserving, defending or celebrating is (if at times with gritted teeth or a broken heart) to strive to forgive to the last breath.

Christendom had over a thousand years to make its point, its mouth close to the only microphone in town. Any strident demand in our post-Christian age for it to be pushed to the front of the queue might well turn out to be counterproductive. A gentler, kinder voice needs to be used, and thereby we might even find a way of changing Terror itself into hope and reconciliation.

The feelings of solidarity and outrage a Christian feels towards those tragically killed in a terrorist attack should be because human beings have been senselessly murdered. The fact that they were Christians is (strangely, radically, life-givingly) beside the point.

Putting the 'Mass' back into Christmas

Slogans about 'putting Christ back into Christmas' are commonly heard each year as Christians try to encourage secular society to remember the religious origins of the season, even though those origins and the traditions associated with their celebration are far from purely Christian and reach back into customs of the winter solstice and other ancient rites.

Although we know that Christ was not born on 25 December, most Christians (especially non-Catholics) fail to realise that the word 'Christmas' actually refers to the Mass on the feast of Christ's birth – Christ's Mass. So even the secular form 'Xmas' retains the inner religious meaning more than it might seem, and the common American use of 'holidays' (Holy Days) for this season is no escape from religious connotations either.

English is actually full of such linguistic incense. 'Knock on wood' in America or 'touch wood' in Britain refers to a relic of the Cross; 'fingers crossed' is making a small sign of the cross for luck; 'short shrift' refers to making a quick confession (to 'shrive' is to undergo that sacrament); 'red-letter days' refers to the major feast days of saints in the Missal or Breviary which were printed in red; 'Adam's apple' – not so hard to swallow; and even some swear words have Catholic origins – 'bloody' is thought by some to be a shortened form of 'by Our Lady'. Oh, and 'goodbye' is an abbreviated version of 'God be with you'.

To 'put Christ back into Christmas' should not mean a return to a religious triumphalism, a reclaiming of a heritage that makes those of different faiths or none feel uncomfortable. Christ in the cave or stable is a challenge to all cosy belief systems, and a poor, unmarried, homeless young woman having her first child in an emergency situation should be a threat to no one. The magic of the Christmas story, whether believed literally, symbolically or seen merely as a fairy story, is its simplicity and its humanity. For many people Christmas has become more a symbol of the way we complicate our lives: the stamps to be stuck, the shopping to be schlepped. An invitation to return to the meaning of Christmas is, perhaps, an invitation to seek afresh our own origins of innocence and simplicity – the real X-factor many of us spend our whole lives longing for.

Christmas carols

Every year, as November draws to a close, those of us who live in cities or towns start to hear Christmas carols. These jingles are usually synthetic – jazzed up, smoothed out, dumbed down – but nevertheless King Wenceslas, the Wise Men and the Christ-child make their appearance annually through the sound systems and speakers of our supermarkets and shopping centres.

Carols are the background noise to the most frantically commercial weeks in the UK's calendar. They shamelessly cooperate with the most rampantly materialistic impulses we have, and yet, ironically, their words recall us to an utter simplicity of lifestyle: a poor, homeless family taking shelter in a cave. Carols 'smell' of Christmas; they are an irreplaceable part of its atmosphere. I'm aware, of course, that cultural context is part of this. I grew up in a village in Cheshire singing these seasonal hymns at school and church. Frosty air, mince pies, decorating the house, sending and receiving cards, presents piled up around the Christmas tree . . . all these combined to create a magical spell for a young boy in England in the 1960s. But I've met people of all ages from very different backgrounds and faiths who have caught the Christmas bug. 'Silent Night' in a dark church lit only by flickering candles can be a moment of repose and wonder for any harassed human being.

Then there's the act of singing itself. 'He who sings prays twice' is attributed to St Augustine. But even without the religious connotations of that saying I still believe that making music is an amplified experience, a poetic response to life, a reaching beyond the everyday: 'Life and light to all he brings, risen with healing in his wings.' Charles Wesley's shining words might originally have been referring to the Son of God but they can also refer to the very tune that gives them voice every season. Music is a bringer of life, of light, of healing. It can seem to give wings to our spirits. And singing carols can be the one time in the year, outside the shower or the football stadium, when people are free to let rip. The uninhibited exercising of vocal cords brings oxygen to more than the lungs.

The theology in many of the Christmas texts we sing can be pretty uncompromising. In that same carol ('Hark the Herald Angels Sing'), as voices strain on the higher notes of Felix Mendelssohn's rousing tune, there appears, 'Veiled in flesh the Godhead see, Hail the incarnate Deity' – no wiggle room there for the passing doubter or unbeliever. But actually I don't think that matters. The truly important message of Christmas and what makes it so perennially touching is its celebration of goodness and simplicity. History is full of gods (and kings and emperors . . . and popes) who display and wield majestic power, benevolently or cruelly. It is less common to observe a ruler who appears to us fresh from the womb, wriggling helplessly in a cave, soiling a makeshift nappy. Purity of dogma seems less pressing when a hungry baby needs feeding.

'What can I give him, poor as I am? Give my heart,' suggests Christina Rossetti in her exquisite carol 'In the Bleak Midwinter'. The idea of giving is central to Christmas, most obviously in the presents we give to others. But, going deeper, we long to give ourselves to those we love. Our only hesitation is our fear that that gift might not be welcome. The message of Christmas suggests that we are loved first and that our meagre gifts are always what is most desired.

Secular Christmas songs can be included in this celebration

because they share the same values of benevolence and generosity. Chestnuts roasting on an open fire are a pleasure to be shared. 'White Christmas' symbolises cheer and joy for all. 'Faithful friends who are dear to us, Gather near to us once more' – sentiments from that most sentimental of seasonal songs made famous by Judy Garland and Frank Sinatra, 'Have Yourself a Merry Little Christmas'. Even the most non-religious of the popular Christmas songs, 'Rudolph the Red-Nosed Reindeer', contains a powerful allegory of the triumph of the underdog. A defect can be the very thing most useful and lovable. Such a reversal of human wisdom is one of the things which makes Christmas so powerful.

Whether you take the Nativity literally or metaphorically, Christmas has a message for everyone. It is a yearly invitation to welcome strangers and outsiders, to care for the weakest among us, to reawaken a spirit of generosity and warmth towards all.

Of course, many people see the whole story as, well, a mere story. But if it *is* a 'tall story' it's one that reaches up to the heavens. A God whom we cannot see becomes One we can smell – the swaddling cloths were presumably for absorption as well as protection. Into a first-century world of swashbuckling myths, of gods towering over humanity with ideals of riches, beauty, heroic strength and will, squishes a slippery baby born to an unmarried mother in an occupied country. Yes, it beggars belief – and not just in its supernatural elements. No king or ruler, claiming to follow this Child, can strut into the stable at Bethlehem with quite the same self-importance as before. The pompous preaching of history's religious leaders – their moral judgements, their confident bluster, their smug 'expertise' – is a mere footprint in the cowpat they narrowly avoid as they approach the manger.

We all begin our lives helpless in a crib. Each year Christmas can enable us to press a reset button of innocence in the midst of our complex, adult experiences. As the branches of the trees are laid bare, so our own rather ludicrous ambitions can be seen more clearly for what they are. Our crowns turn out to be made of tinsel . . . but no matter. We can smile at our little games of power and their ultimate irrelevance. Each year . . . until our last Christmas, when we ourselves return to a manger in our own swaddling clothes, helpless, soiled and emptied out.

'The hopes and fears of all the years are met in thee tonight.' At the end of December every city, every village, every home can become a 'little town of Bethlehem'.

Sacraments and the sugar-plum fairy

'I saw both the *Nutcracker* ballet and *Midsummer Night's Dream* over the weekend. I was completely overwhelmed. We must cling to these artistic experiences and treasure them because they truly replace religion in so many of our lives.' Thus spoke a dear friend of mine during a phone call. It wasn't the moment to suggest the inadequacy of art alone as a moral compass for life (remember the fervent Schubertiades in the log-fire twilights of Auschwitz), but I did comment that both of those masterpieces involve the thrill of magic, the contrast between innocence and experience, the enchantment yet pain of lost childhood and its memories.

After the conversation I started to think of enchantment in a different sense, in a religious sense, in a sacramental sense. That deeply touching experience my friend had had in the theatre was perhaps closer to a religious experience than he thought. Christ was a storyteller and a miracle-worker (let's leave aside for now whether the miracles actually took place), but he was not a theologian. His appeal was magical. He *enchanted* people and drew them after him like some irresistible Pied Piper. The sacraments (external signs of internal grace) are some spells he left behind to remind us of him.

The Reformers said that there are only two sacraments mentioned in the Bible, Baptism and Eucharist (although Luther himself included a third with Penance) and they were right; but they went on to purge them of poetry, chaining them to the written word alone, devoid of mystery. The Catholics claimed that there are seven sacraments, but theologians over the centuries so entangled them with fine points of dogma and tradition that to omit intentionally one gesture of thumb and forefinger in the intricate rubrics of the Mass was enough to send one to hell. The magic circle had become a noose around the neck.

Magic can be threatening because it is uncontrollable. 'How often should I forgive my brother? Seven times?' asked one of Christ's disciples. 'No. Seventy times seven times,' he replied. The spell is cast; the forgiveness is infinite, illogical, dangerous. 'If someone demands your jacket give him your coat too.' The spell is cast; the generosity is infinite, illogical, dangerous. I agree with my friend that the imagination of art gives birth to magic, whether it's Tchaikovsky, Balanchine or Shakespeare waving the wand. But to forgive even once, to offer even a jacket . . . there is the miracle; and there perhaps religion waits in the wings, prompting, encouraging, empowering.

Reformation: the individual or the community?

People argued about religion a lot in the sixteenth century. A disagreement about the smallest details of a doctrine, shared at the wrong time or in the wrong place, could lead to torture and a gruesome death. One subtle and hard-to-pin-down distinction between Catholics and Reformers intrigues me, as I think it can apply to the world of music and concert performance: does the human being relate to God primarily as an individual or through the community known as the Church, and formerly known as the people of Israel?

The individual or the community? Well, it's both of course, but Martin Luther's focus on the individual, which we see reflected in his attributed statement, 'Here I stand, I can do no other', was one of the most important influences in human thought and led eventually to the full flowering of the Enlightenment. Without this idea of the primacy of self-expression or conscience (with its allowance and celebration of the idiosyncratic, the offbeat, the heretical even), my musical world would not exist. Developing a personal voice is essential for a soloist or composer. Take Beethoven. Despite being attached to the rigour of Classical forms, he took delight in bending and breaking them. He was a lapsed Catholic who combined the genius and confidence of individualism with a vision of the universal. He hadn't the slightest fear of questioning authority, however venerable it might be.

With the Abbé Liszt, his Catholicism worn as a cloak around him, the plot thickens. No one developed the idea of artist as individual, as star, more than him. Sitting in profile to the audience, playing from memory, alone on stage, adored by his (mostly female) fans, he was the antithesis of the medieval artist as an invisible servant – of God, of the Church, of society. Indeed Liszt spent the latter half of his life living out the spiritual contradictions of this as he went in and out of retreat, in and out of the limelight. Was his cassock a sign of submission to the Church or a theatrical costume? Probably both.

Is an orchestra an example of Catholic community and a soloist of a Protestant individualism? Is a conductor a kind of authoritarian papal figure or a radical, prophetic voice? Does Bruckner's fervent Catholicism reveal itself in his music? Although it is possible to hear in his vast symphonies a kind of monumental, cathedral-like utterance, we hear too the Austrian composer's reverence for Richard Wagner, a lapsed Lutheran and a textbook example of larger-than-life individualism.

As the future of concerts becomes ever more uncertain, there is a new, pressing need to make a connection with the community as we seek to develop new audiences for the next generation. Promoters now often organise pre- or post-concert talks and orchestras have extensive outreach and education programmes, but all music-lovers need to become evangelists, convincing people that live concerts are a more thrilling experience than sitting alone, ears blocked with headphones.

The individualism that flowed from the Reformation colours every aspect of modern life, but it has its limits. No musician is an island and G. K. Chesterton's description of tradition as the 'democracy of the dead' is apt when we seek to bring to life works from the great canon of masterpieces. The individual or the community? Well, after we've tuned our instruments and the audience has settled in their seats we realise, with joy, that it is both.

Crack!

The Second Vatican Council called the Mass 'the summit towards which the activity of the Church is directed; at the same time it is the font from which all her power flows' (*Sacrosanctum Concilium* 1:10). For Catholics it is there around every corner of their lives: fifty punctuating rest-stops through the year's Sundays, as well as baptisms, confirmations, funerals, marriages . . . and, for many people, that casual midweek Mass caught hastily between a business meeting and a half a sandwich. Libraries of volumes have been written about every aspect of its practice (its liturgy, its theology, its history, its music) over many centuries. It was one of the most hotly disputed topics for debate (and, it has to be said, torture and killing) during the Reformation period – and not just between Catholics and Protestants. Reformers fought bitterly among themselves regarding this issue.

In the course of the centuries, every word, particularly of the 'moment' of consecration has been dissected within a jot and tittle of its life. 'This is my Body': yes, but at which *exact* point does the wafer of wheat and water become a spiritual nuclear bomb? If the priest died before saying the word 'body' (or said just the 'b' of that word), would the elemental change have taken place? Such points seem arcane in the extreme, unless you really do believe what the catechism tells you. Then they could be the most important words of Life heard during your brief life on earth.

There is one detail among all the details – one grain of sand on the beach – that I've never seen discussed, except in passing (although I include it in my novel *The Final Retreat*, mused on by the fictional priest, Father Joseph); and it's a point that seems to me of greater significance than a grain of sand – indeed, more like a cornerstone of the whole devotional building. I've been to thousands of Masses in my life so far, and something bothers me every time. At the absolute central point of importance, the moment of consecration, the priest tells us that Christ did something . . . but then we don't do it.

Here are all the versions of the moment in question in the Bible:

> While they were eating, Jesus took a loaf of bread, and after blessing it *he broke it*, gave it to the disciples, and said, 'Take, eat; this is my body.' (Matthew 26:26)
> While they were eating, he took a loaf of bread, and after blessing it *he broke it*, gave it to them, and said, 'Take, eat; this is my body.' (Mark 14:22)

Then he took a loaf of bread, and when he had given thanks, *he broke it* and gave it to them, saying, 'This is my body, which is given for you. Do this in remembrance of me.' (Luke 22:19)

For I received from the Lord what I also handed on to you, that the Lord Jesus on the night when he was betrayed took a loaf of bread, and when he had given thanks, *he broke it* and said, 'This is my body that is broken for you. Do this in remembrance of me.' (1 Corinthians 11:23–4)

Here is the same moment in the Tridentine Rite:

Qui pridie quam pateretur, accepit panem in sanctas ac venerabiles manus suas, et elevatis oculis in cælum ad te Deum Patrem suum omnipotentem, tibi gratias agens, benedixit, fregit, deditque discipulis suis, dicens: Accipite, et manducate ex hoc omnes: Hoc est enim Corpus Meum.
(Who, the day before he suffered, took bread into His Holy and venerable hands, and having lifted up His eyes to heaven, to Thee, God, His Almighty Father, giving thanks to Thee, blessed it, broke it, and gave it to His disciples, saying: Take and eat ye all of this: For this is my body.)

He 'broke the bread', but we don't – at least not at the same moment. In fact, the priest waits until the Agnus Dei to break the consecrated wafer, which is quite a while after the Consecration. Indeed it is after the Eucharistic Prayer, after the Lord's Prayer, after the Sign of Peace – just before Communion. Yet it is quite clear from all the sources, scriptural and liturgical, that the piece of bread at the Last Supper was broken *before* the words were said.

Does this matter? Let us go in imagination to the upper room and watch Christ as he performs this action. It is the Feast of Unleavened Bread in the Jewish calendar, the Passover. He is not holding a wafer and speaking words over it, into it: no, it is much more dramatic than that. In fact, it's pure, brilliant, utterly compelling theatre. *'This'* (breaking the unleavened, crisp bread) 'is my body.' It's the *action* of breaking the bread, not the bread itself to which his words seem to apply. *This* is what will happen to my body: *crack!* He is acting out his self-giving sacrifice in a sort of mime.

And it doesn't end there. *'This'* (pouring the red wine into the cup) 'is my blood.' This is what will happen to my blood. It will pour out from my hands and my feet, and especially from my side. I don't think it is the fermented grape juice sitting at the bottom of the chalice that is so much the object of his 'this', but rather the action of pouring out blood-like wine, capable of staining Christ's garments at supper as it will stain them when the lance pierces his side the following afternoon.

He adds, 'Do this in memory of me.' Do what? Break, crack the bread. This is truly symbolism of a sacrifice more than of a meal. When we *do this*, says St Paul, we 'proclaim his death' (1 Corinthians 11:26). Ah, indeed. By cracking the wafer we literally show forth (act out) his death in the mime he left us, and thus we renew his sacrifice. Furthermore, when St Paul complains of the Corinthians indulging in a meal without 'discerning the body' (1 Corinthians 11:29), maybe he meant it literally. They were concentrating on the supper – on the eating of bread and drinking of wine – rather than on the *breaking* of bread and *pouring out* of wine. They had sidelined the significance of the dramatic re-enactment left to us by Christ – in his broken body, in his shed blood.

I think this is not just a matter of semantics: it changes completely and significantly our approach to the Mass. First, it needn't and shouldn't affect our belief that something happens to the substance of bread and wine, but perhaps it makes such a transformation less of a magical act and more an integrated part of the liturgical experience. It makes tactile sense of the physical properties of the elements chosen by Christ for his unique act of remembrance. It also has an ecumenical dimension. It explores a profound symbolism, which would have intrigued Luther, Cranmer and Calvin. It moves away from specifying too absolutely *when* the change takes place, which might appeal to the Orthodox Churches who find Rome's legalism a stumbling block. For Catholics, it renews the understanding of the Mass as a sacrifice, as well giving us an example of the supreme liturgist in action . . . Jesus Christ.

There is one moment in Scripture I haven't yet mentioned – the account of the journey to Emmaus after the Resurrection, related in chapter 24 of St Luke's Gospel. It is a fitting note on which to finish because Christ's conversation left the disciples in the dark, even though 'their hearts burned within them', and it wasn't through eating or drinking that their eyes were opened. No, before the risen Christ disappeared from their sight, we are told that 'they came to recognise him in the breaking of the bread'.

The ghastly story of Lazarus

During Lent we hear read at Mass the story of the raising of Lazarus from the dead by Christ. No need to relate it here; it's easily accessible in chapter 11 of St John's Gospel.

Thousands of books and articles and theses have been written on the four Gospels, their differences in style, of authorship, and of the 'voice' of Christ, which distinguishes the three Synoptics (seeing together) from St John (a different view). Not even a thousand words here, but two specific problems I have with the Lazarus story: first, I don't think it could have happened; and, second, the way it's told reveals a side of Jesus's character that is deeply unpleasant and therefore, for me, unlikely to be authentic.

Let's take the second point first. Jesus is shown displaying private grief in public in the shortest verse (John 11:35) in the Bible: 'Jesus wept.' No problem with that. To see the human side of Jesus is something to be treasured. But looking more closely, it strikes a false and duplicitous chord. He weeps over his dead friend and then (knowing he will do it only moments later) he raises him to life again. The weeping has to be a pretence.

He's already played games with his disciples earlier in the chapter by suggesting that Lazarus is only asleep not dead and that he will go to wake him up. But then he snaps back to reality: 'Lazarus is dead, and for your sake I am glad I was not there, so that you may believe.' This is strange; moody, petulant, theatrical. He lets him die so he can bring him to life, 'so you may believe'. Then he pretends he's mourning his dear friend, and then calls him out of the tomb. The whole episode shows a manipulative person playing cat and mouse with those who trust him implicitly – lying even, if not in words then in actions.

Beyond this, the question remains: did Jesus raise a man from the dead called Lazarus? Internal evidence apart (and St John likes to show how careful he's being with the 'facts' – we're told that Bethany is less than two miles from Jerusalem, and given the detail of the stink of decay after four dead days in the tomb), this is the most prominent, public miracle recorded in the New Testament. It was witnessed by a large crowd and, according to the author, its effect was so powerful that it became one of the reasons the chief priests wanted to arrest Jesus. People were following Christ because they'd seen the spectacle of his raising Lazarus to new life. If this were true, it is completely inconceivable that the episode would not even be hinted at, never mind described, in the rest of the New Testament. Beyond all occurrences related from Christ's birth to his death this miracle proved power and divinity. But it's simply not mentioned elsewhere, only in this one place.

The Gospels are fascinating documents creating a new literary form. They are not straight biographies. They do not attempt to give a chronological or exhaustive string of facts and details. They aim to convey a life-affirming message that excited their authors and is meant to excite us. And they were intended to be evidential documents proving points of supreme significance. If Lazarus were truly raised from the dead, Matthew, Mark and Luke (and Paul, whose epistles predate the Gospels) would have known about it and nothing on earth would have been able to stop them telling us about it.

Assumptions about the Assumption

One day on tour, with groans, stiff joints, and a sour stomach, I hauled myself out of bed to go to an early Mass, despite having a morning dress rehearsal followed by an afternoon concert. It was the Feast of the Assumption and my lethargic, bad mood was intensified by the priest who turned out to be one of those clerics immersed in the sort of Catholicism unquestioned until the 1960s. He spent a lot of the sermon quoting Pope Pius XII who, in 1950, defined the doctrine the Feast was commemorating. The Pontiff's ominous declaration that those who wilfully refused to believe it were no longer in a state of grace (and thus on the way to Hell) did not lift my spirits, despite the early-morning sun streaming through the stained-glass windows.

Believe *it* – what? The problem with this doctrine is that it is so nebulous and vague that one might wonder what sort of denial would actually be the cause of such a loss of grace. Pius declined to declare whether or not Mary died before she was assumed body and soul into Heaven; and no theologian has fully been able to define what the body means in post-earthly, eternal terms. It left me thinking that the defining of this dogma in 1950 was all about power – the power of the Papacy in a difficult moment of world history (the spread of communism, nuclear bombs, rebellious youth), demanding obedience, even if we were not told what we were meant to be obeying. We were asked to affirm the messenger rather than his message.

Too often the Catholic Church has taken fluid devotional ideas and customs and tried to bake them into dogmas or doctrines. Limbo was one of these and it was eventually cast aside as indigestible; one wonders if purgatory (another loose and undefined idea *almost* but not quite found in Scripture) might not be far behind? The Orthodox Churches speak of Mary's 'dormition', her going to sleep, and they wisely refrain from further comment. But pigeonholes are beloved in the Vatican, and if the birds remain quiet they are well fed and looked after.

The writer Anne Rice wrote about leaving Christianity behind while holding on to Christ. That is a complex topic (and my attendance at early Mass indicates that I don't yet share her conclusions), but there do seem to me to be some who have left Christ behind while holding on to Christianity.

The three greatest fears

There are three fears that most humans have and that Christ faced during his Passion: suffering, disgrace and death. Almost everything in our lives that causes distress or terror can be traced back to one of these three roots. Whether you regard the story of Christ's death as a legend or as a true event, as irrelevant or as central to existence, its meaning involves an innocent man grasping these three nettles in ways that might help everyman to grasp them too.

Why do these three things make us so afraid? I think it's because they threaten to negate three vital and instinctive desires: the desire for joy and flourishing (suffering), the desire to be loved and accepted (disgrace) and the fundamental desire to live (death).

Physical suffering is something we all understand, even if its distribution among the human race seems grossly unfair most of the time. From a twinge in the dentist's chair to the most excruciating pains of torture it sounds a strident chord we instinctively long to silence. Mental suffering, ranging from overtiredness to the horror of a severe nervous breakdown, is much harder to understand. It is an invisible nettle, consciously painful but often with no visible wounds.

From the time we are born we learn by imitation, reward and punishment. Our youth is shaped at home and at school by these techniques of control as we are formed into members of a family, a community, and much of our adulthood is spent trying to undo the negative aspects of this. We habitually do things in order to please, to be praised, flattered, honoured, approved . . . and the fear of being ridiculed or despised is probably behind every neurosis.

And then it all ends with death. We understand somewhat the death of others, the bereavement of family and friends, but our own death? *Me* about to become 'un-Me'? We can't really take it in. Whether we believe that the end of life is the simple snuffing out of a candle, or the lighting up of a new house containing many mansions, the very idea of it is ungraspable, like mercury sliding across our palm.

Good Friday: Christ undergoing *suffering* – flogged, punched in the face, struck over the head with a pole, crowned with brambles.

Good Friday: Christ undergoing *disgrace* – mocked as so-called 'King of the Jews' when his own religious leaders were calling for his death; someone who claimed power to raise the dead and now hung naked and helpless on a cross.

Good Friday: Christ undergoing *death* – even facing doubt in the presence, if not the existence, of God.

If God can suffer, if God can be disgraced, if God can have a problem believing in God then maybe all of us have a chance, especially those who no longer feel able even to ask the questions. And if Good Friday is not the end of the story . . .

Is he musical?

If I may use this quaint euphemism, whispered in the late-Victorian years when even homophobia dare not speak its name, I actually did know I was 'musical' before I knew I was musical. From the age of four onwards I was deeply, vitally aware that I was attracted emotionally and romantically to boys rather than girls. Of course the explicitly sexual dimension of such an attraction came later, but I knew, when it did come, that it was a branch sprouting from the same root that in turn had grown from a seed at the oldest, deepest part of my being.

It is strange looking back at those childhood years where memories are muddled like crumpled papers at the back of musty drawers. I had no traumatic experiences – no dead spiders – but I did share with most homosexual children growing up at that time (the mid-1960s) a strange instinct for survival that meant hiding, denying, pretending, and hoping that somehow it could be different. The delicate awakening of tenderness, before 'homosexual' was a word known or pronounced, had to be crushed in the panic of recognition – waking into a nightmare rather than out of one. It really was like pulling the flower out of the ground as it bloomed, the torn roots remaining deep in the soil.

One of my greatest fears in early life was that I would be discovered to be gay – by friends, neighbours, teachers or relatives. It was a fear that grew as I grew, and as I felt the sting of playground jokes and savoured the stale, sour comments of grown-ups. It was holding on to a terrible secret: an insect captured inside a jam jar where the lid could come off at any moment. The default setting in society at that time was that in revelation one faced rejection. It is still the case in many parts of the world today. Silence is death; but speech is worse. Where most parents plan and wait impatiently for their children's wedding day, for the same parents the revelation that a son or daughter is gay can mean an end to communication, a banning from the home, an erasing from the family. The gay child can find that he or she has lost *two* families: the parental home and the chance to form a future relationship protected and nurtured by society.

The first message of explicit negativity I heard towards being gay came from my religious beliefs as I entered my teenage years in an Evangelical church. The teaching was that something growing within me (which *was* me) was disgusting and must be kept quiet, cured, squashed, punished . . . anything would do. Reading my Bible I would fear opening the scorching pages of Romans 1 or 1 Corinthians 6. These brief passages shine with a terrible light for a gay person, until we look at what they aim to illumine rather than at the light itself. Just as we can now see clearly the inadequacy of St Paul's teaching on women or slavery and excuse his historical limitations, so we need not blame him for his lack of understanding of the concept of same-sex love. He was looking through a window at first-century Rome and Corinth with first-century Jewish eyes from a perspective of religious and cultural separation that had lasted for centuries. It is virtually impossible that he could have seen gay couples in faithful, committed partnerships, and it is certain that he saw all kinds of orgiastic, abusive behaviour that would often have been linked to pagan rites and beliefs. What else could he have written in his situation?

When I became a Catholic the teaching on homosexuality remained the same, although being unmarried now became a respectable, even glamorous option. Priests, nuns and monks were all able to live safely without being asked, 'Why aren't you married?' or 'Have you got a girlfriend?' I even considered the priesthood myself, partly to avoid having to answer honestly such terrifying questions. Yet I remained a musician, accepting the Church's prohibition, buried under my work, avoiding 'occasions of sin', destroying certain friendships before there was any chance of them developing into anything intimate – in many ways a happy yet somehow shrunken life.

It was when reading Pope John Paul II's book *Love and Responsibility*, published in 1960 when he was an auxiliary bishop in Kraków, that I first began to think again about this issue. You cannot offer such a radiant vision of love and human relationships to your readers and then exclude those who happen to have 'green eyes'. Once you have affirmed, as he did controversially and courageously for a Catholic bishop of his time, the sacredness of the human body and its self-gift in the sexual act, you have opened a floodgate of recognition for all who have both bodies to reverence and 'selves' to give.

'It is not good for the man to be alone,' said God in the opening chapters of the Bible and of human history – the one blemish in an otherwise unblemished world, where everything was 'very good'. Such an affirmation of companionship at the beginning of time is fresh and inspiring still. Combined with new discoveries about sexual orientation in the natural world, it opens up a radical challenge to previously confident assessments of the morality of gay relationships. To share a life of intimacy with another is the way the vast majority of men and women, regardless of their gender preference, are meant to live whole and holy lives. Such relationships are about more than making babies. They are about making love, because to do so is to be fully human, with sensitive, 'musical' hearts attuned to vibrations that animals may hear but only men and women can hold. Celibacy is of value only as an affirmation of what is renounced – the best given up freely because it is the best gift one can give. If celibacy is not rare, and a totally free donation, it has the whiff of something slightly perverse about it – literally, 'contrary to nature'.

We are subject to natural law as part of creation, but we are also able to contemplate it and relish it. It is the great epiphany of reality: what is actually there, not what we would like to be there, or what our forebears have told us is there. It can be full of surprises and it has no favourites. The one who confidently claims natural law as an ally in arguing for the sanctity of life might end up finding it an annoying foe in a discussion on homosexuality. When the world in which we live tells a different story from what we were taught, we eventually have to break free. It isn't so much that law changes, but that the Church (from St Paul onwards) simply has not had the vocabulary to discuss an issue it neither named nor understood. (The idea that a person could actually *be* homosexual, rather than a badly behaved heterosexual, has been accepted by the Catholic Church only in the past thirty years or so.) Law is living and flexible: always growing, adapting, changing shape; never abandoning its roots but never rigid either. Christ not only boiled theology down to the simple statement 'God is love', he also distilled the complex religious laws of his time to love of that same God and of neighbour as oneself. The spiritual liberty and simplicity resulting from this new, unified vision led, in theory at least, to the breaking down of the divisive barriers between men and women, slave and free person, Jew and Gentile. It is tragic that it took Christians at least 1900 years even to begin to explore or live this freedom in practice. The prison gates were open but we remained inside, either cowering in the corner or standing with arms outstretched, blocking the exit. Both responses came from fear, and both were betrayals of the Christian message.

Ultimately the only real argument against homosexual equality is a belief that God has told us it is wrong. All the other reasons given (destruction of the family, seduction of the young, unnatural behaviour, a genetic disorder like alcoholism) are attempts to find a common, secular currency to barter for what is an a priori, religious judgement. But the coins are fake and are being rendered obsolete by common sense and daily experience. Actually I believe that the religious arguments are wrong too, and that, as with slavery, the churches will have to re-evaluate their teaching on this issue. That will probably take decades, but in the meantime the churches cannot expect gay, non-Christians in a secular world to abstain from sexual relationships from their teenage years up to the end of their lives. They cannot exclude those same people from either marriage or a formal, legal commitment and then complain that such relationships are unstable. Straight couples are no strangers to marital collapse, even with the cement of children and society's affirmation to encourage them to hold firm, so why should we expect even higher standards from gays?

To use 'musical' as a euphemism for homosexual is rather flattering when you think about it. It suggests a sensitivity, a creativity, an ability to attune to beauty. Of course it was originally an ironic, snide use of the term. A real man might whistle *at* work, or bawl a song in the pub *after* work, but to be touched or moved by music below the surface seemed weak, lacking in the moral fibre of that tough, tearless type that was the male ideal. It is not an accident that music and the arts were always a tolerant environment for gay men. It was a world where an appreciation of the 'feminine' was not seen as weakness, and where strength did not have to manifest itself in violence and coarseness. (It also became a safe place for gay people to hide and to flourish among like-minded friends in the years – not that long ago – when blackmail and prison were an ever-possible threat.)

Perhaps we can go even further. The modern performing artist is really a direct descendant of the village entertainer, found in the earliest human communities. This person, at least while on stage, was an outsider, someone disguised or different, looked on with admiration and envy, or even fear and discomfort, as he transported his audience to realms of fantasy, amusement or glamour, away from the mundane and humdrum. The entertainment involved could be singing, dancing, acting, conjuring, storytelling . . . a whole host of different things. It was the perfect place to indulge a sense of the extravagant and exuberant, as well as offering ideal camouflage. A mask, a costume, an affecting melody, a graceful leap were all perfect alibis for those whose affections danced to a different tune – a Scheherazade-like escape from the 1001 knights in the community ready to pronounce and enact the death sentence. If the gay artist could hold the audience captive he might avoid being captured himself. This is not to suggest that gay people are inherently more sensitive or artistic than straights, but everyone draws on a central emotional core in the act of creativity, and when the normal outlet of intimacy is blocked, the heart will find alternative ways to express itself, sometimes with enormous intensity.

Since the start of the twenty-first century there has been

an increasing impatience with the lying and loneliness of the closet, and gay people have found a new vocabulary of love and confidence. They want to commit themselves to each other in mature, stable partnerships or marriages. The eccentric bachelor uncles and spinster aunts are not content any more to be guests at other people's homes; they want to host parties with their own families – and what fun parties they turn out to be. The floodgates are open, but we find that the water is good; we can swim, we needn't fear, we can embrace and be embraced by the waves. People are realising increasingly that their best friends, their children's best friends, their neighbours and colleagues, their politicians and admired public figures are gay. Gay liberation will have arrived when, as a term and concept, it has become archaic. That will be the point when understanding and tolerance have been transformed into the familiarity of friendship – the love that has no need to speak its name.

In earlier times . . .

Same-sex marriage is still a problem for many and an abomination for some. Aside from the moral issues relating to prohibitive religious texts there is an uneasy sense for many that it is a change from the way things have always been done, that somehow one of humanity's treasures is in danger of being devalued. Has marriage always meant something that is now to be unmeant? I don't think so because . . .

In earlier times, indeed for most of recorded human history, marriages were arranged to continue a bloodline, to obtain the neighbouring farm, to curry favour with an enemy. Money was the principal motivation, and the lack of a dowry for a woman often meant the inability to marry.

In earlier times for male monarchs teenagers were the
   preferred spouse. The first wife of Richard II (1367–1400)
   was sixteen when they married and his second wife was
   only seven. These were sacramental marriages when the
   Catholic Church had full control of such matters at the
   height of Christendom's power.
In earlier times people had lots of children because they
   needed to, for financial reasons and because so many of
   them died in infancy.
In earlier times life expectancy for adults was low and to be
   married for twenty years was a lifetime. You had children,
   then you died.
In earlier times marriage presupposed that women were
   weak, without rights, without education, without jobs
   and without choice of spouse. Indeed, the word 'husband'
   implies someone in charge. It's derived from Old Norse
   húsbóndi, 'master of a house', and the original sense
   of the verb was to till or cultivate the land.

So when someone claims that gay marriage is an abuse of language, or at least a change in the way marriage is understood,
they are right.

Sodom and Gomorrah: straight,
upside down, inside out

There are two stories about Sodom and Gomorrah in the first
book of the Bible. Here I'm talking about the other one, not the
one about homosexuality (which is not actually about homosexuality anyway) but the wonderful, semi-comic bargaining
exchange between Abraham and God. One can almost see the
third-rate actor warming to his role as he tries all his persuasive

skills to change the mind of the Boss: 'If I may be so bold . . . if I will not anger my Lord', an eye rolled towards the audience.

The Cities of the Plain are to be destroyed. 'If there are fifty, forty-five, forty, thirty, twenty, ten good men there, will you spare it?' pleads Abraham, as if reducing his merchandise in some cosmic clearance sale. His wheedling is to no avail. No good men could be found (perhaps they should have tried women) and the Boss orders fire and brimstone, sufficient for full destruction. A Hiroshima moment.

It's a nightmare passage for the fundamentalist. Surely this conversation cannot literally have happened like this? It makes sense only as both a parable and as an early step in the learning curve from a primitive understanding of God as vengeful to an eye-opening (soul-opening) view of God as compassionate and therefore as *approachable* – a view now commonplace in the three religions that claim Abraham as father. At least this 'tyrant' will engage in a conversation. Maybe next time we can persuade him . . .

But then there is another parable. In St Luke's Gospel another Jewish teacher unfolds another outrageous tale. 'Suppose one of you has a hundred sheep and loses one of them. Doesn't he leave the ninety-nine in the open country and go after the lost sheep *until he finds it*?' Wait a minute. Abraham was hoping that ten goodies would produce a merciful change of heart. Jesus is claiming that God's heart is already so merciful that rescuing one baddie is worth risking the safety of the ninety-nine goodies. This is Sodom upside-down.

But in our times the story of the destruction of Sodom and Gomorrah has been reversed in a different, darker way: Sodom inside out. In Auschwitz God appeared to destroy the good men while keeping intact the city and the evildoers – at least for far too long. This monstrous injustice and suffering has sown doubt in the hearts not just of fundamentalists but of all human beings of faith and none. Elie Wiesel famously dug deep into this mystery in his book *Night*:

> Then came the march past the victims. The two men were no longer alive. Their tongues were hanging out, swollen and bluish. But the third rope was still moving: the child, too light, was still breathing . . . And so he remained for more than half an hour, lingering between life and death, writhing before our eyes. And we were forced to look at him at close range. He was still alive when I passed him. His tongue was still red, his eyes not yet extinguished.
>
> Behind me, I heard the same man asking: 'For God's sake, where is God?' And from within me, I heard a voice answer: 'Where He is? This is where – hanging here from this gallows . . .'

Such a story deserves a period of silence after it, but permit me a short coda. Archbishop Desmond Tutu had his own Abrahamic moment during one of the regular angry arguments in the Anglican Communion about the issue of homosexuality when he claimed he would rather go to Hell than worship a homophobic God. I was impressed and began to wonder whether, instead of bargaining, Abraham should simply have said to God, 'If you won't spare Sodom then I'm going down there right now and you can destroy me along with them if you wish.'

When God in our stories and parables begins behaving with compassion, there's a good chance we will do so too because we will finally have heard the still small voice above the fire of human vengeance and the earthquake of human cruelty (1 Kings 19:11–13).

Abortion: can I go there?

Dr Kermit Gosnell, a former abortion provider, is serving life imprisonment without the possibility of parole plus thirty years. He was accused of performing illegal abortions, killing live (sometimes screaming) babies by inserting a pair of scissors into the back of their necks. When police raided his premises they found unimaginable levels of filth with severed body parts in milk jugs, in orange-juice cartons and even in cat-food containers. Women had been left bleeding on blankets, medical equipment was outdated, untested and encrusted with dust . . . oh, and a flea-ridden cat was found wandering around from room to room.

When this case was in the news I was asked accusingly by a couple of people why I'd not made any comment on this case, either in my blog or on Twitter. They suggested that the lack of sufficient coverage or interest in the press was the result of a 'liberal' conspiracy. Indeed, I had heard nothing about Gosnell and I thought it was surprising that something so luridly sensational and so macabre (morality aside) had not become daily front-page news, but I didn't think that social media was the place to discuss such a sensitive and complex topic. 'So write something about it on your blog and about abortion in general,' challenged one person. So I did.

I am not a journalist and I spend only a few minutes a day reading the news but as one accuser's anger with me rose I began to get a glimpse why, as unspeakable and evil as this story was, some people in the media wanted to speak less rather than more about it. Furthermore, it is not impossible that legal justice itself could have been affected by letting abusive protestors appear to win their case. 'I told you so' is never an easy argument by which to be influenced, and when truth stares us in the face we can still turn away.

About twenty-five years ago I read about some pro-life activists and researchers in America (I wish I could remember the name of the organisation) who had begun to wonder why their cause was so unsuccessful. Why was abortion legal in virtually all the developed countries of the world? Why did otherwise reasonable, kind, decent, compassionate, hard-working doctors still refer women for terminations? And, more to the point, why did those women not see that what they were doing was taking the life of an unborn human being, their own child? In the course of their study they made some interesting discoveries. Women *did* know what was going on when they sought to end their pregnancies, but a more powerful instinct kicked in: to keep the child was seen subconsciously as some sort of suicide. Having an abortion was like an extreme kind of self-defence; the foetus seemed to them an aggressor threatening to take away their life. These researchers realised that the old style of pro-life activism – accusing, morally absolutist, aiming to shock, aiming to shame – was ineffective, even counter-productive, because it ignored a deeper psychological truth about the mind as well as the body of a pregnant woman. When self-defence is involved reason rarely matters.

Of course, abortion is not just a medical issue. It touches on sex and on religion, both potatoes of the hotter variety. Most, though not all, of those who oppose all abortions do so from a religious viewpoint. They believe that the foetus has an immortal soul from the first moment of its conception and thus deliberately to destroy that life is murder. I think that without religious faith it is hard to accept a zygote as equivalent in value to a fully formed child. I understand that a non-religious person is going to see a scale of development in the nine months of pregnancy just as, in law, there is a scale of seriousness and culpability in criminal acts.

And then there's the question of miscarriages. Around one

in five confirmed pregnancies end this way, not to mention the countless millions of earlier miscarriages that appear in a tampon or toilet bowl. Human life might be precious to God but it's often messy, and to destroy the life of a foetus or a mother is not unknown in the 'Divine Plan'. We might cause unplanned pregnancies but the Creator seems to permit millions of unplanned terminations. It's not that people who support abortion think that it's ever a *good* thing to end a pregnancy; rather they think it's a *worse* thing to let it proceed: weighing the balance of rights, weighing the balance of suffering. As a Catholic I have a problem with that logic but I see its logic for someone who doesn't have religious faith. And I see that any discussion of this issue that doesn't engage respectfully with that difference of perspective is doomed to fail.

Nevertheless, even without a supernatural perspective, we all draw *some* lines in the sand. Everyone would accept that an hour-old child wriggling in its mother's arms should not be killed. But wind back the clock . . . How many seconds, minutes, hours, days, weeks? Where is the line? On which Thursday at 8.53 a.m. does this lump of flesh become a human being? In 1990 the UK law changed the legal limit for an abortion from 28 weeks to 24, and, because of the increasing viability of survival of a foetus at this lower figure, there has been talk of another decrease to 20 weeks. If this is about saving lives more than scoring points (on either side of the debate), this seems to me to be a reasonable progression. One of the uncomfortable facts in the Gosnell case was that if some of the babies he killed (and for which he was convicted of murder) had still been in their mother's wombs, he would have been legally protected. Can we really allow our law to be as myopic and morally contradictory as that? Can just a few inches and the hiding wall of a stomach make something acceptable that otherwise would be first-degree murder?

No one actually wants to have an abortion, and everyone, from mothers to doctors to politicians, would be happy if the procedure were never carried out. But an extreme case such as Gosnell is not a moment for pro-lifers to start pouring out vitriol on the medical profession or the media to try to change minds and laws. Such an attitude hasn't worked for fifty years now and in countries where abortion is actually illegal it is still common. So how do we better prevent unwanted pregnancies? How do we admit that science has moved on and that the understanding of the viability of life might require a change of policy? How do we create a safe, loving environment where vulnerable women can be listened to and supported? How do we work in a secular society, in the words of President Bill Clinton, for a time when abortion is 'safe, legal and rare'? How can we agree to differ and yet move forward?

Why haven't you written anything about Gosnell? Well, I did. A frightful case like this is a moment when attitudes on both sides could harden, or when both sides could begin to talk.

A light that is so lovely

We do not draw people to Christ by loudly discrediting what they believe, by telling them how wrong they are and how right we are, but by showing them a light that is so lovely that they want with all their hearts to know the source of it.

This quotation is from the book *Walking on Water* by the American writer Madeleine L'Engle, who is best known for her science fiction novel *A Wrinkle in Time*. I came across it by chance and it struck a great, powerful, comforting, lovable bell. 'A light that is so lovely' – well, it's been called the 'Gospel', a word meaning 'good news'. The problem is that the news Christians so often want to tell you seems (at least to this feeble Christian) to be far from good, and, as the twenty-first century hurtles along, hardly news any more either.

L'Engle's words are reminiscent of a phrase attributed to St Francis of Assisi: 'Preach the Gospel at all times and occasionally use words.' Another Francis, born in Argentina, demonstrated the effectiveness of this insight during his papacy. Apart from his oft-(mis-)quoted, 'Who am I to judge?', few of his statements are remembered, but people are aware of a 'light that is so lovely' in the simplicity of his lifestyle, his practical debunking of papal pomposity (the descendants of a fisherman should not live in palaces) and his straightforwardness and humour.

I'd like to go a little further. It seems to me that if Christians happen to discover this lovely light outside the walls of Christianity, it should be cause for celebration, not for an awkward and embarrassed fudge. Throughout the Gospels the lovely light appears exactly where we *least* expect to find it: in prostitutes, in sinners, in 'heretics' (the Samaritans), in outsiders (coarse shepherds and cynical tax collectors), in the poor, the sick, the abandoned . . . and it seems to be manifestly absent in the religious types, especially in their leaders. It has no copyright.

And the final clincher occurs in the famous parable of the sheep and the goats. 'Whatever you do to the least of my brothers and sisters you do to me,' said Christ, describing various works of charity: satisfying the hungry and thirsty, visiting the sick and imprisoned, clothing the naked. What is astonishing about this parable is that those whom Christ praises for their acts of charity were unaware that they were doing anything 'holy'. They simply responded to human need, and the need of humans for tenderness and love. If we're going to believe the New Testament, an atheist showing compassion trumps a Christian neglecting to do so. Christ turns religion on its head, but then institutional Christianity so often puts its feet back on the ground again.

Christ's radical iconoclasm is good news to me and is truly a light so lovely that I want with all my heart to know its source even if I don't care that much about its name. I'm not arguing for a dismantling of organised faith: it is through the human communities (churches) who hand on and try to live the wisdom (writings, traditions) of the source that we hear the perennial message in the first place. The risk of merely 'doing our own thing' can mean that we're left with nothing *but* our own thing. And unless we continue to be open to seeing things upside down, we shall probably end up not seeing them the right way up.

One of the Jesuit methods of meditation described in St Ignatius's Spiritual Exercises is to imagine Christ talking to us in concrete situations of time and place. I'm writing this on a plane and the seat next to me is, strangely, not empty any more . . .

You are loved now, as you are, nothing to change, whatever you've done, however little you've tried in the past, however hopeless a better future seems – loved because you were created in love and for love.

I did not come into this world to start another religion: and faith is not theological orthodoxy but radical trust – to the end, despite everything, beyond death, even when trust itself seems impossible.

Please don't take too seriously those who call themselves Christians; they often get my message wrong and their behaviour gets it wronger.

Religion is dead, leaving not so much a corpse as an empty tomb surrounded with a light so lovely, and with blessings as free and as universal as the very air we breathe.

A FINAL REFLECTION

To write is to have read.

More: to speak is to have
Listened, a conversation
With others and with the
Past, reflections frozen into
Words about things which
Flow beyond words.

Seeds flying across my
Garden across many seasons;
Ideas received, embraced,
Rejected, changed . . .
Always changing. Seeds which
Drift away or which settle
Deep down, which grow then
Scatter, branches shaken, down
Driven across the next fence.

Art's stage whisper; the perennial
Communication of music and more.

STEPHEN HOUGH: DISCOGRAPHY
1985–2018

Piano Solo

Beethoven, *see* Stephen Hough in Recital and In the Night

Berg, *see* Tsontakis: Man of Sorrows; Berg: Piano Sonata; Webern:
Variations

York Bowen: Piano Music
Hyperion, 1996

Brahms: Sonata in F minor op. 5 & Four Ballades op. 10
Hyperion, 2001

Britten: Music for one and two pianos
Ronan O'Hora, piano
EMI, 1991 (also included in various Britten collections)

Chopin: The Complete Waltzes
Hyperion, 2011

Chopin: Four Ballades & Four Scherzos
Hyperion, 2004

Chopin: Late Masterpieces
(includes Sonata no. 3 in B minor op. 58)
Hyperion, 2010

Copland, *see* New York Variations

Corigliano, *see* New York Variations

Debussy: Piano Music
Hyperion, 2018

Franck: Piano Music
Hyperion, 1997

Grieg: Lyric Pieces
Hyperion, 2015

In the Night

(mixed recital, including Hough: Sonata no. 2 [*Notturno luminoso*]
   and Schumann Carnival op. 9)

Hyperion, 2014

New York Variations

(works by John Corigliano, Aaron Copland, Ben Weber and George
   Tsontakis)

Hyperion, 1998

The Piano Album

(mixed recital)

EMI, 1993

Russian Piano Music

(mixed recital, including Prokofiev: Sonata no. 6)

ASV, 1985

Stephen Hough's Dream Album

(mixed recital)

Hyperion, 2018

Stephen Hough's English Piano Album

(mixed recital)

Hyperion, 2002

Stephen Hough's French Album

(mixed recital)

Hyperion, 2012

Stephen Hough's New Piano Album

(mixed recital)

Hyperion, 1999

The Stephen Hough Piano Collection

(sampler)

Hyperion, 2005

Stephen Hough in Recital
(includes Beethoven: Sonata in C minor op. 111)
Hyperion, 2009

Stephen Hough's Spanish Piano Album
(mixed recital)
Hyperion, 2006

Webern, *see* Tsontakis: Man of Sorrows; Berg: Piano Sonata;
  Webern: Variations

Works for Piano and Orchestra

Brahms: Piano Concertos 1 & 2
BBC Symphony Orchestra
Andrew Davis, conductor
EMI, 1991

Brahms: The Piano Concertos
Mozarteumorchester Salzburg
Mark Wigglesworth, conductor
Hyperion, 2013

Dvořák & Schumann: Piano Concertos
City of Birmingham Symphony Orchestra
Andris Nelsons, conductor
Hyperion, 2016

Grieg, *see* Liszt & Grieg: The Piano Concertos

Hummel: Piano Concertos
English Chamber Orchestra
Bryden Thomson, conductor
Chandos, 1986

Liebermann: Piano Concertos
BBC Scottish Symphony Orchestra
Lowell Liebermann, conductor
Hyperion, 1997

Liszt & Grieg: The Piano Concertos
Bergen Philharmonic Orchestra
Andrew Litton, conductor
Hyperion, 2011

Mendelssohn: Piano Concertos
The Romantic Piano Concerto, vol. 17
(and works for piano and orchestra)
City of Birmingham Symphony Orchestra
Lawrence Foster, conductor
Hyperion, 1997

Mozart: Piano Concertos no. 21 in C 'Elvira Madigan' and no. 9 in
    E flat
Hallé Orchestra
Bryden Thomson, conductor
EMI, 1985

Rachmaninov: The Piano Concertos
(2 CDs)
Dallas Symphony Orchestra
Andrew Litton, conductor
Hyperion, 2004

Hollywood Nightmares
(includes Miklós Rózsa: Spellbound Concerto)
Hollywood Bowl Orchestra
John Mauceri, conductor
Decca, 1994 [2014]

Chamber Music with Piano

Beethoven: The Complete Sonatas for Violin & Piano
(4 CDs)
Robert Mann, violin
Nimbus, 1988

Beethoven, *see* Mozart & Beethoven: Quintets for Piano & Winds

Brahms: Cello Sonatas
Steven Isserlis, cello
Hyperion, 2005

Brahms: Piano Quintet op. 34
(with String Quartet op. 51 no. 2)
Takács Quartet
Hyperion, 2007

Brahms: The Three Sonatas for Violin and Piano
Robert Mann, violin
Music Masters, 1990

Brahms, Schumann, Frühling: Trios
Michael Collins, clarinet
Steven Isserlis, cello
RCA Red Seal, 1999

Franck & Rachmaninov: Cello Sonatas
Steven Isserlis, cello
Hyperion, 2003

Frühling, *see* Brahms, Schumann, Frühling: Trios

Forgotten Romance: Grieg, Liszt, Rubinstein
Steven Isserlis, cello
RCA Victor Red Seal 1994 [2008]

Grieg, *see* Mendelssohn, Grieg & Hough: Cello Sonatas

Broken Branches: Compositions by Stephen Hough
Jacques Imbrailo, baritone
Michael Hasel, piccolo
Marion Reinhard, bassoon/contrabassoon
Steven Isserlis, cello
Tapiola Sinfonietta
Gábor Takács-Nagy, conductor
BIS, 2011

Hough, *see* Mendelssohn, Grieg & Hough: Cello Sonatas

Liszt, *see* Forgotten Romance: Grieg, Liszt, Rubinstein

Mendelssohn, Grieg & Hough: Cello Sonatas
Steven Isserlis, cello
Hyperion, 2015

Mozart & Beethoven: Quintets for Piano & Winds
Berlin Philharmonic Wind Quintet
BIS, 2007

Danses et Divertissements
(includes Poulenc: Sextet for piano and wind quintet op. 100)
Berlin Philharmonic Wind Quintet
BIS, 2009

Rachmaninov, *see* Franck & Rachmaninov: Cello Sonatas

Rubinstein, *see* Forgotten Romance: Grieg, Liszt, Rubinstein

Schumann, *see* Brahms, Schumann, Frühling: Trios

Strauss: Cello Sonata in F, op. 6
(with works for cello and orchestra)
Steven Isserlis, cello
RCA Red Seal, 2001

Children's Cello
(mixed recital)
Steven Isserlis, cello
Simon Callow, narrator
BIS, 2006

Vocal and Choral Music

Bird Songs at Eventide
(songs from the Edwardian era)
Robert White, tenor
Hyperion, 2003

The Prince Consort: Other Love Songs
(including Stephen Hough's song cycle, *Other Love Songs*)
The Prince Consort
Linn, 2011

Hough, *see* Vaughan Williams: Dona nobis pacem; Hough: Missa Mirabilis

Vaughan Williams: Dona nobis pacem; Hough: Missa Mirabilis
Colorado Symphony Chorus
Colorado Symphony
Andrew Litton, conductor
Hyperion, 2015

Acknowledgements

Many of the reflections in this book germinated from articles that were first published in newspapers (*The New York Times*, *The Times*, the *Guardian*, the *Evening Standard*) and magazines (*Gramophone*, *Limelight*, *BBC Music Magazine*, *New Statesman*, the *Tablet*, *Radio Times*, *International Piano*, *Prospect*). And then I kept a blog on the *Telegraph* website for over five years, writing over six hundred articles. I combed through these transient musings and reworked some ideas which still interested me. The reflection on 'Elgar and Catholicism' was originally a talk for BBC Radio 3, and 'Is he musical?' appeared in an anthology of essays published by Bloomsbury, although both have been trimmed here, expanded there. There are probably some other outlets which have slipped my mind and which I should acknowledge. One often forgets as one transforms . . . but, one hopes, is forgiven.

Special thanks to Rt Revd Lord Harries, Alain de Botton, Peter Doig and Gordon VeneKlasen, New City Press, Farrar, Straus and Giroux, and the estate of Madeleine L'Engle for permission to use quotes from their writings and publications. And even more special thanks to Jill Burrows, Kate Ward, Belinda Matthews, Jonathan Galassi, and my agent, David Godwin, for advice, suggestions, encouragement, enthusiasm and more.

Index

Mozart, Wolfgang Amadeus, 36, 60,
113, 164, 186–7, 201, 209, 221, 222,
242, 267, 286, 416, 422
Don Giovanni, 242
Piano Concerto no. 9 in E flat (K.
271), 419
Piano Concerto no. 21 in C (K. 467),
59–60, 68, 85, 163, 419
piano concertos, 36, 104, 234
piano sonatas, 158, 213
Mozarteumorchester Salzburg, 418
music therapy, 59
musical memory, 63–4
Musical Opinion, 216

Nashville, 338–9
National Gallery, London, 10
concerts, 262
Naumburg International Piano
Competition, 69–71
Nazi era, 28, 45, 241, 261–2, 269, 297,
309
Nebraska, 342
neglected composers, 10
neglected works, 10
Nelsons, Andris, 122, 418
neoclassicism, 193–4
Netherlands Philharmonic Orchestra,
126–7
Netherlands Radio Philharmonic
Orchestra, 127
new age spirituality, 66
New College, Oxford, 313
New York, 11, 29, 42, 44, 48, 52, 54, 70,
170, 192, 200, 241, 263, 265, 304–5,
321, 326, 336, 342, 362
9/11 attack, 362
see also individual venues
New York Philharmonic, 51–2
New York Times, 340–41
Newcastle, New South Wales, 128
Newman, Cardinal John Henry, 27,
179–80, 184, 281
The Dream of Gerontius, 180–81,
218
Ney, Elly, 261–2
Nicholas, St, 11
Notre Dame de Fidélité, Jouques,
111

'O Little Town of Bethlehem', 380–81
Ogdon, John, 280
O'Hora, Ronan, 415
O'Leary, Father Daniel, 348–9
Open University, 169
opera, 15
Oramo, Sakari, 420
Orchestra of the age of Enlightenment,
72
orchestral standards, 73
Orlova, Alexandra: *Tchaikovsky: A
Self-Portrait*, 57
ornamentation, 159–60
Orthodox Churches, 283, 388, 391
O'Sullivan, Father Benjamin, 323, 327
Oxford, University of, 179, 313

Paderewski, Ignacy Jan, 39–40, 166,
322
Padua, 127
Paganini, Niccolò, 194, 238
page-turning, 93–8, 103
Paik, Anna, 307
Paradis, Maria Theresia von:
Sicilienne, 267
Paris, 150, 177, 220, 221, 224, 225, 244,
246, 249, 274, 285–6
Paris Exposition 1889, 243
parlour songs, 73–4
Parsons, Geoffrey, 8
Pascal, Blaise, 19, 345–6, 368
Passover, 387
Patel, Upen, 106
Paul, St, 387, 390, 394–6
Paul Hall, New York, 92
pentatonic scale, 243
performance anxiety, 87–90, 100, 102,
111, 125
performance practice
authenticity, 73
historic, 72
licence, 75–6
performer–composers, 20–21, 101, 230
performers
and emotion, 57–8
and repetition, 84–5
and risk, 108, 117
Perlemuter, Vlado, 156, 273–5
Petri, Egon, 87